T0063061

Total Tripping

Mexico

CARL LAHSER

Order this book online at www.trafford.com
or email orders@trafford.com

Most Trafford titles are also available at major online book retailers.

Printed in the United States of America.

ISBN: 978-1-4907-4449-0 (sc)
ISBN: 978-1-4907-4450-6 (e)

Trafford rev. 08/27/2014

www.trafford.com

North America & international
toll-free: 1 888 232 4444 (USA & Canada)
fax: 812 355 4082

from Mexico:
poems and scenes

Carl Lahser

Contents

This is a collection of my more significant visits to Mexico over the past 20 years. Included are observations and commentaries on customs, weather, people, plants, birds and other items of interest to me that may be useful to future visitors.

1

Mr. Cuul in Yucatan

Chapter 1

#CANCUN: December in the Tropics

The following is a narrative and poetic visit to the Islands of Cancun, Cozumel, and Isla Mujeres in the state of Quintana Roo, Mexico, and to archeological sites in the states of Quintana Roo and Yucatan. It is an account of what we saw rather than what there was to see.

The title comes from the Yucatec Maya word "*Cuul*" for foreigner. That we are able to visit Yucatan is, in part, due to the Maya prophetic allusions to "open roads". These prophecies resulted in curtailment of Maya rebel activities. They also suggested the coming of modern technology, freedom of movement, and of communication between the Maya and outsiders after a hundred years of the Caste Wars.

Summer and winter seasons did not vary much in temperature or tourist load but the birds, flowers and sea shells showed a marked seasonality.

Most of the popular tours we took are discussed along with the natural and political history of the region. The discussion will never replace a trip to the area but it will hopefully give the uninitiated a view from a different perspective.

Preparation for a trip is part of the fun. Ask your friends about any region in question and you will get opinions but probably not a lot of facts. Your travel agent will have current prices and transportation and tour options and will provide brochures. Public libraries have encyclopedias, travel guides and magazines that can provide great pictures and general information. Current guidebooks included *Insight Guides, the Michelin Green Guides, Berlitz Travellers Guides, Fodor's Travel Publications, Fromer's Comprehensive Guides,* and specialized guides for shoppers, the handicapped and for traveling on a shoestring. Not much available for the nature traveler.

Once you have a general idea where to go and what to see you can try natural and political histories. For Yucatan I read *Incidents of Travel in Yucatan* by Stephens, *Conquest of Mexico* by Berler, *History of the Conquest of Mexico* by William H. Prescott, *Unfinished Conversations* by Sullivan and the *Area Handbook for Mexico* by the Foreign Areas Studies of The American University. Picture guides to Tulum, Cancun, Cozumel, Coba, Chitzen Itza and several books on the tropical flowering plants were found in used book stores. I read applicable parts of Graf's *Exotic Plant Manual* and Carcasson's *Field Guide to the Coral Reef Fishes,* Stevenson's *Key Guide,* and *Caribbean Seashells* by Warmke and Abbott. I took along copy of *A Field Guide to the Birds of Mexico and Central America* by Davis and a waterproof copy of *Fishwatchers Guide* by Chaplin.

Saturday, 11 December 1993. The sun would not rise until about 0730 but my wife, Carol, and I were up at 0330 to begin our first trip to Mexico. We had made a time-share swap for a week on Cancun. The taxi arrived at 0430 to take us to the airport.

We arrived and checked in at the Northwest Airline counter with our passports. Our flight 737 left San Antonio, Texas, on time at 0610 bound for Memphis, Tennessee.

It seemed strange to have to go 800 miles northeast to Memphis to get to Mexico. Looking at a map, the island resort of Cancun is 800 miles south and 1000 miles east of San Antonio. It is 1000 miles south of Memphis, but Memphis was the hub where all Northwest flights shuffled passengers. This route was cheaper and faster than going through Mexico City.

I like flying at night. It's peaceful and quiet and, usually, uncrowded like this flight. The predawn crispness and torpor from interrupted sleep make the waiting less aggravating and easier to get back to sleep. The airlines maintain a cabin pressure of about 10,000 feet. This means you have about a third less oxygen than on the ground and feel the need to sleep. Only the crew is on oxygen to stay awake and alert to fly the plane.

I prefer a window seat over or just behind the wing. The ride is smoother over the plane's center of gravity, it's easier to doze leaning against the window and there is usually something to see during the waking moments. Night flying is a time of stark contrasts. Unless it's a moon lit night clouds are not readily visible but lightning is easily seen for many miles. Sunrise and sunset can be spectacular at altitude and by changing altitude you can see multiple sunrises and even see it set in the east or rise in the west.

These first two poems offer personal pictures of flying at night.

FIGHT FLIGHT TO MEMPHIS

San Antonio's nocturnal sights
outline an invisible world in light
as we leave the ground.
Horizon to horizon -
a myriad golden dots
with red and green spots
on a frozen of background.

We banked gently to the right
to head northeast
and found the black of night
with magic spots of light.

Each town and city is a different show -
a pale string of New Braunfels,
the bright pool of San Marcos and
Austin's golden glow.
There's Bourne, Fredricksburg, Waco
and, in the distance,
Redneck City -
Dallas, don't you know.

The day breaks
and night's beauty fades
into the dull reality of day
in its pale blue shades.

SUNRISE at 30,000 feet

At 30,000 feet it's thirty below.
The night sky is black with stars all aglow.

A bloody red streak appears in the east,
then arcs of violet, then blue.
A splash of green, then yellow, then orange
as the spectrum order marches through.
A veil of purple clouds hides the sun ball
until small red holes are made.
The red streak grows and becomes a red disc
and the spectral colors begin to fade.
Washes of purple and pink
flood the north and south
and the sky begins to turn blue.

Meanwhile, down on the ground
the lights of town are extinguished,
their nocturnal duty through.

Fitzgerald's phantom false dawn can be artificially induced when flying eastward approaching the rising sun. Even the rising of the sun can be manipulated, forcing the sun to both rise and set in the east by changing altitude. A normal sunrise can be spectacular at altitude.

The plane began descending over Arkansas and entered the approach pattern to Memphis in the early morning sun. The Mississippi River was still high and its water glowed in the early dawn silhouetting drowned trees in the floodplain along the river. We touched down in Memphis at 0743 as the low sun cast long shadows. This poem was drafted on the approach to Memphis.

COWS CAST LONG SHADOWS TOO

Flying low into Memphis
the early morning sun
caused the trees to cast long shadows.

So did the power poles
and water tanks
and cars
and eighteen wheelers.

The shadow of the plane
fell lightly on the low white clouds.

A lone milk cow
standing in a meadow patiently, grazing
cast a long shadow too.

The Memphis airport was clean, spacious, and comfortable compared to airports like DFW and Washington National, but we were just passing through and anxious to be on our way. Our route would be over still flood ravaged Tennessee, Mississippi, and Louisiana, just east of New Orleans and then 600 miles across the Gulf of Mexico. The shallow water along the Louisiana coast was dotted with oil platforms. The weather was clear and smooth for the flight across the Gulf.

Receding flood water leaves unique patterns of sand and silt streaks in fields and bottom lands. Oxbow lakes trace the path of river beds of earlier times. Flood waters sought and found new and easier paths to the sea. River bends were cut off forming oxbow lakes as the following poem illustrates.

OXBOW LAKES

Oxbow lakes are reminders of old river beds.
Curving streaks of sand and water show how
the course of rivers have changed
stable for only a geologic moment called now.

The Gulf Coast was thinly overcast. A hundred miles out the weather cleared and an hour later Cancun could be glimpsed under a bank of clouds hanging over the Yucatan coastline. We flew east of Contoy Island and Isla Mujeres then south along the twenty kilometers of hotels on Cancun beach. Our plane banked to the right and entered its final approach southeast of Punta Nizuc and the Club Med facility. We flew low over the mangroves of Laguna Nichupte' and landed at 1137.

Immigration and customs were surprisingly efficient for the tropics or anywhere for that matter. We bought some pesos and were in a taxi for the eight mile ride to town by 1215.

The twelve kilometer taxi ride along the Hotel Zone of the island yielded this first impression of Cancun recorded below.

CANCUN

Buildings of russet and azure and beige
stand stark against a clear blue sky.
Pastels not muted but sharp and crisp.
Clean air is the reason why.

Twenty kilometers of hotels
built on a barrier island of sand,
near perfect weather and a beautiful beach.
Cancun - a very pleasant island.

The first touch of the mañana syndrome was on arriving at the Tucan Cun Beach Hotel on the Playa Ballena. We were told that our room would not be ready for about three hours.

We were approached by a local entrepreneur offering a new time-share alternative and the offer of lunch and half-price tours. Several hotels were selling vacation plans with prepaid rooms for some period of years. We ate lunch on them and listened to their spiel. Then we took advantage of their half-price tour offer and booked tours to Chichen Itza, Isla Mujeres, Cozumel, a submarine cruise of Chanikar Reef and a rental car for a day.

The sun was setting when we got back to the hotel. We moved in and went out for lobster and Mayan lime soup. Our first day ended with a walk on the dark starlit beach.

December 12. I was up at 0530 to exercise and jog/wander on the beach. The morning was a clear, humid 65° F. After my warm-up exercises I jogged a mile south on the beach before turning back. On returning to the hotel I sat on the seawall and drank a pot of tea while watching the sun come up through a cloud bank on the horizon. It was Sunday, a day for rest. We went across the street to Kukulcan Mall for typical state-side breakfast.

TROPICAL BEACH MORNING

The Caribbean's flat
with a few low waves making
a swish-slopping sound.

Low purple clouds float
in a fading orange sky while
pelicans and gulls dive down.

A couple, standing hand in hand,
wait patiently for the rising sun
to begin its round.

The sky turns blue
and the clouds disappear.
The beauties of the dawn abound.

A half hour bus ride the length of the island took us to Cancun City for some shopping. The market was a square block of T-shirt shops, pottery and other tourit items.

Back at the hotel, after lunch and a siesta, and I went snorkeling in the surf in front of the hotel. I have astigmatisms I can't focus on anything I can reach under water. I was happy to find that my bifocal mask still worked. I probably looked funny wearing the mask across beach but at least I didn't trip over things. I preferred wearing Levis and a long-sleeved shirt for snorkeling for protection against cool water, corals, jellyfish, etc.

The beach was a soft tan coral sand that does not get terribly hot, even in the afternoon sun. The water was clear with a visibility in the surf of maybe ten feet. Breaking waves picked up and dropped the sand but there is almost no silt to cloud the water.

The beach had a bench that dropped about six feet to a flat scalloped forebeach. At the focus of each crescent a channel funneled water back to sea under the breaking waves creating an undertow. The excess water feeds a strong current flowing south parallel to the beach.

SNORKELING ON CANCUN BEACH

Out off the beach beyond the breaking waves
a shoal of silverside minnows moves as one.
It suddenly behaves like a predator is near.

Slipping into sight like a shadow from graves.
Just so! Sight of a two foot barracuda
awakes a memory primordial

I looked up and found
I'd drifted a quarter mile down
the beach riding on the onbeach current.
Over a sandy channel
I could feel the undertow tugging on my feet.

13 December. A ride on a city bus and a stop at McDonalds prepared us for the trip to Chitze'n Itzá or Chichen Itza. We left on Monday at 0730 and proceeded 120 miles west on a new toll road. Someone recommended renting a car for the trip, but there is an extra $20 rental fee to cross the state line and a $50 for the toll.

The road was flat and bypassed all of the little towns. A few houses appeared in clearings well off the road. There were also a number of abandoned slash-and-burn fields where the jungle was retaking the corn fields. The brush or "jungle" was a mix of second growth trees and grasses including Gumbo-Limbo, Cecropia and wild papaya. A few large snags of old sapote trees showed cross-hatched scars where local Maya Indians had collected chicle over the years. The forest growth was relatively uniform as a result of damage by a Class V hurricane in 1985 with 200+ mph winds.

Lunch was at a hotel in the village of Chiche'n Itz'a, a so-so buffet. I loaded up the camcorder and two 35mm cameras and we walked to the ruins. The weather was warm and pleasant for a tropical December day. They charged extra for camcorders but not for 35mms.

CHITZE'N ITZ'A

Maybe it was the new toll road,
or the hotels that diminished the effect.
or the stone temples standing in a fenced field
while a thousand tourists strained their neck.
Or a hundred years
of archeological investigation, restoration, sterilization
and commercialization that I reject

The
impact
was soft -
soft like going
to a museum instead
of a church. People lived
here 1000 years and died and
are dead and gone except for Indian
children begging pesos and monuments in stone.

Our guide was very well prepared and had a good presentation. We saw a lot - the Temple of a Thousand Columns, the Soldiers Temple with its steils and big Chocmul, the Pyramid of the Chairs which was being renovated, the Temple of the Eagle and Tiger, the Temple of Venus, the handball court with its multiple echoes and terrible history, the Grand Pyramid with its inner and outer temples, and the sacrificial well.

All of my video tape was over exposed but the 35mm, especially the panoramic shots, were very good. TV specials on Chiche'n Itz'a were made with no one else around and on the proper dates so that the sun did its thing for equinox and the summer and winter solstices. It was distracting to see 500 tourists and hear several languages at once tell the story of the Maya Empire history and culture.

I climbed the exterior and interior of the Great Pyramid. The tunnel to the inner older temple was steep, damp and warm. It was about 40 inches wide and five feet tall. Steps were 8 inches wide and slippery. Lighting came from several low wattage bulbs. Sight of the red stone chocmul and jaguar were worth the climb.

One of the major impression was a hiccup in time, the attempt to stop these monument's slow return to jungle and dissolving into the earth.

Great Pyramid

The Mexican government was in charge of the study and restoration of this and other archeological sites. Most early archeological work was privately sponsored and some of the artifacts had been removed from Mexico.

CLIMBING THE GREAT PYRAMID AT CHITZE'N ITZ'A

The
steps are
narrow and
the slope is steep
ascending the nine
levels of the great pyramid.
Tiny plants growing in crevices-
grasses and ferns, forty species of
broadleaf weeds - taking it back to the jungle.

Temple of Columns

The bus flew out of the sun along the toll road with only a short break to pass out cokes and beer. Tropical night falls suddenly, almost like flipping a switch. The sun disappeared into the jungle, and it was dark.

NIGHT ON A TROPICAL BEACH

A no moon sky
with pale clouds drifting by
while bright stars twinkle.
Polaris is too far north to be seen
The sea is phosphorescent.
Waves break in a flashing crescent.
The beach seems to faintly glow,
in the starshine to the water's dark, dark green.

A cruise ship with a million lights
passes silently like a blight
on the far, dark horizon. A skimmer glides
by squawking to the warm-cool breeze.
In the distance, hotels fight the nights
and show their red aircraft hazard lights.
A ghostly couple passes, an apparition framed
against the pitch black sky and sea.

We had supper and wandered through the shops and boutiques in the huge, air conditioned Kukulcan Plaza mall located conveniently across from the hotel.

The sky was black and stars twinkled for me for the first time since the Canadian subarctic in June. A storm was passing off shore with a light show of lightning but I could hear no thunder.

The storm cleared the air so that Tuesday's sun could come up out of the sea into a bright, clear day.

Tuesday, December 14. Morning was cool after the off-shore storm. Lightning had flashed most of the night but no rain had dampened our roof. My morning jog was doubly rewarding - I found a number of shells in the drift line deposited by the high tide and onshore wind.

MORNING ON CANCUN BEACH

Its light enough to see a couple walking
hand in hand
kicking an impertinent wave.
A sliver moon is talking
to the sun still behind the horizon
in nights cave.

MORNING ON CANCUN Beach 2

A lone pelican cruises the surf
while two Tropicbirds
circle for altitude.
A weak sun peeks through thin clouds
to see who is on its turf.
The pelican crashes into the sea
and surfaces with a pouch of food.

A bright orange sun disc burns
through the scud
and the orange reflection appears
upon the choppy flood
silhouetting the lone pelican.

A cruise ship took about fifteen minutes to pass silhouetted against the early morning clouds. It was probably heading to Cozumel where two or three cruise ships were usually anchored.

An early morning jet flight climbed out of the jungle into the rising sun and turned north. Most of the flights go through Mexico City, but there are a number of chartered and scheduled airlines from Miami, Houston, Memphis, and even South America.

Europeans and the Japanese had just discovered the Mexican resorts. The Mexican resorts were newer and less expensive than many of the older South American resorts. There were few multilingual tour guides in Cancun. Other than English I heard two couples speak German and one

Japanese. Just wait and the tourist will come. Multilingual ability will be part of guide certification.

After my jog and a pot of tea I woke Carol. We had breakfast at the 100% Natural Restaurant - fresh fruit and a western omelet with black beans and white cheese. This beat McDonalds special the previous day.

A city bus took us to the car rental office. We rented a Volkswagon with a standard shift.

We filled the car at the only Pemex government monoply gas station in town and got lost in Cancun City looking for the road south.

A four lane road passed the airport then settled down to a well maintained two lane blacktop. Each homestead had its own "sign" for where to turn off or what trail to follow - a stick piercing two plastic jugs; three red streamers on a tree branch. I don't know where they went, but we didn't.

We passed an aquarium and a crocodile farm. Turning around we found that the aquarium was closed.

The crocodile farm, a garish pink building announcing, Crococun, was open. Saltwater crocodiles were raised, displayed, and harvested. There was also a 15 acre zoo featuring deer and other local animals in a jungle a setting.

Next stop was three miles down the road at the Dr. Alfredo Barrera Mar'in Botanical Garden. This was a 150 acre research and teaching center operated by the Center for Research for Quintana Roo (CIQRO) with its main office in Puerto Morelos. Several cenotes or collapsed limestone caverns and several Yucatec Mayan archeological sites were included.

A typical native homestead had been erected including a dooryard garden with typical crops such as papaya, banana, maize, limes and some medicinals. There was a well and a one room sleeping hut with hammocks and handmade wooden storage containers. A separate kitchen structure was used for cooking and other food preparation to prevent burning down the main structure.

The Garden also had a native plant and tree nursery and an orchid farm.

A large blue Morpho butterfly flashed in the shade and a noisy blue Yucatan Jay glided across the trail. Iguanas crashed through the trees and underbrush. I heard a drumming sound nearby and followed the sound to see the bright red head and dark body of the large Guatemalan Ivorybill Woodpecker.

As a teaching center many of the trees were labeled with the common and scientific name and medicinal use. A number of technical publications were offered for sale but the majority of them were in Spanish.

This park maintained a considerable biological diversity, but no parrots or other life I had half expected to see in the Yucatan jungle. The jungle and its inhabitants were not like TV and travel brochures advertised.

Native kitchen

We drove on down to and through Puerto Morelos, Playa Paraiso and Playa del Carmen. These were once small fishing villages. Now they were a mix of government-built concrete block or corrugated tin houses with thatched roofs, moderate hotels, and fancy resorts that brought tourists and progress. Each town had a modern school building that doubled as a hurricane shelter.

Rain was threatening and we were hungry, so we waited out the rain at Puerto Aventuras with lunch. A Mexican movie company shooting scenes around the harbor had to stop for the rain too.

The intent had been to drive south to see the ruins at Tulum but it was after five when the rain stopped. The sun was low as we drove back north for Cancun. Several species of flowering trees along the road were brilliant in the late afternoon sun. Bats of twilight flitted about several places along the road consuming insects.

Busses, cars and trucks passed us in the twilight. We finally passed a motor scooter after chasing him several miles. VWs still don't like me.

A storm to the north had flattened out the sea and there was still lightening in the distant clouds. A light, cool breeze drifted off the water as I sat on the seawall and absorbed it all.

Later, I went for a walk along the water's edge.

Cancun Sand

The beach is all public - yea!!
and I jog on the coraline sand
that doesn't get hot in the sun.

The sand is a cool, hard
as pavement under the retreating wave.
Just above the waterline lies
a two foot wide strip of sand
a soft slurry like fresh cement.

As the water drains
the sand is cool and crisp like meringue.
This crust dries and
breaks up into loose blowing, skittering sand.

I guess I jog differently.

Cancun Beach

Tropical sunsets are supposed to be outstanding, but sunset was on the other side of the island, and it was the wrong time of year. In the winter the sun sets and it gets dark. We arrived on the new moon so there were no moonlit nights either. But the black nights were star filled and the sunrises were worth getting up for.

15 December. Wednesday was the day we scheduled a trip to Isla Mujeres, an island four miles north of Cancun Island. I took two cameras, my prescription mask with snorkel, and tennis shoes. My fins were left behind. They were big enough to slip over tennis shoes and push a scuba tank. I felt they would not be needed on a shallow reef trip.

At breakfast I ordered rolls and hot tea. Getting hot tea was a challenge of language and patience. For some reason the waiter did not appear to believe anyone would be serious about drinking hot tea in Mexico. People drink hot coffee, don't they? Why should there be any difficulty getting a cup of tea? Just a little literary license there - he did not really bring a beer, but it was the third time around before a tea bag and hot water arrived together.

MAÑANA TEA

"Cafe, Senior?"
"Hot tea, please."
"Que?"
"Una taza de te caliente, por favor."
"Oh. Si, Senior. Right away."
Hot water arrives but no tea bag.
Time passes.
"Mozo, por favor."
"Senior?"
"Traigame una taza de te.?"
"Si. Si. Right away."
The water is luke warm when the tea bag arrives.
"Mozo, por favor."
"Senior?'
"Traigame una taza de aqua caliente?"
"Que?"
"I want hot tea, dammit!"
"Oh. Si, Senior. Right away."
He brings me a cold beer with a sly grin.
"Salute. And to Hell with the tea."

We took a bus to Playa Linda where the ferries and cruise ships to Isla Mujeres were docked. On our tour boat were pastry and punch for the passengers but a lot of the pastry went to feed a flock of terns and gulls. Two white Tropicbirds were circling, looking for a morning thermal. Their long, forked tail feathers worked like scissors controlling the soaring as they climbed higher over the beach. They accompanied us across the channel and over the fleet of Cuban fishing boats.

TROPICBIRD

a white-tailed Tropicbird rides
on thermal currents of air
scarcely moving it soars
its long, forked tail streaming out behind.
It chides a Cuban fishing boat
for belching diesel smoke.

Our ferry was a large, double-decked party boat which took an hour to cross the seven mile channel. About two-thirds of the way across the channel thirteen Cuban fishing boats were anchored south of the island waiting out a storm in the Gulf. These were rusty old trawlers and longliners that used a smoky, low grade fuel oil.

Isla Mujeres was the site of the first Spanish contact with Mexico. Francisco Herna'ndez de Co'rdoba landed on the island in 1517. The island name may have come from the figurines of the fertility goddess, Ixchel, that were found near a Mayan temple on the south end of the island.

There was part of an 18th-century hacienda that was supposedly built by the pirate, Fermi'n Mundaca, to impress a beautiful, blond captive.

The island had a several nice beaches, good snorkeling and diving sites and the village of Isla Mujeres.

The ferry docked at El Garrafon National Park near the south end of the island near the lighthouse and ruin of the Maya Temple of Ixchel. The park had a small protected reef with a well marked trail for snorkeling called "a natural tropical aquarium". There was a bath house, concessions, and several caged nurse sharks that were fed to amuse the touristas waiting for the ferry.

SNORKELING ISLA MUJERES

An underwater park on Isla Mujeres.
A living reef ringed with markers
to keep people from hurting
themselves or the reef.

A near perfect park with
thirty foot visibility,
ten foot depth,
no stinging corals
or dangerous marine life.
A living reef for many to see and enjoy.

A rounded, stony coral head serves as
a cleaning station where green parrot fish

hang, tail down and operculum flared,
while a black and white cleaning goby
picks parasites.
Several other fish patiently wait their turn.
A mottled squid leaves the coral.
It senses me, turns white
and jets into the distance

Garrafon Beach

After two hours at the park, we boarded the ferry for a short trip up the coast and a picnic on the beach. The buffet was nothing special, but it was served out under a big canvas pavilion on the sand. An outstanding dish was a basket of Habinero peppers that were really too hot to eat.

Several women and children were selling shells laid out on the beach - Tritons Trumpets and local starfish and sea urchins. Conchs all had the edges filed and a hole in the tip where the animal had been cut loose and eaten.

I took a walk up the beach and picked up specimens of several species of beach-worn shells that were not offered for sale.

After lunch we sailed and docked at the town of Isla Mujeres. We were escorted on a quick tour of several tourist shops then allowed a couple hours on our own. We found several shops that had good local art at relatively high prices. This little town and island would make an interesting few days visit.

Downtown

I asked if anyone sold conchas or caracols (sea shells) and was directed to two vendors on the seawall. They had a few local shells but most of the shells were in sea grass baskets packaged in the Philippines.

CARIBBEAN SHELLS

"Isla Mujeres shells for sale, Senior."
"Pretty lady, buy some shells from me.
A pretty basket of shells for you."
(Packaged by a Moro in Zamboanga on the Sulu Sea.)

The trip back was a 90-minute occasion to play adult games - Limbo contests, tequila slammers, and participate in a variety of beer drinking contests for bottles of tequila. Interesting.

We docked at sundown. Supper was at a seafood restaurant where we had Mayan lime soup again. It was a chicken based soup with lime juice much like Chinese hot and sour soup or the Philippine singalob.

Thursday, 16 December. Today's diversion was a trip to the Osland of Cozumel. The bus left from the Kukulcan mall and drove to Playa del Carmen for another ferry ride. The beach area north of Playa del Carmen was several miles of tropical picture postcard views.

Two large ferry boats made a two hour round trips to Cozumel on alternate hours. Three wheel bicycles were used to carry all the cargo out onto the dock to be loaded on board.

The trip took almost two hours acompanired by a school of raballo or flying fish. The ferry docked at the marina of Puerto de Abrigo. This was near where, in 1519, Cortes launched his campaign that eventually defeated the Aztecs.

The island had numerous ruins and jungle sights to see, a rougher ocean shoreline on eastern shore and a more protected western coast. We had about four hours and took the easy way going to Chankanaab Park for lunch and the afternoon on the beach. This island deserves several days to see it well.

Cozumel Is

The park had a small, well managed museum and botanical garden, a beach for sunning, and umbrellas for the less hearty, a swimming area, a reef just off shore, and a large observation pool, a restaurant, and three vendors of snorkeling equipment and diving trips. A lot of people were in the park, but it was not really crowded.

The botanical garden and jungle had iguanas and butterflies and lots of birds. When we first arrived we were met by a little bird in a coconut tree, the rare Cozumel Bananaquit restricted to only Cozumel and Holbox Islands.

The Cozumel Bananaquit

We just arrived at Chankanaab Park
when a little bird landed in a coconut tree.
Black striped head and a white throat,
the Cozumel Bananaquit nibbled
coconut flowers and posed for me.

I picked up several shells on the beach along the seawall at Puerto Abrigo before we left. They were typical of rock dwellers or inhabitants of the sea grass.

Friday, December 17, was a leisure day so we shopped and took a submarine ride to the reef off of Punta Nizuc. A Class V hurricane of 1985 did a lot of structural damage and the reef was still recovering. Biodiversity and a balanced commumuiy was being restored and new species of corals were growing on dead, broken coral. Some species had not been seen in many years.

Local thinking about the hurricane damage was like that of the "disaster" of the Crown of Thorns starfish invasion of the Pacific reefs. "It will take a hundred years for the reef to recover." The principle damage is caused by loss of species diversity and the weakened structural integrity when only a few species dominate. Removal of these dominant species by the hurricane actions allows many species to return. This new population will have rebuilt the reef in ten to fifteen years. The fish will come back once their reef habitats are restored, and the shells and sea grasses will return to the flats once the protection of the reef is in place.

Supper on the last evening of a vacation should be something special. We dined over the water on the lagoon side with a sinking sun and sliver moon just a couple hours from setting.

We sipped virgin pina coladas and watched the sun and moon set while waiting for the lobster to cook.

Lagoon Evening

Waiting for the lobsters to cook
we watched the sun set
behind the mangrove trees
in a short burst of color.

A silver sliver moon
who trailed the sun by two hours
reflected off the lagoon
framed first by the orange glow
then by the black of night.

Two moons,
Pina Coladas
and you.
Memories are painted just so.

18 December. Saturday morning was last minute shopping, pack up and checkout. A cab took us to the airport. Mexican immigration was as efficient as on our arrival and the plane was on time. We left Cancun about 1300 on a sunny afternoon and I thunderheads forming to 40,000 feet and casting shadows on the stratus clouds below.

Afternoon Flight

Cloud shadows on clouds.
A thunderhead intercepts
late afternoon sun
darkening the fleecy white clouds below.
An afternoon sky viewed from above.

We had a two hour layover in Memphis for immigration and customs and left Memphis as the sun was sinking.

SECOND SUNRISE MISSED

A grey sky greeted our Northwest Flight
leaving Memphis on December 18, 1993.
We left the ground four minutes late
and a second sunrise we would not see.

The Captain made a valiant try to catch the sun
as he climbed at 4000 feet per minute.
The cloud layer was thick and it turned to night
as soon as we were in it.

A slash of red topped the cloud bank
and it looked like we had won
but this slash of red was all we saw.
The sun was gone and the day was done.

We arrived in San Antonio about 2000. Home ‘til next time.

Chapter 2

#Cancun Summer 21-28 May 94

May 21. A second trip to Yucatan began at 0430 on May 21st. Our Northwest DC-10 to Memphis left at 0600. It was still dark in San Antonio when we left the ground heading northeast. We hung the sun up and, from our sunny vantage at 28,000 feet, watched the dark ground come alive and the lights belonging to the night wink out.

This trip was different in several aspects. My 24-year old son, Charles, was with me while my wife, Carol, stayed home. This was a summer trip at the full moon and the previous trip had been in the winter at the new moon. We would be staying on the lagoon instead of the beach.

Memphis approach and departure scenery was different than it had been on the previous trip in December. The world was green with new crops and pasture. The flooding of the previous fall was over and the effects had largely disappeared.

TENNESSEE FARMS

New Fields

Fields of sandy loam
wrested from the forest mottled
and streaked tan and brown
where the flooding Mississippi deposited
Minnesota silt and sand.

Old fields

Mottled tan fields with curving berms
marking constant elevation
retarding soil erosion
and retaining life-giving water.

Windbreaks
Green strips of wind breaks planted
to slow the cold, wet winter winds and
provide wildlife with habitat and food.
Farm and Home Administration
specials from the 1930's.

Abandoned farmstead
A small, square clapboard house
with rusted tin roof
sitting in a field of green
surrounded by FHA trees.
No trace of man's recent use

Old Homestead
A house just so
with trees just so
and out buildings just so
mark Farm and Home Administration houses
financed by the government
just so.

The flight across the Gulf was smooth and uneventful but several of the passengers were concerned that the steward allowed two blue-haired ladies to sit in the exit row.

A small jet a couple miles and 5000 feet below us and a full tanker waddling towards the Yucatan Channel broke the monotony.

A counterclockwise spinning low pressure cell was sitting over the eastern Gulf and a cloud bank of thunderheads marked the coasts of Cuba and Yucatan. Our approach to Cancun was from the west over Holbox Island and the port town of Chquilo.

Airport formalities went smoothly and we were on our way to the Cancun Clipper Club in less than a half hour. They showed us to a small room with two double beds. I remarked that this was much smaller than I expected. They checked our reservations and moved us to a suite - 1200 square feet, two rooms and two baths with a full kitchen. Gotta watch them people.

The Clipper Club was in a convenient location. We were a block from the Convention Center and the Plaza Caracol Mall. There was a pool and an outdoor gym with Nautilus equipment.

We got tour tickets for half price through the hotel and booked tours to Xcaret, Chiche'n Itz'a and Tulum. We thought about renting a car and seeing the archeological site at Coba' but chose to go to Isla Mujeres instead. I asked about a birding trip to Contoy Island but found the price was $400 US.

Oleanders, plumeria, bougainvilla and Hibiscus were in bloom. The orange and purple Oleander Moth that looks like a wasp was a common sight. There were no mosquitoes and the weather ranged from 70-90 F. It was clear except for haze on Wednesday. An eclipse Wednesday evening covered a quarter of the moon that began about 2000 and finished by 2200.

The first evening, as we were sitting around the pool, the following poem was played out.

THE TROPICBIRD AND THE MOON

The
afternoon
moon
was two days from full and three hours out of the sea
when a Tropicbird
with long, forked tail
and coal black wings
came soaring,
soaring,
soaring
and
flew over
the moon.

Night on the Beach

May 22. Sunday was orientation day. We began by walking along the beach at Playa Caracol. Then we hit several malls and a hundred shops. I sold several copies of my poetry book from the first trip to Cancun. The evening was occupied by a Margarita party sponsored by the hotel.

May 23. Our Monday trip to Chiche'n Itz'a began at 0500 with exercise and watching the sun come up. A 0630 bus to Plaza Kukulkan arrived at 0645. The restaurant where the tour passengers gathered did not open until 0700 so we went across to and through a hotel to the beach for a half hour walk before breakfast and the tour. Several varieties of "sea beans" and false black coral were on the beach but no shells.

The tour went along the old road through the old towns of Leona Vicario, Nuevo Xca'n, Xca'n, and Chemax. Tiny side roads or trails let Army patrols access to smaller villages such as San Diego.

Patchwork House

It was strange to see a thatch roof and a microwave dish on the same building.

I noticed the blue Africanized honey bee trap boxes hung along the road. The driver did not know their significance. These "killer" bees did not appear to be a problem in the Yucatan.

Burned vegetation indicated where fires had been set to clear land for a couple crops of corn and bananas and, maybe, sugarcane.

Yellow butterflies and smaller white butterflies were especially numerous near Chemax. I thought the kids could collect them for sale but the Mexican law says this cannot be done until a survey has been completed and the indigenous people don't have the money to begin the survey. Maybe the Maya Indians could get a waiver like American Indians do.

The Old Cancun Road

The old road from Cancun to Merida
has two ten foot lanes and no shoulders
much like the Mayan roads or sacbeh of compacted marl.

Every village is protected
by "sleeping policemen"
or speed bumps ("Vibradores" in Spanish)

"Killer" bee survey boxes decorate trees
and charred areas burned for slash and burn farms
preparing for today's crops and tomorrow's jungle.

These villages seem to lurch through time. Tropical flowers and butterflies provide color. The modern schools result in minimal formal education and a dilution of the Maya culture. Army patrols stand on the edge revolution. There are ambiguities like primitive dooryard gardens edged with empty soda cans and thatched roofs with microwave dishes.

The bus passed thorough the colonial city of Valladolid and a few more small towns.

Valladolid

Founded in 1529 this colonial city
painted itself Vatican white
to honor the Pope's visit
to Mexico in 1993.
The Pope went to Merida instead
but the Valladolid is still white.

A rest stop near the village of Kaua was on the schedule. The walls of this old hacienda enclosed about an acre. The main building was occupied by a gift shop and restaurant. Perimeter walls were covered with bougainvilla. A separate building for the kitchen and restrooms stood behind the main structure.

A cenote and cave complex was located at Balancanche a couple miles north. Maybe I will see them on anothert trip.

We drove another twenty minutes before finally arriving at the museum at the main entrance to Chiche'n Itz'a.

A large tourist market occupied the space in front of the museum. The museum was minimal and labeled in Spanish. I had not seen this museum on the previous trip.

Archeology Site

The tour guide covered the great pyramid and the ball court in a half hour. The rough outer wall of the ball court was pointed out as having been constructed as a place for iguanas.

IGUANAS OF CHICHE'N ITZ'A

The outer walls of the pok pok court
was kept rough as homes for Iguanas
that the Iguanas would bless the court.

They still do.
Iguanas are still climbing these walls
and the walls of the sacrificial well
and the surrounding jungle
and bless an occasional stew pot.

Charles at the Great Pyramid

Ball Court

The echoes in the ball court were stressed. Maya leaders who had gone to meet with Dr Sylvanus Morely at Chiche'n Itz'a in 1932 were not awed or impressed with the echoes. These Mayan accepted the echoes as confirmation that the ancient cities were enchanted places. The souls of their ancestors lived underground and were waiting for the awakening. The echoes were direct communications with their ancestors.

Temple of the Chairs

Road to the Sacred Well

Nothing was said about the Soldiers' Temple, the restoration of the Temple of the Chairs, the Temple of a Thousand Pillars, the Temple of Venus or the Temple of the Jaguar and the Eagle. We were given 45 minutes to see anything else we wanted.

A quick walk took us to the sacrificial well where Charles traded his talkingTimex for several Maya figures. Then we climbed the inside and outside of the great pyramid.

The guides were not certified like they had to be in London and many other tourist locations. This results in visitors often getting a guide with poor language skills or a distorted story. Certification is something that Mexico should seriously consider.

Return to Cancun was a straight shot down the new toll road. This divided highway had two eight foot wide lanes each direction and a scant three foot shoulder on each side. Busses and trucks took up the full lane stripe to stripe. Toll for a car was $52 US each way. Speed limit was 100Km or 60 MPH. The toll road bypassed everything.

The tour Tuesday went to Xcaret. This was about 100Km or 60 miles south of Cancun, a nice day trip. It was even better by bus where I didn't have to do the driving. The park site covered about 500 acres of jungle with a museum and archeological sites. Its primary claim to fame was the caleta or natural aquarium where you swim or snorkel through about 2000 feet of caves filled with brackish water. There was also a beach, dolphin pens and a dolphin show. For a price you could swim with the dolphins.

The museum structure was a large square about 300 feet on a side. Its central patio had a 20 foot water jet. Many good architectural models of most of the prominent Maya sites and a show of local artists works were on display. The gift shop had T-shirts, snacks, and snorkeling equipment, a good selection of educational toys and one of the best selection of books I found on the Yucatan.

The water temperature was about 75 and everyone was required to wear a life vest. The water was brackish and mostly 4-5 feet deep. Visibility under water in the caves varied with temperature and presence of salinity density layers. It reminded me of the Maui wells on Guam and the Hawaiian Islands where fresh drinking water is skimmed off the heavier brackish water layer.

The route was lit by vents bored through the cave roof - not quite the romantic "sunlight streaming through cracks in the ceiling" in the brochures. There were several exits into sunny outdoor pools. Fish life in the cave was limited to silversides and Sargent Majors.

Xcaret Temple

Entrance to the *Caleta* or caves

The site supported a farm, horse pens, a breeding farm and small zoo with Peacocks, ducks, geese, chickens, guinea fowl, iguana, Spider monkeys. I talked to the musicians playing "native" music for the crowd. They were from Mexico City and were playing Quecha music from Peru. Their public did not seen to know or care.

The trip back was uneventful arriving at the hotel about five. It was still light so I walked the beach to point at Punta Cancun.

PUNTA CANCUN

Walk the beaches of Cancun
to the east or to the north -
those tan beaches of coral sand;
beaches where children play
and lovers walk hand-in-hand;
clean beaches with a dozen
kinds of sea beans
and fifty species of tiny shells;
past hotels that line the beaches;
quiet northern beaches of
Playa Caracol and Playa Tortugas
on the Bahia de Mujeres;
Caribbean beaches facing eastward
where the surf breaks and sings to the world -
and you come to Punta Cancun,
a headland of eroded fossil coral
rising twenty feet above the sea.
The point contends with the waves from the Caribbean
and its lighthouse signals
warn naive ships,if they value their hulls,
Peligro - Danger,
and it protects the Bay of Women.

The beaches in front of the hotels along Playa Caracol on Bahia de Mujeres were quiet at sundown and the tide had just turned from the lowest point. I stepped from the sand to the rocky headland and found a small automated lighthouse on the point. While low waves slopped on the beach on the bay side of the point on the Caribbean side large waves were breaking with a force that shook the rocks. The hotel guards recommended that I be careful since the rocks could be dangerous.

The stump of a tree about five feet in diameter rested amongst the eroded fossil coral boulders.

My path back from the point was a sidewalk through one of the hotels. Something ran across my path. A few feet further and I saw a kit fox standing in the weeds like it expected a handout. I don't know if animals in Cancun have rabies but wildlife that expects to be fed in the hotel zone could be a problem,

Charles and I went to Kukulkan Plaza for two warm-up jazz concerts preceding the big Jazz Festival on the next weekend. Joao Henrique and his group from Brazil were up first. It was not the best of modern jazz. It was extremely loud and made worse by the very bad tinny acoustics of the mall.

Henrique was followed by Mike Mulvain from Los Angeles. Mulvain took almost an hour tuning his piano to perfection. He played well but the acoustics made his piano tuning a waste of time.

We left the concert early and tried the 100% Natural Restaurant for supper. I had tacos that were unusual but ok. Charles' spaghetti had a weak soupy sauce that looked like what you might get when rinsing out the bottle of Ragu. Their music was played so loud you had to shout at the waiter.

This was the night of the full moon and an eclipse would shadow about a third of the moon's surface. The eclipse was not well publicized. It was a beautiful clear night for the event that began about 2000 and over about 2200. Nobody paid much attention.

Five snowy egrets, spooked from the lagoon, flew overhead.

Five Egrets

It was evening by the pool
at the Cancun Clipper Club and
the full moon claimed the sky.
Pool and hotel security lights
softly lit the scene with flitting reflections.
Five egrets spooked from the lagoon
flew over the pool, white against the sky
challenging the eclipsing moon.

The morning of the 25th was hazy and stayed that way all day. Everything in Cancun was normally pastel but this haze cut visibility to about a mile and the pastels faded into the haze. I had thought there might be some good summer sunsets but the sun settled into the red-orange margin of purple late afternoon bank of clouds.

I had talked to several hotels about using my first book of poetry and prose about Cancun for advertising with no luck. I sold some individual copies but not in bulk. I had an appointment this morning to see the manager of the Clipper Club with no luck and the same for the Hard Rock Cafe that advertises green tourism. I made an appointment to drop copies at the office of Sr Pastacinni, who owned Plaza Caracol and honorary Italian ambassador, and to the editor of *Cancun Tips.*

With no more appointments for the day we went on a snorkeling trip from the hotel to Chantakar reef, the second longest reef in the world. A dive boat picked us up at the hotel at noon and flew across Laguna Nichupte. The captain slowly traversed the narrow, mangrove lined Canal Nizuc because of heavy traffic from the skidoos and other tour boats and then cruised by the seagrass flats to Punta Nizuc and Club Med. We docked at Paradise Island, an artificial island that serves as a hub for snorkeling and the submarine and jet ski tours.

I still prefer to snorkel in a wet suit or long jeans and a long sleeved shirt. This costume kept the stings of jellyfish off my arms, the sun off of my back and kept me warmer in cool water. I wore tennis shoes under my extra large fins. This dated from my walking across a coral reef in tabys and from all the sandburrs on many beaches.

The snorkel trip went very well. Visibility was about 20 feet. We swam out about a quarter mile to the edge of the reef and worked along the reef face. I found that my bifocal mask still worked tolerably so I had both near and far vision without my glasses. We snorkeled for over an hour and headed back in to Paradise Island.

The reef was recovering well from the last big hurricane in 1985. I saw at least eight species of corals plus purple sea fans, yellow sponges, false black coral, two species of sea cucumbers, a few shells and two species of sea urchins- short black spines and short pink spines. The most common fish were schools of Goat Fish dabbling in the sand, French Angelfish, species of Tang, Surgeonfish, parrotfish, wrasses and masses of fry.

I just had to try a deep dive at the edge of the reef and found that about ten feet down my ears really hurt. I used to go to 30 feet and stay down almost two minutes.

Personal Observations on not Snorkeling for Several Years

Years ago I would slip on worn Levis,
a sweat shirt, mask, snorkel and
tennis shoes and snorkel for hours.
I could free dive to 35 feet and
stay down for two minutes.

Today I found that if I could see it
I couldn't reach it and
what I picked up was a blur.
I could not stay down a whole minute.
My ears hurt below ten feet.
My legs told me an hour of flippering
was more than enough.

I may be getting old
but I prefer to think
I'm just out of practice.

We were back at the hotel by 1700. After a shower and a nap we caught the bus and went out for supper. Charles suggested that we try Planet Hollywood for supper.

a Welcome Surprise
PLANET HOLLYWOOD

I'm not sure what I expected
at Planet Hollywood
but the experience
was a pleasant surprise.
Eclectic decor without being garish.
Staff galore, well trained
and with distinctive clothing.
Comfortably cool without annoying drafts.

Music and videos present
but not so demanding you could not talk.
Real class. and excellent food.
What can I say, I'll be back.

There are literally hundreds of eating places along hotel row. Some have good food. Many are expensive. Some are just loud and glossy.

Thursday morning I took an early walk along Playa Tortugas. I was watching the fishermen with their castnets (*tulagi*), children playing in the surf, sea birds and other seaside songs. The sounds of the surf and background sounds of the street. The growl of delivery trucks. The squeal of bus brakes. Snips of conversation. A beach boy sweeping the sand smooth in front of a hotel. Sight and sounds of early morning are always interesting. Some sounds seem to be common world wide.

morning sounds of Cancun

Yee! Yee! Yee! Yeee! of the Mexican Grackle
Someone learning the guitar
on the beach at 6 AM
The TV news in Spanish
Engine growls and the howl of brakes
on busses and trucks
The sizzling noise of tires
on the asphalt street
All drowned out by the singing of the surf

Some sights and sounds are unique to a place or circumstance. Singular combinations of sounds can make a place memorable and, may someday trigger a memory of this trip, this place, this time. This also applies to sights - golden sunrises; bloody red sunsets; blue sky; brilliant stars glittering against black velvet; colorful birds silhouetted against jungle green; flitting jewels of butterflies; a lone fisherman at dawn with his castnet walking the beach on the incoming tide.

Tropical Fisherman

A lone fisherman,
his brown body burned darker yet by the sun,
bare footed,
in shorts and New York Jets T-shirt.

He walks the beach in the false dawn
with a castnet draped over his left shoulder
at the ready.
Two quick steps into the surf
and the shapeless net
springs like a snake
its large, round mouth biting into the sea.

Net sounds -
a small thunk of weights thrown hard
at the waters surface;
a slerissh sound
as the netting cut the surface;
a quiet hiss tiny bubbles trapped by the net breaking the surface.

Stopped by the rope around his wrist
the net settles.
When pulled in, the net contains
flashing silver in its folds.
The fisherman walks on silently thankful
for the bounty and beauty of the sea.

A trip to the archeological site at Coba had been proposed for **Thursday** but our guide did not show up by 0900. He had partied too hardy the night before. He was hung over and his girl friend was mad.

Instead, Charles and I caught a bus for Downtown as Cancun City proper was called. The driver let us off near the Italian embassy to drop a copy of *Cancun* for Sr Pastacinni. Next stop was a two block walk over to Cancun Tips to deliver another copy of *Cancun* to the editor.

Business done for the day, a two dollar cab ride took us to Puerto Juarez and the ferry to Isla Mujeres.

The fare was ten pesos each for the 40 minute ferry ride. Sand patches and dark areas of coral or sea grasses flashed beneath us. A large, round moving dark spot appeared - a ray crossing a sandy area. A car ferry crossed our bow headed for Punta Sam, a port just north of Puerto Juarez. Two charter boats rigged for marlin were returning with no trophy flags flying.

As we approached the dock on Isla Mujeres some of the more enterprising vendors jumped on board before we docked.

A short three block walk took us across the island to the northern beach. The streets were made of paving blocks and most of the cars were light weight. Mopeds and bicycles were the primary traffic.

There were few shells so we walked back. For lunch I had lime soup and fried bananas while Charles had a steak sandwich. We both ordered watermelon water to drink, Aqua de Sandia.

After a few shop stops we took a taxi to the lighthouse on Punta Sur, the southeastern tip of the island. The taxi skimmed the east coast past the Navy barracks and past a mile or so of wind blown barren areas.

The lighthouse was just that, a small, automated lighthouse. The lighthouse keeper lived in a house on site and sold cold drinks, table cloths and shark jaws and kept watched over the archeological site.

A couple hundred meters south of the lighthouse stood the ruins of the Temple of the Women. It consisted of a small raised platform with one partial wall still standing. This was surrounded by the stones that were once parts of the other walls. Spaniards purportedly had found terra cotta figurines that were fertility fetishes for Ixchel, the fertility and harvest goddess. Hence one possible origin for the name, Isla Mujeres. (Another suggestion is that Pirates left their women on the island in relative safety when they headed out to attack Spanish shipping.)

The sites historical marker was in tatters from various storms and had not been repaired.

The temple presided over the sea from an impressive point rising forty feet from the crashing waves. The view was of a rocky coast, sea caves and magnificent blue sea. The water was shallow and dotted with reefs. Cancun hotels defiled the skyline about five miles to the south. A couple was sitting on a rock shelf at the end of the island enjoying the scene, the solitude and each others company.

Temple of Ixchel

The Temple of Ixchel

If this were indeed the Temple of Ixchel
then maidens wishing children
would here temporarily dwell
and, as in Diana's temples of ancient Greece
consult a number of young, learned
and helpful priests
and, as from many a restful vacation,
return blessed with procreation.

The marine park at Garrafon Beach was a ten minute walk down a dusty trail through thorny vegetation to the highway and another five minutes down the highway past a couple of abandoned houses.

We went swimming but there was a breeze and a two foot swell that made snorkeling rough. A ray was seen flitting along the bottom but not many other fish. The ebbing tide was about to turn and the fish were hiding. We got out and changed clothes as the park was closing and caught a taxi for the five km ride back to town. The driver picked up a singer with his guitar who practiced several songs on the way back to town. A ferry was preparing to leave so we hurried aboard and were back in Cancun by 1730.

The hotel had a native (?) fiesta scheduled for the evening. The menu had roast pig, a chicken dish, fresh fruit, black beans, achote rice and an avocado dip. Drinks were half price so we each had a couple Pina Coladas without rum. Entertainment was a trio that performed two Indian dances and played native music. Neither the music nor the dance were Mayan. The flute music was from Peru. One of the dances was the Aztec legend of Popocatepetl and Ixtacchihuatl and how the lovers were turned into volcanoes near Mexico City. The other dance was the Aztec legend of the Quetzel bird. Apparently the other guests did not know the difference but the hotel should not call it a Maya fiesta.

Friday was the last full day and we were on our way to Tulum and Akumal. Tulum was the largest Mayan coastal city and located 96 miles south of Cancun.

We stopped about 90 miles along for a rest stop. I was taking a picture of an Oriole nest when a local native said these were "Nepa" or pajarotte (little bird). Nests of the Altamira Oriole were common hanging from power lines and trees along the highway. Along the Amazon similar nests were an indicator of an open stream bed or river where the nest hung out over the water. The bird was a possible relative newcomer since Yucatan has no streams. Roads and power line right-of-ways provided the same edge effect and Yucatan was a few hundred miles less of a migration flight.

Hundreds of swallowtail butterflies, <u>Papilio</u> <u>polyxenes,</u> were "puddling" or taking water from puddles and muddy spots at the rest stop. I picked several from the bus radiator along with a Queen butterfly, <u>Anosia</u> <u>berenice</u>, that looks much like the Monarch.

Tropical almond trees (<u>Terminalia</u> <u>Catappa</u>) were in fruit and the butterfly bush (<u>Budhinia sp.</u>) was also covered with red-orange blossoms. Mostly, the stop was for sodas and souvenirs before we got to the shops at Tulum.

Temple of the Descending God

Tulum was unique in that there were only three walls. It was built on a thirty foot limestone bluff overlooking the sea. The walled area covered several hundred acres and had a number of native stone structures. Entrance to the site was single file through a Judas gate in a wall about fifteen feet high and almost as thick. Watch towers were located on the two inland corners of the wall. Several thousand peasants had lived outside the gate to provide food and other products that kept the thousand or so soldiers, priests, scholars and royalty going. Our guide was not very knowledgeable and preferred to speak Spanish.

The first structures we visited were tombs dedicated to the temple of the sun. They, like most of Tulum structures, were closed to public and were being restored. Next was the Temple of Frescoes which had a number of paintings still visible and a sundial in the inner court that had been used to determine the equinox. Many of the frescoes have fertility connotations. We passed Temple of Columns and House of Halach Uinik with a carving of the Descending God, "the first skin diver" according to our guide. It and the Temple of the Descending God near the Castle were probably related to the sunset.

Tulim Castle and beach

The path wound over what had been the market place. A few stone platforms and foundations were still visible. The House on the Cenote sat on an outcrop above a shallow cave with a spring. The cave roof was home for a hundred or so cave swallows. The guide said the park was closed at night because wild animals still came there to drink at the cenote including Jaguar.

Swallow in Cenote roof

Several small shrines and the Temple of the Wind stood on a high bluff over looking the beach. These were not explained but they had obviously been used because the rock access was worn and polished and slippery to the unwary foot.

Below this was a small beach that had been used as a natural harbor for the royal trading fleet. The beach was now occupied by bathers.

The Castle was located on a hill south of the beach. It was the largest complex in Tulum and primarily used for ceremonies. The complex contained several temples, alters and ceremonial platforms including the Temple of the Ascending God. Below the Castle was a narrow cut in the bluff that had provided protection but now allowed access to the sea.

Tulum was a holy site during the Caste War. It was located about sixty miles northeast of Santa Cruz, the rebel capitol and thirty miles from Chun Pom, the home of the Maya rebel prophet, Florentino Cituk. The Tulum structures were smaller and crude compared with other temple sites like Chiche'n Itz'a.

In 1842, John Stephens was one of the first Europeans to visit and describe Tulum. Explorers did not return because of the rebel scare.

In 1895, a group from the Columbian Field Museum anchored off shore. They were afraid they would be attacked and did not land.

Several other expeditions did not land because they did not trust the rebel intentions. Howe and Parmelee from Harvard spent two days exploring the ruins in 1911 but left when fresh signs were found. The pair were apparently trying to remove some artifacts.

Drs Sylvanus Morely and Jesse Nusbaum, sponsored by the School of American Research in Santa Fe, spent a few hours in Tulum in 1913. Hearing of a peace agreement Dr Morely returned for four days in 1916 sponsored by the Carnegie Institution.

Prince William of Sweden visited Tulum in 1920 and was met by a small group of Mexican soldiers that showed them through the ruins.

It was 1922 before a relative peace that permitted investigation of the site.

After only an hour at Tulum we reboarded the bus for the twenty five mile ride to Akumal. This was a bay protected by the reef with a narrow white sand beach. Thousands of sea turtles formerly came to this beach to lay their eggs. It is now home of several beach resorts. We had lunch and were allowed an hour to swim. I walked a mile of beach and found no shells. I did find a used plastic syringe. We tried to snorkel but the tide was turning with turbulent water due to density layers and sand/silt. The hotel freshwater pool offered a welcome rinse. We reboarded the bus about 1500 and were back in Cancun by 1730.

Supper on this last night was at the Hard Rock Cafe. It was much like Planet Hollywood in being a pleasant surprise. It was full but not crowded and the food was good and moderately priced. It is definitely my kind of place.

A Saturday morning walk down the beach to Punta Cancun essentially finished the trip. We packed up and checked out.

While waiting for transportation to the airport I called Ms Green, the editor of *Cancun Tips*. She said they were not interested in my book and did not know how they would use poetry. We discussed several of my observations and she gave me the number for the Sian Ka'an Biosphere Reserve. I called this number and talked with one of the staff.

We were on the plane by 1300 and in San Antonio about 2200.

AFTERTHOUGHTS

A Mayan proverb says, "He who makes an enemy of the earth makes an enemy of his own body." In my opinion that at this time Cancun and Yucatan have several environmental and infrastructure problems with fairly easy solutions. The longer they wait the more expensive the solutions will be to implement.

1. Air pollution. Presently there is no serious smog problem but there was one day in the 14 days I spent there. Most of the vehicles are old, many are diesel powered, and there does not seem to be any emission standards. The old vehicles have squeeling asbestos brakes. Set and enforce air emission standards.
2. Noise. People do not like noise. It's time to for controls when some of the clubs can be heard blocks away. Set and enforce noise standards.
3. Montazuma's revenge did not appear to be a problem. However, a good water and sewage treatment to meet US EPA standards would be good advertising for the tourist dollar.
4. Although the tourist industry preaches green or environmental tours none of the tours I took stopped to look at the vegetation, etc. and the guides could not answer most of my questions.
5. Guides need a certification program to weed out the baloney and pass on accurate information.

2

Puerto Valarta

HEY MOMMA,
WHEN WE GOIN' AGAIN?

by

Carl Lahser

Mexico City and Puerto Vallarta
in December 1995

Fore play.

We had been putting off visiting Mexico City. The opportunity finally came for a couple days in Mexico City on the way to Puerto Vallarta.

"Getting there is half the fun" is usually true for me. Planning and research time is set aside to find what can be seen prior to the visit. After visit research both identifies and explains more about what was seen and often uncovers things missed on site. I never seem to have enough time to get ready, but it usually falls together at the proper time.

This trip was to Mexico City and Puerto Vallarta in December 1995. I reviewed guidebooks for Mexico including Fodor's Mexico, Frommer's Puerto Vallarta, Manzanillo and Guadalajara, and an old copy of Frommer's Mexico and Guatemala on $15 and $20 a Day formed a basis for the trip. Berler's The Conquest of Mexico which is a modern review of Prescott's History of the Conquest of Mexico and The Political Economy of Mexico by Glade and Anderson gave some insight into the history and development of that country.

For natural history, I looked at Bailey's Manual of Cultivated Plants and Hortus Second and Flowering Plants and Ferns of Arizona by Kearny and Peebles, A Field Guide to Pacific Coast Shells, A Field Guide to Western Birds, and Butterflies of the Western US by Oppler.

For health and safety, I checked the US State Department Traveler's Advisory for Mexico and the Armed Forces Medical Information Center's Monthly Disease Occurrence (Worldwide).

I made airline reservations on Aeromexicana in August to Puerto Vallarta (PV in California slang) planning to leave San Antonio on Saturday (2 Dec) returning on Saturday (9 Dec). In November Aeromexico cancelled our return flight because of overbooking for holiday traffic for the Festival of the Virgin of Guadalupe (the patron saint of Mexico) on 9 - 12 December. This was, in a way, opportune since the weekday flights were about ten per cent cheaper. I rescheduled the flight to leave Thursday (29 Nov.) with two days in Mexico City before continuing on to PV and returning on the following Friday.

Hotel reservations in Mexico City were made at the Calinda Geneve Quality Inn using their 800 number. The difference in the air fare paid for one night's room.

We had a timeshare condo reserved for Puerto Vallarta at the Sheraton Buganvilla through Resort Condominiums International (RCI).

Mexico City.

Thursday. Aeromexico's Airbus A320 aircraft left San Antonio on time. We flew south and crossed the Rio Grande River east of Laredo, passed over Monterrey and, near Ciudad Victoria, saw the lake backed up by the Vicente Guerrero Dam on the Rio Soto.

The A320 was the best riding airliner I had flown on to date; very smooth and quiet. The meal and beverage service was outstanding. I was favorably impressed with the professional appearance and demeanor of Aeromexicana's cabin crew and the ground crew. Of course, this is subject to change.

About thirty minutes north of Mexico City, we crossed a range of mountains, and the clouds took on a gray-brown color. We had been in and out of the clouds several times when the snow covered peaks of Popocatapetl and Ixtaccihuatl came into view.

These mountains are both over 17,000 feet above sea level and have a permanent mantle of snow. In Aztec mythology Popocatapetl was a warrior who was in love with Ixtaccihuatl (the sleeping lady) before they were changed into mountains.

We began our letdown through a white haze into the Valley of Anahuac (the Mexico City basin) passing over numerous suburbs for almost ten minutes. Visibility varied from two to ten miles. We finally flew over the downtown with almost 2000 churches, historic and modern buildings, buildings of pink and blue and orange and lavender, and numerous parks and boulevards just before landing at the Bénito Juarez International Airport on the eastern edge of the Federal District (D.F.).

A sparrow hawk (Falco sparverius) sat on one of the taxiway signs, and a Blue Heron (Ardea herodias) checked standing water between the runways. Both the runway and taxiway were rough.

The plane stopped, and we were transported to the terminal on a mobile lounge. Baggage and customs were painless, and we were in a cab to the hotel thirty minutes after landing.

The ride to the hotel provided an insight into the crowding in Mexico City. We passed "Sabor Bergerking" and several Dansea snack bar chain outlets on the way. Only one Pemex gas station was passed. Gas stations were not on every corner like in the US.

One of the largest cities in the world it is home to an estimated twenty-two million (22,000,000) residents. Most of the dirty industries, such as a PEMEX refinery, were closed or moved out of town. The intent was to clean up the environment of the Valley of Mexico and to attract skilled workers out of the city. The strategy helped somewhat, but people moved in from rural areas faster than the far fewer skilled workers moved out with industry. The sky was blue overhead but brown-gray with air pollutants up to about forty-five degrees above the horizon.

Another strategy to move traffic has been to make many of the streets one way and adding more lanes by reducing the lane width to 8 -10 feet. Most of the lane marks were obliterated so they drive where there's room. The main streets have four or six sections of two or three lanes divided by tree planted dividers.

Mexico City drivers were patient and remarkably courteous considering their historic reputation of driving with the horn. They would be in deep trouble in any US city where every driver thinks he owns his lane.

The average speed around town appeared to be about 25-30 KPH, but with three or four lanes weaving about it looks like chaos. We, personally, saw no accidents and noted few dented fenders. Although none of the vehicles looked like a real air polluter, smog accumulates. It's probably for the best that forty percent of the cars are inoperable at any one time. There was also a couple thousand pounds of untreated sewage volatized in Mexico City's air every hour.

We checked in about 1430 (2:30 PM). The Hotel Geneve was built in 1912 and had a reputation for patronizing service. It was bought by Quality Inns, remodeled, and given an attitude change under the name of Calinda Geneve. An old slow elevator, skeleton key locks and a full service staff gave a 19th century atmosphere.

We arranged tours for the afternoon and the next day as an orientation to Mexico City and to see the maximum in the time available. The first tour was to begin at 1500 with a ride thirty miles north of town to the pyramids at Teotihuacan. A city tour of the Zocalo, national palace and cathedral and the "floating gardens" at Xochimilco were reserved for Friday.

The driver and guide picked us up in a VW van then picked up four other people at other hotels - a man from India, a woman from Columbia and a couple from Arizona who were Mexican citizens.

The route was roughly north along the Metro line on Avenida Insurgentes to Highway 85.

Most of the hills were covered with housing. Several quarries were evident where limestone and red lava were being removed in vertical lifts.

Dry fields of corn and okra were waiting to be burned. Burning crop waste seemed strange in an area where air pollution was so bad. Smoke from burning fields gags San Antonio at times. Plantations of prickly pear cactus sold prickly pears or "tunas" as an agricultural crop. Blue agave, Agave atrovirens, was grown to produce pulque, fermented agave nectar.

The first stop was at a handicraft center with silver, onyx and obsidian art. Tablecloths made of "henequen", fibers from Agave fourcroydes, were also sold.

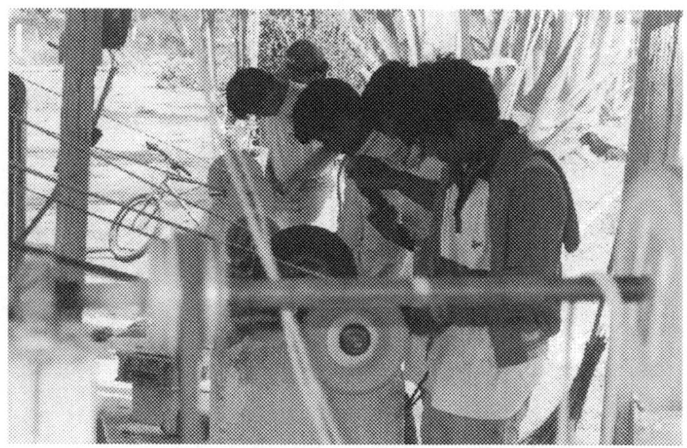

Obsidian Cutters

The management demonstrated the making of pulque. The flowering stem was removed from the center of a large Agave plant and a hollow scooped out where a lightly sweet nectar was collected. In about 24 hours the nectar ferments into agave wine or pulque or distilled into a brandy.

A natural paper was collected from the skin of the agave leaf and agave fibers are extracted to make rope and the coarse fabric called henequen.

We arrived at the north entrance of the historical site about 1600, two hours before closing time. The site was begun about 300 B.C. by a relatively unknown culture that claimed the site was the center of the universe. The area had prospered, and the population peaked about 500 A.D. at about 125,000 inhabitants. Its importance declined and the site was abandoned about 700 A.D. when it was taken over by the Aztecs. The eight square mile site contained two large pyramids, numerous platforms for palaces and temples, and a Temple to Quetzalcoatl.

The tour began with a walk through a partially reconstructed palace. Only the foundations and lower sections of the walls remained but some murals and carvings survived.

This exited down a flight of steps to the Avenue of the Dead. Over a mile long and about a hundred yards wide, the Aztecs called it the Avenue of the Dead because they thought the mounds along the street were tombs.

Avenue of the Dead

The Spanish left the site intact since it was abandoned and no structures were clearly visible. Villages, like Cholula and Pachuca, in the area promised more loot and slaves. The massacre at Cholula is story for another time.

The smaller Pyramid of the Moon dominated the scene being at the north end of the Avenue of the Dead. The pyramid was only about 180 feet tall, but the climb was difficult because the steps were of irregular height and only about eight inches wide.

OTHER PEOPLE'S PYRAMIDS

(Tiotihuacan)

Aztecs slaughtered and sacrificed
friend and foe alike
but they respected the gods

and the dead.
The Spaniards killed in the name
of the Church
and destroyed whole cultures
as a million heathens bled.

**Climbing the Pyramids
at Tiotihuacan**

Sailboats are not the only thing to tack
Its also for adventurous people that
common sense may lack
and want to climb the pyramids.

The steps are about eight inches wide
so the easiest route is serpentine
or diagonally from side to side
to climb the pyramids.

The easy part is going up.
You look around and then start down
then Whoops!
Its a long way down the pyramids

The number of steps and terraces were based on a calendar of ten thirty day months per year and a fifty-two year cycle. I had a hip replaced ten months before and was determined to climb the pyramids to prove that I was in good shape. The altitude added to the challenge since the site is about 7,000 feet above sea level. Many people huffed and puffed just walking around.

I turned back at the top terrace. The top was covered with boulders in no particular order and was poor walking. I shot several pictures of the site and tacked back down across the steps to the Avenue of the Dead.

Live men and children stalked the Avenue selling silver bracelets, carvings of obsidian and other souvenir items. I avoided all of them and found the guide at the base of the Pyramid of the Sun.

I climbed on top of the foundations of the temples that lined the Avenue and was going to take a picture and leave. The guide and a fellow passenger were going to the top, and I couldn't resist a challenge to do something extra dumb. The guide bounded up the steps carrying my camera bag, and I hobbled along behind, sometimes on all fours, puffing all the way.

The steps to the top terrace were the most difficult with a hump in the middle so you began climbing almost straight up and finished almost horizontal. From there it was not far to the top.

Pyramid of the Moon

The temperature was about 70F, the sky was cloudless and the view from the top was outstanding. The Pyramid of the Moon to the north, the Temple of Quetzalcoatl to the south, cactus and desert to the east and west, were framed by the setting sun and by a half-moon about an hour before the zenith.

When we got back down, my fellow passenger wanted to see the rest of the site and said he would meet the van at the south gate. I was pooped and two Cokes dehydrated. I had had enough for one day.

The trip back to the hotel was through the dark. We passed an island of floodlights, the prison where a former president and his brother were being held on drug charges.

The driver found our way to our last stop on the tour, the new Basilica of Guadalupe at the north end of Avenida Insurgentes. The

Basilica was designed by Pedro Rameriz Vasquez. Construction began in 1964. The Basilica was completed and dedicated in 1976. Located on the site of the Aztec Temple of Tonantzin (the mother of the gods), the Temple was replaced by a small Catholic chapel which was replaced in 1531 by a larger chapel to commemorate the appearances of the Virgin Mary to a recently converted Indian on 9 and 12 December, 1531.

TEMPLE PLACES

It seems strange that the Basilica
was built on the site of a church
built on top of a chapel
built on top of an Aztec temple
that had been modified over time.

Anthropologists say that a site
suited as a city or temple
is reused for that purpose
like a crook returns to the scene of the crime.
A hill is a hill that fact persists
regardless of culture or clime.

The original chapel was over utilized and had been damaged by earthquakes. The second chapel was replaced by a larger, more ornate basilica in the 18th century. The basilica was damaged by several earthquakes and fire and had become structurally dangerous.

The new Basilica seemed to have a life of its own. Two processions, including people who had walked on their knees from their villages arrived while we were there. We had seen one pilgrimage along the road near the pyramids. Services appeared to be around the clock.

A collection of stores surrounded the entrance to the site and carried numerous religious artifacts. Beggars occupied locations on the steps leading to the square in front of the Basilica and the steps leading to the Shrine. Vendors of all kinds had stalls around the square.

The architecture was complex and the size was heroic, but I was really too tired to enjoy it. Because of the time of day the tour did not include the nearby colonial cemetery.

We returned to the hotel about 2000 and went out for supper. Streets and restaurants were full but not crowded. It was late November and cool but flower beds along the streets contained blooming pink and lavender azaleas, blue irises and red roses.

Dia de Guadalupe

The Virgin Mary produced
a red rose to prove her visitation.
Red roses bloom on December 12
to mark this celebration.

The red rose is the flower of the Virgin of Guadalupe.

Supper was at a nearby night club - tough steak and Mexican beer.

Friday. We were up early. We would have been up shortly anyway because construction work began down the hall about 0700 and continued until about 2100. We had a continental breakfast and started a city tour at 0800.

This time it was just us and the guide and a driver. We went through the hotel dining room and out the back door across the street from the central police headquarters. There were about a dozen police were dressed in green uniforms with riding boots and spurs armed with flak jackets and automatic weapons. No parking was permitted and the police even looked carefully at vehicles that stopped to pickup or drop passengers.

As we drove north along the Avenida Insurgentes, the guide pointed out hotels and monuments. We turned on to the Paseo de la Reforma at the Glorieta Cuauhtemoc with its 31 gilded angels, passed the Glorieta Colo'n, then turned east on Juarez at the old art deco National Lottery. A block to the west was the Monument to the Revolution. Several hotels and other buildings damaged in the earthquake of 1985 were still standing awaiting demolition. They were filled with squatters from the countryside.

To the east on Juarez was the new glass and steel National Lottery building. We passed Alameda Park, the Belle Artes (Palace of Fine Arts) with murals by Rivera, Orozco and Siqueiros, the Bank of Mexico and La Torre Latinoamericana (the Latin American Tower).

Avenida Juarez became Avenida Madero. At the intersection with Avenida Lazaro Cardenas was the Casas de Azuleos or House of Tiles. This colonial building covered in blue and white tiles was built in the late 1500s for the Counts of the Valley of Orizaba near Veracruz.

Further down on Madero was the Iturbide Palace. It was built for Don Augustin de Iturbide who proclaimed himself Agustin I, Emperor of Mexico in 1822. He reigned less than two months.

Zocalo

At the Zócalo, we walked across a plaza that must occupy ten acres. The area got its name, Zócalo, from the Mexican word for base or pedestal. In 1843, a pedestal was constructed for a monument that was never built. As a result, the main plaza in many Mexican towns is called the zócalo.

Street photographers were taking pictures of people and their kids in the plaza chasing and feeding a flock of pigeons.

The National Palace, on the east side of the Zócalo, was begun by Hernán Cortés after he defeated the Aztecs. It was built on the site of the main Aztec pyramid using stones from the pyramids. Spanish viceroys and Mexican presidents lived in this structure until the Emperor

Maximilian. He and modern presidents used it as an office building. Maximilian designed the Avenida de la Reforma leading from his castle in Chapultepec Park to the Zocalo after the Champs d'Élyées in Paris.

Inside the stairwell of the National Palace was a mural by Diego Rivera illustrating the history of Mexico completed in the 1950's. A number of smaller murals were painted between the doors on the second floor porch around the central patio but Rivera died before completing all of the murals.

To the north of the Palace, the base of Templo Major, the Great Temple of the Aztecs, was recently discovered during some demolition. More excavation and some restoration will continue long into the future.

New Cathedral

The Metropolitan Cathedral was also constructed from the stones of the Aztec temples. It had a number of chapels and outstanding carvings around the main altar. There were crypts below the Cathedral floor. Part of the problem with tours is they have their schedule to keep and ten minutes to walk through the Cathedral was much too short.

Beggars sat outside the door of the Cathedral. Around the corner, on Avenida de Cinco de Febrero, day workers patiently waited with signs advertising their specialty - painter, electrician, etc. Unemployment all over Mexico was high as was the rate of inflation. These combined to bring about a large underground business community that worked for cash or barter and rampant tax avoidance.

The van took us back to Reforma. We passed the Plaza de Garabaldi, known as the plaza of the mariachi. Groups and single singers and musicians waited for work. This was recommended for an evening visit for the music.

The next stop was at the Central Crafts Market. It was interesting but looked like the semi-permanent San Antonio flea markets. The prices and variety were little different from the Mercado in San Antonio where there was no duty and no shipping problems.

It was noon, and I told the driver we would like to find a place for lunch. Their reply was, "in a minute". This must have been a Mexican minute because we went to the Museum of Anthropology for an hour. An hour allowed us to see the Aztec room only. The museum was a massive structure with separate halls for many of the cultures that originated in Mexico.

This was but one of a number of museums in Chapultepec Park. Others included the Museums of Modern Art, Natural History, Technology, National History and an 18th century Castle. There was also a lake, an amusement park and a zoo.

We managed to get a Coke before continuing our Mexican minute to Xochimilco. While we drank the Cokes we sat and watched a performance of the Totonac Indian voladores. It is originally from El Tajín between Tampico and Veracruz. Five men climb a 20-meter pole. Four of them sat on the edge of a platform while the fifth danced and played drum and whistle. The music stops and the four launch themselves backward into space and swing around thirteen times as ropes attached to their ankles unwound and the four approached the ground. This was a fertility rite where four macaw-men make invocations to the four corners of the universe and bring the sun and rain with them. Back on the ground they hit the crowd for donations.

Our tour passed the Castle. The Castle was an Aztec fortress and built into its present form in the 1780s. It was used as a military college during the time of the Mexican War when the US Marines captured Mexico in 1847. At the base of Chapultepec hill, along the Reforma was the Niños Heroes, a monument to six cadets who jumped to their death rather than surrender to the Marines. In the the 1860s, the Empress Carlotta would watch her husband, Maximilian, parade down the

Reforma to the Zócalo. She also designed the grounds and gardens that surround the Castle. The Castle was still used as the official home of the president.

Our route passed through University City, the former Olympic Village, and led down Friendship Boulevard lined with the statues donated by various countries after the Olympics. We flew past the exclusive Jardines del Pedregal (Lava Garden) protected ecological zone and residential area where the Xitle volcano erupted 2,000 years ago, the round Cuicuilco Pyramid near Tlalpan, the colonial community of San Angel and finally arrived at Xochimilco. The tour schedule did not allow time to visit these areas, but they were supposed to contain interesting features to be investigated during future trips.

Xochimilco

Xochimilco or "field of flowers", was fifteen miles south of the Zócalo. It is one of the few areas of the Valley of Mexico to survive from Aztec times unchanged. A shallow silty lake was modified into las chinampas or floating gardens between 1300 B.C. and expanded by the Aztecs between 1300 and 1500 A.D. There were five lakes in the Basin: Xaltocan, Zumpango, Texcoco, Xochimilco and Chalco. The swampy southern areas were changed into productive farmland producing up to 7300 kilograms per hectare of corn. The term chinampas came from the Náhuatl chinamitl or fence of cane and from chinampan, within the fence. Channels were dug by the young chinamperos, and the spoil transported on flat bottom boats to become piles used as garden plots. A chinampa was outlined with poles and reinforced with willow stakes and matting to retain the soil. This farming method has been studied by many countries.

The Aztecs were not pleasant landlords so the natives of Xochimilco supported the Spaniards in the final invasion that defeated the Aztecs.

The signs leading to the gardens read, "Los Embarcaderos", the boats. We boarded one of maybe a hundred "Trajineras", the hand poled tour boats. Tourist do not actually get to see the farming areas.

It was Friday and few of the boats in the passenger fleet were occupied. However, the canals seemed crowded with boats - boats with troubadours; boats that sold food and jewelry; water-borne photographers with old, hand made cameras that waited along the water's edge; boats with old women who sold flowers. A few boats were hauling laborers as well as cement and other construction materials.

The banks extended three to ten feet above the water level and were interlaced with tree roots and other vegetation. These gardens are not floating by any means.

A pleasant hour on the canals returned us to the docks. Another thirty minute ride took us back to the hotel by 1530. The Mexican minute was over, and I was starving.

Lunch was of regional Mexican food at one of the hotel restaurants. We intended to go out for supper later, but a couple hours later I had a bout with enteritis which lasted most of the next week.

Saturday. We packed up and checked out of the hotel by noon. The Tagamet I was taking did nothing for the heartburn and neither did a bottle of Maalox.

A cab to the airport started us on the next leg of our trip.

The plane took off towards the south and circled over the remainder of the lakes and water supply for the city. We passed across the southern part of the city and turned northwest. There were a number of large quarries and reservoirs covered with water meal (Lemna sp.) We passed over Toluca, then over dry farmed lands, then over a series of east-west oriented ridges and deep canyons. Just north of Cuidad Hidalgo was Lago de Cuitzeo on the Rio Lerma. We continued WNW across the Parque National Lago de Camecurao. We passed to the south of Lago de Chapala 35 miles south of Guadalajara. The water level in the lake had dropped 20-30 feet. It served as the water supply for Guadalajara and a source for local irrigation. One of the major causes of the low water level was the illegal pumping up stream on the Rio Lerma. Lake Chapala was still one of the sacred lakes of the Huichol Indians.

South and west of Guadalajara, big green valleys extended northwest into the Sierra la Primavera Mountains. Lago Atotonilco Reservoir was southward down the Coahuayana River between the Sierra Manzanillo to the east and the Sierra de Tepala to the west.

The plane turned almost straight west across the rough Sierra de Tepala Mountains just south of the Rio Ameca. The Ameca looped north and then swung southwest entering Bahia de Banderas north of Puerto Vallerta.

Several valleys were spotted with what appeared to be oil well drilling sites. Further west, logging roads led to large clear-cut forests. The clearings supported cattle. The narrow roads were marked with light colored landslides and mines.

The Pacific, actually Bahia de Banderas, came into view as we let down along the Rio Ameca. The bay is one of the largest in the world measuring 19 by 25 miles. It was a stopping place for food, water, and firewood for the 16th century Spaniards on their way to the Intendancy de Vieja California (Baja California) or the Isla de Perlas (Island of Pearls) in the Sea of Cortez (Gulf of California). We followed the Rio Ameca to a beautiful landing on its one runway. The approach was from the north towards the center of downtown.

Vegetation visible from the plane left little doubt we were in the tropics. Tall Coconut palms (Cócos nucífera), toxic red castor beans (Rícinus commúnis), local mahogany trees (Cercocárpus betuloídes), cecropia (Cecrópia palmáta), Huisache (Acacia smallii), Hibiscus (H. chinensis and H. rosea), Bougainvilla of several colors and other tropical plants grew in disturbed areas or as ornamentals around the airport.

Baggage handling was efficient, and we were out of the terminal in about 15 minutes.

Puerto Vallarta.

As we walked out the door, we were approached by a representative of the "Puerto Vallarta Condominium Assn.". He was really a shill for one of the time-share condominiums offering taxi and breakfast but wanting a $20 deposit to make sure we would show up. The deposit was a new twist.

A twenty peso ($2) cab ride took us to the Sheraton. We checked in, and our luggage was taken to the condo management office where they wanted to set an appointment to sell their condo timeshare program.

Eventually we got to the room - a bedroom, bath, kitchenette and a living room with two day beds. Cable TV carried mostly stateside programs. One channel was a Denver station that was reporting on their recent snow storm.

I was not hungry so I drank a coke and crashed. The beach and unpacking could wait for a while.

Sunday morning I was up about six. The hotel was less than a mile from the center of town. La Inglesia de Nuestra Señora de Guadalupe (the Church of our Lady of Guadalupe) clanged its bells in the call to early mass at 0600. This happened every morning and served as the alarm clock for the central PV area.

I did my morning exercises, had a cup of tea and went out to look at the beach. A quiet walk along the beach just after low tide looking for shells did me a world of good.

The beach of Bahia de Banderas was composed of cobbles and well worn rocks. Some appeared to be petrified wood. Most were of volcanic origin including lava, breccia, and granite. There were also wafers of red sandstone and small chunks of gray and white marble.

The only birds that were up with the sun were the numerous Great-tailed or Mexican Grackles (Cassidix mexicanus) around the hotels, a lone Anhinga (Anhinga anhinga) flying across the bay and a flight of six White-tailed Tropicbirds (Phaenthon aerthereus) looking for a thermal along the beach front to boost them to soaring altitude.

The base halves of California oysters (Ostrea lurida expansa Carp.) remained on the seawall or "malecon".

On an abandoned concrete pier four species of shells were found at or near the high water mark:

Acamea fenestrata Reeve	(the fenestrate limpet);
Acamea testudinalis Esch.	(plate limpet);
Littorina aspera Phil.	(Periwinkle)
L. scabra (angulifera) (Linne)	(variegated periwinkle).

An upper valve of an immature Ostrea fisheri Dall (Fisher's oyster) was found on the beach.

A number of shells were offered for sale as local shells including a large Little Deer Cowry for 200 NS (the new or devaluated pesos, about

$20 US), Hexaplex erythrostomus, and several Olives, but the vendors did not know anything about the shells.

Seeds or "sea beans" on the beach included young coconut (Cocos nucifera), tropical almond (Terminalia catappa L.), mango (Manganifera indica) and black mangrove (Avicennia nitida). Jungles to the north and south provided a ready source for these beach artifacts. Some, like the mango, was probably local refuse that found its way into the bay. Thanks to a lack of gulls and shore birds a shrimp was found on the beach. It looked like a Peneid about two inches long colored tan with olive drab spots.

BANDARAS BAY

Bandaras Bay is second in size
on the whole Pacific coast
The bottom is rocks and boulders
with few shell of which to boast

I returned in time to sit through a presentation on the Sheraton time share concept. The primary difference was that the week in the condo could be traded in for two weeks in the hotel. In return for our time we were given breakfast and cut-rate tour prices.

We took a cab to the market beside the Cuale River at the end of Ave de Rodriquez and spent a couple hours shopping.

When we returned to the hotel I was still not feeling well. About eight on Sunday evening my wife was concerned with my lack of appetite and dehydration and called the hotel medical emergency number. The doctor said he would see me at 2200. He diagnosed bacterial enteritis, gave me an IV for dehydration, a course of medication (buscapina, percodan and chloramphenicol) and told me to avoid spicy, greasy food and alcohol for a week. This regimen did the job and cost $90 which was nonrefundable by our HMO, Humana, because I did not call then ahead of time.

Monday morning I was almost back amongst the living, and we scheduled a tour of the city and the local jungle.

While we waited for the tour I noted that the hotel landscaping was over-planted with its theme of coconut, philodendron, ficus and hibiscus.

It also lacked some of the other common tropical plants such as Geiger trees, Flame trees, Ixoria and Frangipani. These trees and shrubs were found in the landscapes of other hotels and public areas.

Our tour bus picked up clients at other hotels, then proceeded along hotel row describing them as we drove. We passed by the 555 boat slips in Marina Vallarta and airport. After crossing the Rio Mascota we turned inland to the village of Ixtapa.

Ixtapa was a farming and bedroom community about ten miles north of downtown PV. Minimum wage for workers was supported at 15 NS (about $2 US) a day. Tenants could become owners of condos and apartments in public housing by living in the unit for thirty years.

Public schools were free and mandatory through grade 10. School hours were 0700-1300 or 1400-2000 to allow children to work to help support the family. The state and national universities were free on completion of grade ten. Two years of English was mandatory. There were also schools for many private and church sponsored schoolsfor those whoss could afford the fee. Several of the private schools were bilingual, dividing instruction between Spanish and English. Most of the schools required uniforms.

The stop in Ixtapa was near the old Catholic church on the zócalo (Remember that word?) Most of the town businesses were around the square. There were also small businesses such as raspa and lemonade vendors, a photographer and jewelry displays.

The plaza, like the streets, was constructed of paving brick. A bandshell dominated half the plaza and basketball court occupied the other half. A variety of tropical vegetation including coconut trees, Flame trees, Ficus trees and red and yellow Hibiscus, decorated and separated the areas and provided shade for benches around the plaza. I rested for a few minutes on a bench on the rincõn de viejo, a corner where old men while away their days watching the girls.

On the west side of the plaza sat a church covered in a tile mosaic. There were twin bell towers but the upper bells were present in only one. (Catholic churches usually have different styles for each of their bell towers so that the church will not be perfect.) Different from many, this church had a clock and a flag pole between the towers. It was furnished with wooden pews and bare walls.

THINGS THAT ARE AND AREN'T

Jerusalem Palms and Travelers Palms
are not what their names imply
Jerusalem Palms are cycads
and older than palms, by the way
Travelers Palms are banana trees
whose leaves have a special splay

About twenty minor archeological sites are registered around Ixtapa but these are not on the tourist routes and not of casual interest. Some could be developed but I won't hold my breathe.

The next stop on the tour was Viejo Vallarta, "Old Town". A port on Banderas Bay was established in 1587 under the leadership of Captain Pedro de Unamuno. No proper community existed before 1851. Sr Guadalupe Sanchez Torres, who lived in Cihuatlan, Jalisco, made a living by shipping salt to the local mining operations. He decided to move his family and arrived on the bay on 12 Dec, 1851. He named the spot Las Peñas de Santa Maria de Guadalupe after the big rocks in the bay now called Los Arcos and the feast day of the patron saint of Mexico. The village of Las Peñas grew to about 1500 people by 1880 and became a municipality in 1918. Its name was changed to Puerto Vallarta for Sr. Ignacio L. Vallarta. Vallarta was the governor of state of Jalisco and had materially aided the defeat of General Zapata. Population in 1990 was about 250,000.

Streets were made of paving tile with ten foot lanes and narrow or no sidewalks. Most of the commercial buildings were multi-story with residences on the top floors. Most of the buildings had ends of reinforcing rods extending out of the roof to show that the structure was not yet completed and deserving of a tax break.

A flying drive along the Malecon pointed out statues of the boy on a seahorse and two dolphins There was one of Sr Vallarta in the main plaza near the bandstand.

We made two stops for shopping and a two-minute stop to see "Gringo Gulch" where many Americans had high-priced homes. Elizabeth Taylor's Casa Kimberly with its foot bridge to Richard Burton's house was highlighted. (Tours of the house were available.)

We made quick photo stops at Conchas Chinas, Camino Real, the Inter-continental Presidente hotel.

Beach and fishing

There was no good spot to stop an see Los Arcos. These huge stones fell off the mountain into the bay and gave Las Peñas its name.

A short stop was made at Mismaloya where a shipyard operated in 16th and 17th centuries. Two ships had been built that were used in the settling of California.

Mismaloya was also the site of the filming of *Night of the Iguana* with Elizabeth Taylor and Richard Burton.

Gringo Gulch Liz and Burtons

The tour stopped for lunch at El Edén. Located about three miles up the Mismaloya River, the site was built for some scenes in the first *Predator* movie with Arnold Swarzenegger. It had no phone or electricity but outstanding atmosphere and food.

We sat overlooking the river and watched butterflies cruise the gorge. I saw a Pale Swallowtail, Papilio eurymedon, along the road. Several large blue-white Morpho butterflies, both black-and-white and black-and-yellow Zebras, several species of sulfurs and an Orange Tip cruised the walls and puddled. The rock walls near the water line were covered with ferns. Trees included gumbo-limbo, cecropia, mahogany. Soil along the road was a tan loess. A termite nest in a tree 30 feet above the water marked the high water line for the rainy season. A large, bright red dragonfly chased mosquitoes and other small prey. No birds were heard or seen.

We returned to the hotel late. Deciding to eat out, we took a cab to Archie's Wok. The cab took the long way towards the mountains to Ave Libramiento, the bypass route for Highway 200. The road dove into and through a tunnel a couple hundred yards long. This was one of the most air polluted tunnels I ever experienced. We finally arrived at Archie's. The Thai food including my fruit curry was very well prepared. Music was provided by a flutist and a couple kids passed by the open window offering gum for sale.

Mismaloya River

Tuesday's trip was to San Blas for birds and a swamp trip. San Blas was about 90 miles (150KM) north of PV and about 25 miles (40 KM) west of Tepic, the capital of the state of Nayarit. Our bus followed the relatively new Highway 200 and crossed the Rio Ameca just below its junction with the Rio Mascota at Las Juntas. Near Mezcales

Los Archos

we turned into Neuvo Vallarta, an exclusive group of condos and homes. The area was impressive but the passengers did not show up. Ponds in the delta of the Ameca River were covered with ducks and shore birds and surrounded with patches of moonflower.

We passed through Bucerias and began to climb over a band of hills, the Sierra de Vallejo, and then up the valley. Ranges of fog-shrouded hills were covered by a variety of tall trees and several species of palms. Scattered farms raised tobacco and pineapples. In the jungle near Las Piedras was a site where some of the scenes from *Predator* were filmed. The new resort of Rincón de Guayavitos catered primarily to the Mexican nationals.

Most of the 47,000 acres of farm land was irrigated from wells using center pivot systems. Some citrus, mangos and papaya were produced and new specialty crops such as oriental vegetables were being raised for the California market. New cash crops were needed because the decline in smoking in the US had decreased the tobacco crop by 60 percent. There was one large cattle ranch where corn was raised for cattle feed.

At Las Varas, a road lead westward towards Jacocotan, Santa Cruz and San Blas. Several small towns existed along the way, each with its public school and public building. Many large farms had disappeared and had been replaced by smaller family farms and cottage industries such as adobe brick making. Adobe brick sold for about 200 NS per thousand and producing a thousand bricks was a good day's work for the family. These same bricks would cost about $600 in San Antonio.

Arriving at the embarcadero (dock) we split into two groups of ten and climbed into two "pangas", shallow draft aluminum boats with 40 horse outboard engines. The first hour and a half we would cruise through a mangrove forest looking for birds, turtles, crocodiles, and alligators. There would be a visit to an alligator farm and then a short ride to Tovara Springs for lunch before the return to the bus.

The trip began down a channel under a canopy black mangrove trees with interlacing branches that blocked out the sun. Ferns and bromeliads grew on the branches. Salinity changed the dominant tree to red mangrove and the overhead cover thinned and a blue sky appeared.

Mangrove tunnel

This quiet waterway wound through tall grasses and large mounds of spider lilies. Occasional trees sported hanging vines and colonies of bromeliads with red bloom stalks and dainty blue flowers.

Turtles sunned themselves on logs or the banks with most of them hitting the water as we approached. The water was clear but dark colored with organic material.

A Northern Boat-Billed Heron (Cochlearius selection) sat in a mangrove tree just out of reach. Birds roosted on the limbs of several dead snags along the channel. Anginas and American and Snowy Egrets (Egret egret and E. hula) were not overly disturbed at our approach. A tropical kingfisher flew out of sight. Several kingbirds had their kingdoms staked out. A green heron (Butorides virescens) took wing from the cane while a Great Blue Heron (Ardea herodias) ignored us. A Gila Woodpecker (Centurus uropygualis) beat upon a dead tree.

We passed an opening where grazing cattle and cattle egrets (Bubulcus ibis) were visible. Alligators occasionally took a calf but usually fed on fish and turtles.

Several alligators were seen hiding under the undercut bank and a couple small crocodiles were seen sunning in the shore. Hydrocottyl or pennywort, H. rotundifolia, the size of silver dollars, grew on a floating log.

A flock of Sinaloa Crows (Corvus sinaloae) greeted us at the government alligator farm. Several pens of alligators and crocodiles were being reared for release. Imported broodstock provided a broader gene pool and a number of young are released each year but poaching had kept the population low. Chickens were served as alligator food.

A short ride from the alligator farm brought us to Tovarus Spring for lunch.

Several of our companions went swimming in the cool, clear water of the spring. The pool also supported a number of large (ten pound) blue catfish and pan fish that looked like the Rio Grande Perch.

The water was clear and percolated through the bottom at the base of a hill. The area around the spring margin was rocked in and a restaurant was constructed along one side. About a dozen tables were located under a portál. Lunch was either steak or fish. This facility also lacked utilities except running water pumped by a gasoline generator.

Light blue Morpho butterflies cruised the spring. Bright gold and pale yellow sulfurs and several beautiful Orange Julias (Dryas julia) butterflies puddled in the water left on the headwall by the swimmers.

About 1400 we reboarded the pangas and returned to the bus. We entered the town of San Blas and turned south and up hill at the main intersection. Houses along the road had cactus and weeds on the roof and laundry hanging on the front porch.

Near the top of the hill was the remains of an old stone church. Further up on top of the hill sat the walls of the fortress, La Contadura. Its canons had commanded several miles of coastline and surrounding sea. It now provides a view of the town, acres of coconut trees and the coastal wetlands. The lighthouse at Playa Del Rey could also be seen.

San Blas had been a port for Spanish galleons trading with the Philippines. The fort was built to protect San Blas from pirates. It was destroyed during the war for independence in 1811.

Kids were all over racing the bus up the hill. They would take candy but not money. Their parents looked on money as charity. However, the kids would sell local wild flowers for hard money.

Back down the hill the road went along the beach past Matanchen Bay and Las Islitas Beach and Playa Los Cocos. These beaches had a reputation of being some of the best surfing beaches in the world. The best waves were expected in September and October. The roadside was lined with beach barbecue shacks, now uninhabited.

The trip back snaked through the gathering dusk. There was no sunset to talk about. It just got dark.

Wednesday morning I was still not feeling top shape. I was up early so I went out on the beach to hear the church bells and watch the near-full moon set. The moon settled into a cloud bank on the horizon around the bay beyond Los Arcos near Yelapa. It was light by the time the moon disappeared but the sun would not appear over the hills to the east for another hour.

We went across the street from the hotel to a restaurant called the "100%" for one of their fruit and yogurt specials. My wife took a $2 taxi to one of the shopping malls.

I gathered up my cameras and notebook and took a bus to El Centro for one and a half pesos ($0.15 US). The bus had about a dozen plastic seats sized to hold two very small people. This was similar to seating five adults in the backseat of your car. The busses ran frequently and stopped wherever someone wanted on or off. The ride was less than a mile and took about five minutes.

I got off on near the center of the malecón and watched several pelicans flying in formation. They came in close to the surface of the bay in a perfect section landing formation then individually crashed.

Malacon

Several groups of tourists were being guided along with their guide explaining the significance of the boy on the seahorse and the frolicking dolphins. Several tourists asked me to shoot a picture of them with their camera against these landmarks.

I crossed the street to the Palacio Principal (city hall) and stopped in at the tourism office. Between my broken Spanish and their elementary English we found what I was looking for. I picked up several brochures.

The zocalo was on the south end of city hall and a nativity scene was set up on the porch. I arrived in time to see a procession of elementary school children dressed in a white peasant costumes arrive, complete with donkey, and go through the nativity ritual. Then each child was given a basket of candy and escorted off by their parents.

Christmas decorations were being installed on the power poles and strung across the streets.

On the southwest corner of the zocalo near the statue of Sr. Vallarta were several shoe shine stands and an old man selling raspa with bees buzzing around the colored syrups. I ambled past and turned down Ave. Morales towards the Cuale River. At least four people wanted to give me a meal and cut rate tour tickets for looking at one of the condominium timeshare deals.

Zocalo and Cathedral

Cuale Island was choice real estate with exclusive restaurants, boutiques and the Cuale Museum.

The museum had a good facility and well arranged displays. I bought a copy of their booklet <u>*Mesoamerican History*</u> by Ana Mendizabal published by the PV City Council.

Eastward the walk led through a block of boutiques and shops. Copper pictures, silver jewelry, wooden masks and water color paintings were offered for sale.

Exit from the island was across the river on a rope-and-plank suspension foot bridge to Avenida Constitucion. The bridge rippled and swung as a woman with a reluctant child by the hand came across. I crossed over and back just for the experience.

I wandered around the old part of town. Many of the homes had been converted into clubs or restaurants. None of the small hotels had a vacancy sign. Basilio Badillo led me west to Olas Altas and more shops. The Olas Altas Acuario or Aquarium was primarily a shop that sold aquarium fish and supplies.

Recrossing the river I went back north along the seawall and found a shop operated by the Huicol Indians. The shop contained displays of Huicol clothing and a medicine hut. Hand crafts included bead-studded sculptures where the beads were pressed into bees wax, T-shirts with Huicol designs, yarn paintings, baskets and pottery and books on the Huicol culture. The Indians live in the Sierra Madre Occidental at altitudes of 3,000 to 10,000 feet. Their strong religion based on peyote still prevails.

A short two block walk brought me to Ave Juarez where the buses ran north. I caught a bus back to the hotel.

We watched the sunset over the southwestern tip of the bay and the Tropicbirds returning to roost on top of the hotel. A string of pelicans were heading south across the bay looking for their friends the dolphins that kept track of the shoals of fish. After sunset we had dinner at the hotel.

AN AERIAL ARMADA

A flight of ten pelicans
ride the thermals down the surf
Fifteen tropicbirds circle downwards
towards their night roosting turf

LONG NIGHT MOON

The full moon made its appearance
an hour after the sun had set.
It took that long to climb the eastern hills
and caused the tropicbirds to fret.

Thursday I stayed around the pool and beach while my wife went shopping. The temperature was in the 70's and cool if the breeze blew or the sun slipped off leaving me in the shade.

We had reservations for the hotel fiesta for the evening. Since I was not supposed to drink or eat spicy foods, the evening was spent watching the other revelers. Marichi bands were good. They were followed by a comedian that conducted a series of drinking games. A bandit with tequila bottles made the rounds with a photographer passing out tequila slammers. The buffet was served about 2100 and I had fruit and several deserts. We left about 2200 as the party was getting in high gear. About midnight I was awakened by a fireworks display whose explosions reverberated off the hotel walls.

Friday morning we packed and checked out leaving the bags in check. The plane did not leave until 1400 so we went to downtown for a lobster dinner and some last minute looking.

A taxi took us to the airport a little past noon as we began the trip back to Texas. The plane took off on time. Twenty minutes later we were over Lake Chapala with Paracutin, the infamous volcano, visible above the clouds to the south.

We were in the Mexico City airport about two hours waiting for the plane to San Antonio. The boarding gate changed twice in that time.

The sun was setting as we finally left. The mountains of Mexico were dark until we passed over Monterrey and Saltillio. The land was black again until we neared the US border southeast of Laredo. Numerous small South Texas towns glowed like jewels and a lightning display enlivened the sky to the northeast.

We landed a little after 1900 and were through customs and home in another hour.

Hey, Mamma, when we goin' again?

3

Looking for the Phantom Crown

Cordoba,

Fortín de las Flores

And

Orizaba

Veracruz, Mexico

by

Carl Lahser

Introduction

The following is a narrative of a quick trip to Veracruz. We took this trip to visit the land where the first contact between the Spanish explorer Hernán Cortés and the Totonacs took place in 1519. This is also the land of the Phantom Crown of His Imperial and Royal Highness Ferdinando Maximiliano, Archduke of Austria and Emperor of Mexico and his wife the Empress Carlotta came to Mexico. I wanted to see tropical jungle, vanilla orchids, and coffee fincas (plantations) with colorful tropical birds that Maximilian saw a hundred and thirty years ago but I know that time brings changes to the land.

We had been planning the trip for several months. Reservations were made at Fortín de las Flores. This is a small town midway between Córdoba and Orizaba and 140 km west of Veracruz.

By way of preparation I reviewed *Day Trips to Archeological Mexico* by Robert Wood for directions to archeological sites around Veracruz. We looked at several travel guides to Mexico and found only one, *the Lonely Planet Travel Survival Kit to Mexico*, that more than mentioned Fortín, as it is locally known.

"The charm of nature is that everything is with the rest … but distinct, individual and complete in itself." That which is expected differs from being there. It is a challenge to describe it to someone who has not been there. Previous experiences and the words of others color expectations. The expectations relate to the actuality like experiencing night by closing yourself in a closet. Night can be described as black but this description will not convey the moon and stars, the subliminal sounds of air currents and the night creatures, the sense of being unconfined by walls but being more intimately surrounded by the night. Sorry you were not part of the experience.

The Trip

The Mexicana Airlines flight departed on the cold wet morning of 12 December 1997. Our flight was unremarkable as we flew over a thick layer of clouds. We had left 40°F weather in San Antonio and arrived in Mexico City at the same temperature plus snow warnings. This did not bode well for a sunny tropical vacation.

A few minutes northeast of Mexico City we could finally see the ground. We were passing over the pyramids of Teotihuacán and Popocatépetl, 40 miles southeast of the airport, could be seen shrouded in a veil of steam from recent eruptions.

Immigration was in Mexico City. Our luggage was checked through to Veracruz where we went through customs.

The plane came down through a heavy layer of clouds and rain fifty miles west of Veracruz. Rain intensified over the tan and green checkerboard of the coastal plains and muddied the distant blue of the Gulf. We passed over dark green wandering watercourses and orange groves and lighter green fields of sugar cane on the approach to the airport.

A cold, wet wind blew as we walked to the terminal. A couple of zopilotes (Black Vultures [Cathartes atratus]) were working hard flying with wet feathers in the cold damp air patrolling the airfield. This was not their kind of flying weather.

It was about 5 PM and the temperature was 5° C (41° F), about the same as we had left 800 mile north. The customs inspector said it was the coldest day in a hundred years.

There were several rental car companies to pick from - Budget, FAST, National, Avis, Mocombo, and Hertz. They were all $400-500 US a week for a car with a standard shift including insurance. It was another $100 a week for an automatic so we rented a VW Jetta with standard and AC. I loaded the bags and, after buying a few pesos, we headed west through a light mist looking for the toll road.

A small cemetery sat beside the road. On its white arched entrance sat a wet Black Crab-Hawk (Buteogallus anthracinus).

The first toll was 43 pesos. A hundred km later and 20 km short of our goal, a second toll was 48 pesos. The toll road was a divided highway with two lanes each way, good shoulders and a safety patrol. The speed limit was 110 km/hour. Other than us there were no other headlights piercing the gloom.

Orange groves gave way to grass lands and scattered trees as we entered the foothills. The mist became a cold fog. The road cuts became deeper. Hills became steep slopes of orange volcanic breccia covered with tall, coarse grass. A few vultures were settling in for a miserable wet night and Tree Swallows (Iridoprocne bicolor) were zipping about feeding. Several flat areas supported part-Brahma cattle while Snowy Egrets (Egreta [Leucophoyx] thula) waded in shallow standing water. The sun set or, at least, it got dark and the fog became light steady rain.

Our trip took less than two hours. Mexico City was about six hours further. Empress Carlotta, in 1864, reported fifteen hours by coach to Veracruz and a forty hour's trip to Mexico City.

The Córdoba exit took us through a town of 150,000 people at 924 meters (about 3000 feet) above sea level. Córdoba was originally known as La Ciudad de los Treinta Caballeros (the City of the 30 Knights). It was named for the original 30 Spanish families who settled in Cordoba and manned a fort called Fortín de las Flores (Fort of the Flowers). The fort was established in 1618 to protect travelers along the road between Veracruz and Mexico City from bandits and escaped slaves. Cordoba is now a successful commercial center for processing coffee and sugar cane and a shipping center bananas and citrus.

We drove half way through Cordoba with no indication of where Fortín de las Flores might be. We turned around in case we had missed the sign and went almost back to the toll road before turning around for a third try. I stopped at the one and only PEMEX gas station for gas and asked where Fortín de las Flores was located. This drew a blank until someone concluded that we must have been referring to Fortín, which was about 10 km up the road.

At about 10 km was a sign indicating Fortín and another PEMEX station. The PEMEX attendants directed us to the Hotel Fortín de las Flores Resort about three blocks further on.

The temperature was in the mid-30s as we checked in. The hotel desk was open to the weather. This large tomato soup pink hotel did not normally need heat, and the staff was bundled up in sweaters and scarves.

While we were checking in, a procession for the Virgin of Guadalupe passed the hotel. A marching band, several floats and the local sacred objects passed by. After all, this was December 12 and the Feast Day of the Virgin of Guadalupe.

We were checked into a 600 square foot two-bedroom suite with a kitchen. It had ceiling fan and a wall-mounted AC for cooling but no heat. (The hotel provided us a small electric heater on request.) The room was strictly utilitarian and not what I would expect at a luxury resort. The hotel was advertised as a "resort for the middle class from Mexico City". It had been built in the 1930s and had virtually no storage space. Rooms rented for about $20 a night and were comparable to many $30 a night 60 year old motel rooms in the southwestern United States. Electricity was 120 VAC but there was a warning sign not to use irons, hair dryers, etc. The kitchen cabinets were locked. Cable TV had four Spanish language stations and HBO in English with Spanish subtitles.

The hotel grounds had nice tropical gardens. There was a pool and a billiards table in the portales. A nice outdoor pool was available, but rain and cool put a damper on most outside activities. Landscape plants included coffee trees, gardenias, hibiscus, roses,a big African tulip tree (Spathodea), Bougainvillea, azaleas, cereus, several species of tuberous begonia, Amazon Lily (Eucharis grandiflora), croton, several species of Dracenia, several palms including fishtail (Caryota) and Royal palm (Roystonea).

The on-site restaurant served very good food with good service, but it reminded me of eating in a large open drafty barn. For the first supper I had mushroom and caper soup with sherry and an Aztec crepe with huicotle (otherwise known as black corn smut) with watermelon juice (aqua de sandia) to drink. Carol had tortilla soup with avocado and white cheese followed by a steak and enchilada dinner. Quite good.

Saturday morning at daybreak, I looked out the window and could not see across the street through the fog. It was still cold.

We finally got to moving and, about 0900, went to brunch. They offered fresh juices of tomato, orange, melon, apple and papaya with slices of papaya, cantaloupe and watermelon; scrambled eggs and bacon or hot sausage, enfriolada, empanadas, and cold hot cakes or waffles. There was also cold cereal, yogurt and omelets to order.

After breakfast I went for a walk around the Parque Principal or main plaza. Here were the city buildings including the Palacio Municipal (City Hall). The cathedral opened on to the plaza and was decorated for Christmas. Buildings were painted in shades of blue, periwinkle and lime. Everyone was bundled up like it was cold.

I asked directions to the fort and was told it was in ruins and they could not direct me to it. I asked the location of Maximilian's palace. The palace was about a block from the hotel but was not open to the public. I walked back to the hotel in a slow drizzle.

Cordoba Plaza de Armas

We drove to Cordoba to do some shopping. The city looked different in the daylight. Coffee processing plants smelled of ground coffee.

The street layout was the old logical Spanish system of numbered streets and avenues, but the 18th century streets almost totally failed to handle 20th century vehicles and the quantity of traffic. Parking was at a premium with double parking common. We finally found a parking garage for ten pesos an hour.

It seemed like every other store was a shoe store. Pre-Christmas shopping was evident. The local Sears store had a ten percent off sale. I visited a bookstore and found a few horticulture texts. They only had one copy of whatever title they had in stock.

It was not good weather for exploring downtown. We drove past the Plaza de Armas enclosed by several colonial period buildings and the 18th century church, La Parroquia de la Inmaculada Concepcion. A block of portales housed vendors and several restaurants.

The home of Condes (Count) de Zevallos was also on the Plaza. It was built in 1687 and was the site where the terms on Mexico's independence from Spain had been negotiated on August 24, 1821. Although they would free Mexico, Spain, in its Plan de Inguala, had proposed that a European monarch rule over Mexico. Juan O'Dojú, Viceroy of Spain, and Don Agustín de Iturbide, a former royalist general and the leader of the Mexican rebels, agreed that Mexico should have a Mexican monarch. Iturbide reigned for two months during 1822 as Emperor Agustín I. He lived in the Iturbide Palace in Mexico City until deposed.

After lunch, we drove 12 mile west to Orizaba. We passed back through Fortín at 970 meters (about 3200 feet) and went down a steep swithcback about a thousand feet into sugarcane and banana country. A large sugarcane processing plant showed no activity on a Saturday afternoon. The road passed through the village of Ixtazoqultlan with a Pemex station and several houses, then back up hill to Orizaba at 1219 meters (almost 4,000 feet). Several concrete plants and gravel quarries were located along this road.

Entering Orizaba was was like going back fifty years in infrastructure. Numerous utility lines ran along and crossed the narrow brick streets and narrow sidewalks. Most of the buildings had colonial period roots but many of the best examples had been damaged or destroyed in a bad earthquake in 1973. The majority of the buildings were white or a weathered cream color instead of the bright colors of Fortín.

Orizaba's claims to fame were the Moctezuma Brewery and the labor problems that had contributed to the overthrow of the dictator, Profirio Díaz. The regional population had Mayan origins and is contentious and closely allied with other Mayan groups further south. It was still overcast and cold.

The mountains to the north and west were hidden in clouds. Included was Pico de Orizaba, the highest peak in Mexico and one of the world's most perfect cinder cones.

Supper at the hotel was moved to a drafty second floor room because of a big party. The food and service was still very good in spite of the cold.

I joined Carol in having bronchitus and on **Sunday morning** the bronchitis was worse. We felt better after breakfast and took a 20 miles drive to Coscomatepec, a market town of 50,000.

The first 8 miles was on a relatively good two-lane blacktop road through coffee plantations. Banana trees were grown to shade the coffee trees with their bright red coffee berries and used as a second crop.

It looked like the entire population of the first village, Monte Blanco, was at the soccer field north of town. A couple speed bumps ("sleeping policemen") and numerous potholes kept traffic to a crawl.

Just outside of town road construction began and continued for about six miles through sugarcane fields. Then the road dropped several hundred feet to a sharp 180-degree turn across a river and back up the hill. At the bottom of the hill a large memorial to many accidents was painted white and decorated with flowers and pendants for the saint's day. At the top of the hill was a shrine to the Virgin of Guadalupe near the village of Noria.

Several large greenhouses were located along the road between sugarcane fields. The steep hillsides were a patchwork of banana and coffee fincas.

We entered Coscomatepec de Bravo and turned up the hill towards the market. This was not a market day. This town had some of the steepest streets that I have ever seen. They were not as long as San Francisco streets but certainly as steep. Other than the market and main plaza, the town was mostly residential.

Back in Fortin, Carol was not feeling well and I had a slight fever. I changed our plane reservations to return on Monday afternoon.

On Monday morning, there were patches of blue and the temperature was up to about 50°F, but it was still misty. We checked out and began the drive to Veracruz about 9 AM down the old highway, Mexico 150 libre, a free road. The road was in fair condition for a two-lane blacktop road with no shoulders.

About forty km down the road, in the mirror I noticed Pico de Orizaba dominating the western horizon. The sky had cleared and the sight of the snow-covered 5700m mountain against the blue sky made the trip worth the effort.

Flocks of Tree Swallows were feeding along the road. Vultures were flying at treetop level looking for thermals. Several Pigeon Hawks or Merlins (Falco columbarius) were sitting on the power lines along the road. Several yellow-breasted warblers, possibly the Orizaba yellowthroat (Geothlypis speciosa) flew across the road

The road paralleled the Rio Blanco for about 20 km. Views of the river were mostly of quiet stretches, but there was one view of rapids. They were not exactly white water quality but would have made rafting interesting

Pico de Orizaba

About 50 km from Veracruz, I made a wrong turn and got on VFR 95. This was like the toll road without the tollbooth. It was a good four lane divided highway towards Cosamaloapan and then on to the south. The road was flanked by flat farm and ranch land. It had a three feet high concrete barrier down the center with turn around only every 20 km. There were no towns or access roads, but the highway was crossed by a several bridges. We turned around at the second opportunity and returned to Mexico 150.

The temperature was in the middle 60's F and butterflies were out in force along this stretch of road. A lone Monarch (Danus plexippus) sailed by. Numerous small Whites (subfamily Pierinae) or yellow Sulfurs (subfamily Coliadinae) attempted to cross the road about six inches off the ground, but their flight was interrupted by the concrete divider. A large bright Orange Long Wing (Dryas iulia) crossed about hood height. A large white Morpho floated across the road about ten feet above the roadway.

We got back on the right road and were in Boca del Rio in about half an hour. The blue Gulf water was breaking easily in the shore. Another 20 km through condos and hotels took us to downtown Veracruz. We took the proverbial grand tour enroute to the airport. After asking directions several times and following signs that lead nowhere we wanted to go, we found it. We checked in the car in and went to the lounge for lunch.

Grackles and starlings played along the edge of the ramp. A Purple Emperor butterfly (<u>Doxocopa</u> <u>pavon</u>) patrolled the front of the building about fifteen feet high pausing momentarily in several Minosa trees to display.

The plane left about 3PM, and we were back in San Antonio by 7PM.

4

Flowers of the Air

Monarch Butterflies
in
Mexico
by
Carl Lahser

Green Pilgrimage

Let me seek green byways
away from the pollution
of sight and sound.
Let me hike green valleys
without a trace
of chemical waste.
Let me walk green hills
still untouched
by axe and saw;
sail the blue water;
breathe clean air.
Let me stretch
my legs
my mind
renew myself
if even for a minute.
carl

First Step.

A Green Vacation means me getting out of the office and away from man's handiwork to the natural world to see and do things natural without a lot of fancy equipment. This is a busman's holiday for me since I am a natural resources manager in real life. Bird watching, beachcombing, shelling, gardening and other activities out of doors are actually part of what I do for a living. This trip was to see the wintering home of the Flowers of the Air, Monarch Butterflies in the mountains of Mexico.

Anticipation for this trip began in 1975, when the discovery of the winter destination of migrating Monarchs was first reported to be in the mountains north of Mexico City. The spark was fanned by the 1976 article and accompanying photographs of millions of Monarchs in *National Geographic*. Subsequent research has expanded the number of sites to nine major and a number of minor wintering populations. These refuges are named after the mountain on which the colony was found.

These peaks are in the Trans-Volcanic belt extending from northwest of Mexico City to the Guatemala highlands. Only one, El Rosario, is open to the public. About 120 million butterflies come to Mexico each year from as far a Canada and New England. Mating occurring in such a large and diverse population maintains a healthy gene pool.

I read an article in the December 1995 edition of the *Journal of the Lepidopterist Society* discussing the chronology of the discovery of the sites. I also reread the August 1976 *National Geographic* article and an article on the February 1996 winter kill of Monarchs. These convinced me that now was the time to see this natural wonder.

'96 MONARCH KILL

What irony, to fly 3000 miles
to escape the cold and snow
but die in a freak snow storm
in the mountains of Mexico.
Six thousand square mile of mountains in Michoacan state
shelter the orange and black butterfly
but the jet stream dropped south
and the cold and snow caused
half a million Monarchs to die.
A '92 storm killed several million.
From this they can recover
but not from cutting and burning the forest.
Our children may see them never.

My first challenge was identifying and arranging for transportation to the Monarch refuge. I looked on the Internet and found several sites that discussed the Monarchs and a reference to the Monarch Butterfly Biosphere Reserve System (telephone 1-800-531-7921). I called several local travel agents. Sanborn Tours and a couple others offered five and seven-day bus tours that included the Monarchs.

I finally found that Grey Line Tours in Mexico City (telephone toll free 1-888-212-6410 or 011-525-208-1163 in Mexico City) and Ecogrupa de Mexico (telephone 001-525-661-9121) had one day tours from Mexico

City for $118 and $145 US plus tax. Both also had overnight tours for slightly more money.

Several airlines provided service to Mexico City including Continental and Delta, but Mexicana Airline was the only one that flew directly from San Antonio. Standard fare was within a few dollars for all the airlines. Mexicana had a $275 special fare but it required a stay over Saturday night. I made a reservation on Mexicana for a standard tourist $347 round trip.

Considering the airline schedule a minimum two-night stay is necessary. I made a reservation at the Quality Inn's (1-800-228-5151) Calinda Geneve in the Zona Rosa for two nights for the AARP rate of $59.88 a night plus tax. This hotel was on the expensive side considering the other hotels in the Zona Rosa but a 1-800 number that saved several $8 telephone calls to Mexico City and guaranteed me a room.

The minimum cost was $347 airfare, $135 ($122 plus tax) for the tour and two nights hotel plus food and local expenses. This totaled about $700 for three days out of the office.

A Fokker F-100 departed San Antonio at 1020 on Tuesday, January 21, 1997, and arrived in Mexico City at noon. A layer of clouds was below us until we were south of Brownsville. We flew down the Gulf coast crossing the Rio Soto east of Vincente Guerro dam and reservoir. We stayed well east of the Sierra Madre Oriental until, just east of Ciudad Valles, we turned southwest up the Rio Temporal valley to Pachuca. Cold clouds enveloped us over Lago de Texcoco and on into the airport. From the ground the sky was clear blue with a temperature near 60°F.

Customs and immigration were a breeze, and I was checked in to the hotel by 1300.

A short walk to the Grey Lines (Linus Gris) office and I was booked for a day trip to the El Rosario Monarch refuge. The 150 kilometer (about 90 miles) trip would leave at 0800 Wednesday.

Backsliding a little.

I also booked a tour for the rest of the afternoon and evening to the pyramids at Teotihuacan and the Shrine of the Virgin of Guadalupe. We left the hotel at 1400 and drove northeast along the Avenida de Insurgentes, past the railroad station and on to Highway 85. Crossing the Rio de los Remedios we left the Distrito Federal and entered the state of Mexico.

The highway was lined with barrios containing numerous slump block apartment buildings that were whitewashed and covered with advertising. These structures housed a few of the new immigrants arriving daily that added to the seventeen million already in Mexico City. Several abandoned quarries served as dumps which were being picked over for anything of value. The hillsides were being covered by squatter settlements.

About fifteen miles north of Mexico City are the village of San Cristobal Ecatepec, a federal prison, and the restored Convent of San Augustine Acolman. Dry fields were being burned. The burning of dry corn and tomato plants, while returning nutrients to the soil, added pollutants to the air. Even the ground around agave and cactus crops showed the results of fire.

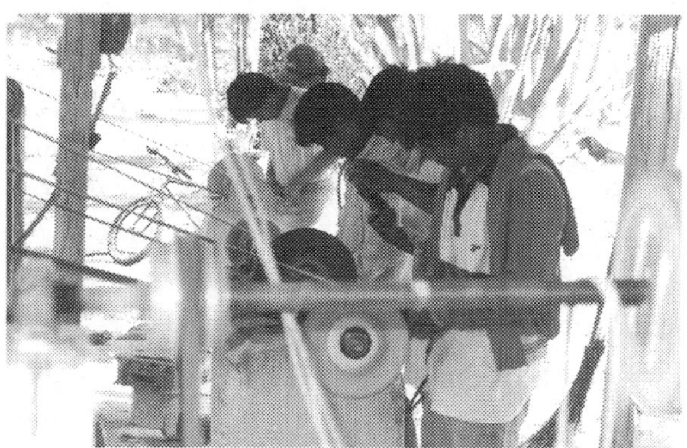

Obsidian Grinders

A male Scarlet Tanager, bright red with black wings and tail, sat on the fence along the road with its mate. These birds usually winter further south. Mature maguey or green agave plants, *Agave americana,* grew in fence lines and were cultivated in fields. The plant matures at about eight years when they are sacrificed to produce refreshing light nectar which can be fermented into a light wine called pulque and distilled into mescal and a light sweet liqueur.

Crossing a small stream we entered the village of San Juan Teotihucan with two large pyramids in the distance.

We stopped at one of the craft centers that demonstrated the uses of agave and the making of obsidian artifacts. One of the young people on the grinding wheel wore a bandana over his nose but most of the artisans had no eye, hearing or respiratory protection from the fine glass particles.

We were encouraged to sample the house pulque, mescal and tequila (with little salt and lime). After inhaling a canned Coke and foregoing an opportunity to buy lace tablecloths, obsidian jewelry and other wares the van took us to the southernmost gate into the Quetzalcoatl and Tlaloc temple. We entered through an Avenue of Shops and crossed what the Aztecs had dubbed the Avenue of the Dead. A city of 125,000 inhabitants had existed between 300 BC and 500 AD The Aztecs had rediscovered the pyramids and ruins around 1000 A.D. The Aztec fear of and respect for the dead resulted in relatively little disturbance of the site until early this century.

Aztec Honor

The Aztec were heroic in battle
and their enemies usually fled.
They greatly respected the afterlife
and honored their enemy dead.

Pyramid of the Moon Teotihuacan

The temple of Quetzalcoatl was a walled quadrangle that covered about ten acres. There were small pyramids were located off Avenue of the Dead and center to the east side. The rounded Tlaloc mound was constructed in front on the older and more elaborate Teotihuacan pyramid. The older structure was decorated with seashell reliefs and serpent heads of the Toltec god, Quetzlcoatl. The smaller Tlaloc temple still retained some of the red plaster that had covered its exterior.

Leaving the Quetzalcotal temple we hurried north up the Avenue of the Dead. I had time to climb the 248 steps up the 216-foot Pyramid of the Sun before we returned to Mexico City.

Our next stop was at the Basilica of Guadalupe. We turned off of Insurgentes Norte on Calzada Misterios and drove along the abandoned aquacia. The hilltop site contained an old graveyard and the first chapel of the Virgin of Guadalupe. This chapel had been begun in 1532 on the spot of the appearance of the Virgin of Guadalupe. It was built on top of the ruins of the Aztec temple to Tonantzin, the mother of the gods.

Pyramid of the Sun

Thoughts from the Top

Ten centuries previous
this view from the top of the Temple of the Sun
might have been my last
sunrise or sunset
or high noon
if prisoner or slave
or maybe my first panoramic view
as child or visitor
or just another glorious ceremonial day
for king or priest.

The second structure (the first Basilica) and a convent were built in the early 18th century. Heavy use and several earthquakes damaged this structure. The new modern Basilica designed by Pedro Rameriz Vasquez has replaced it. The Basilica was completed and dedicated in 1976. The original miraculous picture of the patron saint of Mexico hangs behind the altar. It is viewable even during services from passages beneath the altar. A large square in front of the church rests over catacombs and parking areas.

First Basilica of Our Lady of Guadalupe

The Conquistador's Excuse

The Conquistador's consuming greed
was disguised
and excused by the need
to convert or kill the infidel
who would not accept the Catholic creed.
European diseases
gave genocide God's speed.

We were back to the hotel about 8 PM, in time for the Mexican dinner hour. Regional cuisine, Mexican beer, the music, people talking brought back memories.

Finally.

The trip to the butterflies began at 0830 from the Grey Line office. The guide/driver was in his late twenties with a degree in economic geography. Even in the third world a college degree doesn't guarantee a person meaningful work. He said he liked his job and had been to see the Monarchs several times. Our bus was a three-year-old Toyoto.

Daily weather at the refuge ranges from near freezing to the low 60's. Layered clothing and comfortable walking shoes are recommended. I also took along two 35mm cameras, a camcorder and binoculars.

After ploughing through rush-hour traffic west along Paseo de Reforma and passing through Chapultepec Park, the Reforma became Highway 15, the toll road northwest to Toluca.

Nevado de Toluca

The first few miles passed through conifer covered mountains. The road descended into rolling farm land for about 20 Km. The 15,016 foot snow-covered volcano, Nevado de Toluca, dominated

We had climbed gradually to 8760 feet when we passed through Toluca. This capitol of the State of Mexico has grown from about 150,000 to a half million in the past several years. Manufacturing and other light industry had been moved from Mexico City in an effort to reduce immigration and smog.

We continued on through the picturesque heartland of Mexico. Oxen were still being used to plow the fields and plastic jugs of the scene to the south and west of Toluca.drinking water and bundles of firewood were hauled on donkeys. Buildings were being built one block at a time of slump blocks were manufactured on site.

Corn was spread on the house roof or stored in prefab wooden frames stacked as high as anyone could reach. Shocks of corn stood drying in the fields for use as livestock feed.

A few of the old men still wore plain woolen ponchos and sombreros but most of the men wore conventional jeans and work shirts with tennis shoes and ball caps.

Farming near Toluca

A few kilometers north and west of Toluca the road entered the tree covered mountains. The road became sinuous with sharp hairpin curves. Many of the curves sprouted roadside shrines dedicated to crash victims.

Several signs for butterfly tours appeared as we neared Zitacuaro. We continued on another ten-km to the town of Angangueo where the road turned off towards the Monarch refuge.

Tours usually stop in Angangueo and you transfer to local transportation in the form of stake bed trucks or pickups for the ten-kilometer trip to the community of Ocampo. This Monarch refuge, El Rosario, is located on Campanario mountain and is the only one easily accessible and open to the public. It is the only one with so much as a logging road anywhere near it. Most of the other refuges require one or more days travel by foot or mule to reach the mountain top sanctuaries.

We drove over a rough, dusty road through candling Oyamel (<u>Abies religiosa</u>) trees. Several abandoned logging roads opened onto the main road. There were several small areas of reforestation and signs were posted warning against logging. Nearer the refuge clear-cut hillsides were divided into small fields lined with natural windbreaks and dotted with houses. Fence lines contained numerous maguey plants destined for the local pulque production.

Road to the Refuge

The car forded a small river and entered a group of houses clustered around intersections of this road and smaller trails. About a mile from the refuge entrance we began seeing butterflies.

We shared the dusty road with a donkey loaded with firewood, several women and small groups of children returning home from the morning session of school. Houses were built of rough-cut lumber with corrugated tin roofs. Springs and seeps were channeled into ditches along the road. Power lines indicated electricity was available to at least some of the homes.

The rutted road and ditches immediately outside the parking area were covered with Monarchs soaking up the sun and drinking from standing water and wet soil (technical terms are basking and puddling). Some butterfly mating was taking place.

Woodcutter and Agave

The air was thick with flitting wings. White noise, those low frequency vibrations that mute all man-made acoustic intrusions, filled the air like listening to the wind. Children's laughter and raucous music from a cantina seemed to lose definition like sounds in a snowstorm

We parked and made our way to a canyon of vendor's stalls that lead to the refuge entrance. Two stake bed trucks from Angangueo, each with a load of school children, parked and unloaded their cargo. Teachers organized the kids into small groups for the hike. The kids had backpacks and sneakers and would have looked at home anywhere north of the border.

Monarchs Puddling in Road

Many of the stalls were empty on this Wednesday after noon. They would all be open for the weekend. Beyond the last stall and restroom a chain link fence guided the crowd to the Center for

Ecotourism's El Rosario Monarch Refuge. Thousands of Monarchs passed us along the trail and thousands more were puddling in wet areas beside the trail.

Our driver paid the entrance fee of twenty pesos each and we were assigned a tour guide for the two-kilometer hike. Our new guide appeared to be about 50 and spoke no English. He was dressed in denim work clothes, heavy shoes and a straw hat. On his hat was pinned a butterfly tag he had recovered.

We signed the visitor log at the gate and were on our way. Several signs in Spanish were posted by SEDESOL (Secretaria de Desarrollo Urbano Ecologia or the Secretary for the Development of Urban Ecology). The signs described butterfly migration and life history, warned against catching or harassing the Monarchs, and exhorted the public to protect and conserve this treasure. Some of the Monarchs had traveled as much as 3500 miles to get to these mountains. The kids, shepherded by their teachers and guides, hurried up the path and were never seen again. Monarchs buzzed by and ran into you and, if you stopped, they landed on you. Steps had been fashioned from split logs anchored in the ground. Split log benches were strategically placed every couple hundred feet for catching one's breath. After all, the trail started at near 9000 feet and rose another 1500 feet before starting down.

Entrance to the Reserve

Oyamel tree branches hung down loaded with hundreds of orange and black Monarch visitors.

Monarch Butterflies Basking

The sky was speckled with Monarchs. A background sound like a breeze or light rain pervaded the woods. Lichen covered tree trunks in the sun supported hundreds of basking butterflies. The occasional flowers were sampled for the thousandth time for nectar. Four species of Salvia and several tall composites with white or yellow flowers were in bloom.

Male Monarchs

Monarchs still a little too cold to fly littered the trail. It might have been too cold to fly but a few males took advantage of the situation to copulate. Statistically less than one percent of the population either mated or nectared at this time of year. The main mating frenzy would take place in mid-February. After mating, the males die leaving the gravid females to make the long trek back north at about 20 miles per hour looking for milkweed plants to lay eggs on.

Male Monarchs differ from the females by having a prominent black spot on the top surface of each hind-wing. These spots do not appear on the females.

We reached the top and the trail leveled off for a couple hundred yards. At this point we were above most of the colony. The descending trail skirted around the major concentration of the Monarchs. There were still plenty of butterflies and this area, with a southwest exposure, had more vegetation in bloom. The steps downward were not any easier than the steps coming up. They still required frequent huffing and puffing breaks.

Back at the bottom was a restroom for a peso fee and a place that sold big cold bottled drinks. We patronized these facilities and then hit the vendors for a well-deserved souvenir T-shirt to commemorate the trip.

The ride back to Mexico City was relatively uneventful. A milky afternoon haze shrouded the horizon. Clouds and haze hid the snow-covered volcano that had been so spectacular in the morning sun. The tour terminated back at the hotel about 8 PM

Sun Warmed Monarchs

Monarchs Covering Oyamel trees

A hot shower removed the dust from the trip and a Mexican dinner with optional Mexican beer finished the day.

A ceremony was taking place in the hotel lobby as I was leaving for supper. Military school cadets formed a corridor of crossed swords and numerous young ladies in formal dresses passed through on their way to waiting busses. This was a dining out and celebrated La Quinceañera (15th birthday) or coming of age for the group of young ladies from Columbia.

Leaving

I was a little stiff but a hot shower and stretching exercises took care of most of the aches. The plane did not leave until sundown so I had half a day to goof off.

For *desayuno* or breakfast I stopped at a street vendor near the hotel that sold several choices. A hot drink is genericly called *atole.* Flavored with chocolate its called *champurrado* made with masa harina, milk, water, cinnamon, chocolate and sugar.

Horchata Vendor

This lady also had a sweet rice water, *horchata*, fresh orange juice or coffee. Food was chicken, red or green tamales served by themselves or, more commonly, in a sliced French roll called a torte or sandwich.

Champurrado and a torte for six pesos cost less than a buck. (Back in San Antonio atole is usually oatmeal or other hot cereal.)

A number of antique shops and art galleries were located along Lourdes Avenue near the hotel filled with continental antiques seldom seem in San Antonio. I walked over to the Paseo de la Reforma passing McDonalds, Arbors, TGI Friday, and watching Mexico City wake up and go to work.

Several chrysalis of the Black Swallowtail butterfly were hanging under the edges of concrete benches along the Reforma. White Sulfur and Gulf Frittillary butterflies checked out the flowers in the median parks and raced down the streets about twenty feet above the traffic.

A brown suited policeman asked if I needed assistance. He said he was assigned to the tourist office and offered to help arrange any tour I might be interested in. I found that these officers made 28 pesos (less than $4) a day and they supplement their income in many ways.

Chapultepec Park Photographer

Wandering down the Reforma towards Chapultepec Park I passed the Independence Monument and the Fountain of Diana. At the entrance to the park I asked a policeman how to get to the Anthropology Museum. He called over a soldier with a flak jacket and M-16 but neither one knew where it was or spoke English. They called to a man in a dark leather jacket talking on a cell phone. While this clean-cut newcomer was giving good directions in perfect English I noticed he had a shoulder holster under his jacket with a small machine gun. This was in a public park in the Capitol City at ten in the morning on a Thursday. I later noticed that two armored car deliveries were accompanied by several armed guards with flack jackets.

I wandered into the park and walked to the Chapultepec Castle. I passed a photographer that would shoot instant pictures of children on a wooden horse; fruit sellers that sliced and mixed orange slices and melon strips; and vendors of everything from toys to T-shirts to table cloths. Outdoor statues visible through an iron picket fence looked interesting so I visited the museum of art.

Like the old frog said, "Time's sure fun when you're having flies". The time had come to return to the hotel to check out and then get out to the airport.

The flight back to San Antonio was quiet. The setting sun was off the left wing tip and the rising full moon sat on the right wing tip. It's hard to get lost with that kind of navigational fix. Lights came on in the ranches and villages and small towns as the night crawled across the borderland. We arrived at the gate twenty minutes late. Immigration and customs took another fifteen minutes and I was on the way home by nine PM.

Carl Lahser
25 Feb 97

Migration Preparation

It IS TIME
TO SIP NECTAR
FROM THE FLOWER.
sUMMER IS GONE.
IT IS TIME.
iT IS THE HOUR.
THE MAGIC MOMENT
HAS ARRIVED
TO MIGRATE
FAR TO THE SOUTH
TO THE MOUNTAINS
IN mICHOICAN STATE.

A HUNDRED AND FIFTY MILLION MONARCH
BUTTERFLIES CAN'T ALL BE WRONG.

5

Cabo San Lucas

November 2003

by

Carl Lahser

Cabo San Lucas
November 2003

Introduction. We had a timeshare week to use and chose a resort in the Cabo San Lucas area. Cabo San Lucas is located on the southern tip of the Baja California peninsula in the State of Baja California Sur mostly south of the Tropic of Cancer. The Sea of Cortez, also called the Gulf of California, is on the east and the Pacific Ocean is on the west and south.

From a biologist point of view it could not be much better. There are Pacific and Gulf beaches and marine life, the San Jose River Estuary, oases, and the Sierra de la Laguna Mountains that rise to 6,000 feet. These mountains catch the clouds and accumulate over 30" of rainfall that support a pine/oak ecosystem. The desert is an extension of the Sonoran Desert across the Gulf in northern Mexico. This desert is broken into four distinct sub-regions: the San Filipe Desert to the north and east averaging 2" of rainfall a year; the Gulf Coast Desert on the Gulf side, the Vizcaino Desert on the Pacific; and the Magdalena Plains or Central Desert. There are about 2000 species of native plants including 110 species of cactus and succulents, 300 species of birds, 30 herptiles and about thirty other animals, a number of butterflies, moths and other insects and various ferns, fungi and slime molds. The climate ranges from desert to sub-alpine. There are also interesting geologic features, fossils and archeological and historical sites. Something for practically everyone. The lists at the end of this narrative are by no means comprehensive but include what I saw during the trip.

References for the trip included:

Roberts, Norman, 1989, Baja California Plant Field Guide.
Epple, A.O, 1995, *Plants of Arizona.*
Martinez, Maximino, 1987, *Plantas Mexicanas.*
Davis, L.I.,1972, Birds of Mexico and Central America.
Johnson, M.E & H.J.Snook, 1955, Seashore Animals of the Pacific Coast.
Keen, A.M., 1960, Sea Shells of Tropical West America.

On our way. On 10 Nov 03 my wife, Carol, and I left San Antonio, Texas, about 1030 on Mexicana Airlines. We arrived in Mexico City about 1230. The weather enroute was overcast, but Mexico City was about as clear as I had ever seen it. Bird control efforts on the airport appeared to be working since neither standing water nor birds was visible.

Volcanoes to the South East

We jumped right in the immigration queue with about 400 other aliens. About an hour later we started bugging Mexicana for the where and when of the connecting flight. About 1600 they announced we would be on an an Aerocaribe flight leaving at 1620 from gate 19 or 20.

I noticed that part of the return trip was on AeroMexico. Good thing Mexico does not have a few more airlines. There are direct flights on US airlines through Dallas and Houston that are quicker and much less hassle and less expensive. it will be worth considering next time.

Mexico City Main Drag and Cemetery

While waiting I got a chocolate with water and a churro.

The flight was smooth through hazy skies with a few cumulus building and a high cirrus layer. Lots of lakes in the mountains reflected the late afternoon sun like pieces of a broken mirror.

Cloud Shadows

We flew northwest over several dormant volcanic cones, jungle, farms and small towns in the mountains. We passed north of the large lake, Lago Cuitzeo near Morelia, then over city of Guadalajara and the even larger lake sacred to the Huicotyl Indians, Lago de Chapala. We were feet wet (off the coast) over Las Piedras just north of the islands of the Las Tres and the Islas Marias group.

After 150 miles over a calm Sea of Cortez land came into view - Punta Boca del Tule. We crossed over Rancho la Fortuna and turned south towards the San Jose del Cabo airport. I was surprised that the desert was so green but they had had two hurricanes and a near miss in the past couple months. Palo Verde (Parkinsonia microphylla), Mesquite (Prosopis sp.), Elephant Tree or Torote (Bursera microphylla), and Palo Blanco (Acacia Willardiana) trees with the large Cardon cactus (Pachycereus pringlei) were visible as we descended. There were also spots of with tropical plants like coconut and date palms bright red blossoms of Ocotillo (Fouquieria splendens) indicating the recent rain and Coralvine (Antigonon leptopus).

The airport was small with one runway. It was located a couple miles from civilization, but industrial encroachment had already begun. Bird problems would be seasonal vultures, but there was nothing to attract them but the runway. We drug our collective feet on the arroyo bank at the north end of the runway, touched down about 1720 MST and taxied to the end of the runway.

There we turned around and taxied back up the runway to the parking area. The terminal was landscaped with tropical Bougainvillea, Crotons, Ixoria, Hibiscus, and blue agaves.

The sun set as we were walking in 78° twilight to the terminal. The red brass ball dropped behind the mountains back lighting one of the peaks highlighting the thin cirrus clouds of the subtropical jet.

Los Cabos

Once inside, I got the bags together and found that one of the airlines had ripped the handle off of one bag. I reported this fact and was given some papers to give to the airline back in San Antonio. Experience has shown that the parking at the airport will cost more than the value any settlement. I do it to harass the airlines in the hope they improve their service.

Sunset

We breezed through customs without a search and headed for ground transportation. A condo salesman with a one-time-good-deal intercepted us. If we would listen to his spiel we would get free transportation to and from our hotel and free transportation to the Hotel Palmere with breakfast (Forget it.) a free bottle of tequila (Hmmm.) and a Mexican blanket (Well maybe.) and a free glass bottom boat ride and a free Mexican dinner. OK.

We arrived at the Club Casa Dorado Beach and Golf Resort located in the Amelia de Cabo hotel. We checked in and went down for supper.

There was only one restaurant in the complex. We were told we should have reservations but they would try to seat us. After we were seated the waiter took 20 minutes to ask if we wanted drinks. I wanted a beer AND a glass of water. Ten minutes later the menus arrived along with a beer and a coke. The water took almost 30 minutes to arrive. We finally ordered after sitting there for 45 minutes. Supper arrived at the hour and ten-minute mark and then was nothing special. I guess this was to put us in our place and results from poor management, arrogance, resentment of having to work beneath their perceived social class, and a lack of pride in their work. It occurs in some up-scale facilities catering to tourists where return business is not expected.

During supper a large Black Witch moth (Ascalapha ordorata) was flitting around the dining room. Some people were swatting at it and a few thought it was a bat. Its Spanish name is Mariposa del Muerto – the Butterfly of Death.

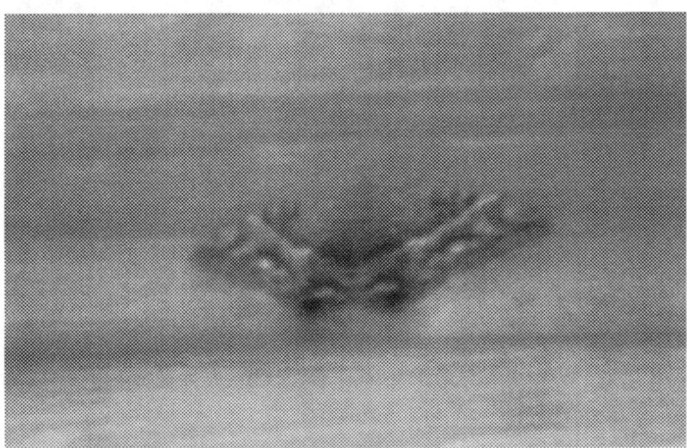

Butterfly of Death

We went down to the beach after supper. It was two evenings after a full moon and an eclipse. A sign was posted saying that this was a no swimming beach due to strong riptides and heavy surf. Disappointing for me. Why go to a beach resort if you can't swim there? At least there was the sound of the surf.

I was up with the sun and took a shot at the gym then a walk on the beach. On the way to the beach I saw a Clavipes Sphinx moth (Aellopos clavipes) with clear wings and acting like a hummingbird.

The forebeach sloped up about 20 degrees to the water and the tide must come up a good ten feet. The sand was tan granite sand ranging from ¼ inch to silt and graded by the waves. Drift lines were outlined in larger sand grains. There were periodic boulders near the low tide level that caused the waves to break and stabilize sand migration along the shoreline.

Clavipes Sphinx Moth on Bougainvillea

Hotel Beach

Several rivers empty into the Gulf in this area, but the channels were dry and sand berms were piled up at the mouth several feet high.

There were a lot of butterflies on and along the beach. Queens (Daucus gilippus). Black Swallowtail (Papilio polyxenes). Gulf Fritillary (Dione vanillae). Dogface (Colias cesonia). Tiny Checkerspot (Dymasia dymas). Long-Tailed Skippers (Urbanus proteus). Beach Skipper (Panoquina panoquinoides). They were clustered around Ragweed (Ambrosia sp.), a grayish composite shrub with yellowish flowers and white pappus.

Rio San Jose

Queen Butterflies on Ambrosia sp.

Brown pelicans (Pelicanus occidentalis) were just coming to work. They settled in singles or pairs about a hundred feet off shore for a few minutes then moved on down the beach. A Magnificent Frigate bird (Fregata magnificens) cruised down the beach.

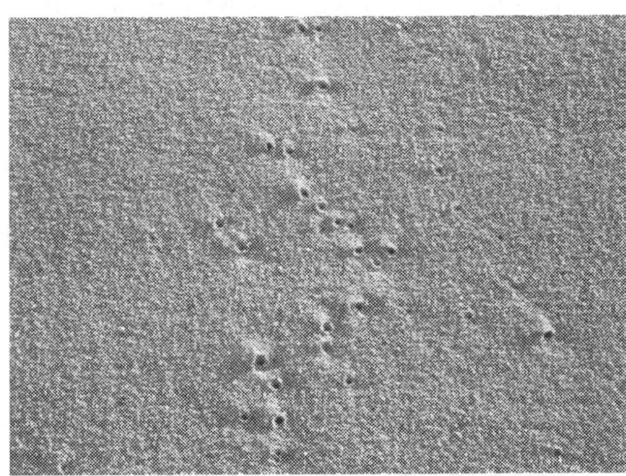

Sand cra burrowbs

The forebeach was peppered with burrows of small sand crabs (Uca crenulata) and larger ghost crabs (Ocypoda sp.) Few shells were in one piece. Shells were mostly rock dwellers like limpets and Crepidula, the big barnacle, Balanus tintinnabulum, and Purple Sea Urchins (Strongylocentrus purpuratus).

Xanthus Hummingbird

Back by the entrance to the hotel a Xantus hummingbird (Hylocharis xantusii) had built its nest in a potted Sheffleria.

They provided us with a cab to the Villa del Palmare condo sales. Now that it was light I saw Esperanza, Moonflower and Woodrose vines, Datura or Jimsonweed (Datura meteloides), and several Huisache or Vinorama (Accaia Smallii) along the highway. We turned on a road past several soccer fields into a group of hotels. There was a wet area with Cattails (Typha domingensis). There was a new addition to an existing complex with residence units running $200,000 to $500,000. They were asking $16,000 for a week timeshare plus membership in Interval International and about $500 per year maintenance fee. Their statistics showed 60% of tourist destinations were to warm areas and most of these were to Mexico. Cabo area was restricted to 10,000 hotel rooms and 15,000 timeshare units so hurry, hurry, hurry. We ate their breakfast but did not buy. We got a half-liter (pint) of tequila and a blanket and tickets for lunch and a boat ride and took a cab to downtown.

Cabo Beach with Cruise Ships

We walked several blocks and looked at several art galleries including the *Golden Cactus* and the gallery of a Texas artist, Kaki Basil. Prices were not bad for good original art. I looked at a lot of T-shirts on the way back to the main street. We decided to have lunch and stopped at *O Mole Mio*.

The condo office booked a couple of trips for us. Thursday we would go to La Paz, and Saturday we would go to Todos Santos. I booked an ATV desert oasis tour leaving in a few minutes. The desert tour was two hours on a Honda ATV. After a few minutes of familiarization and equipping with helmet and bandana the guide and I were off.

The first 10 minutes was basically playing chase the guide. We finally took a break under a 44,000 volts transmission tower on top of a hill with a good overview to the Gulf.

Flowers included a purple Malva Rosa (Melochia tomentosa) in the Sterculia family, Mariola or Oja de Liebre (Solanum hindsianum), a yellow composite, a large leafed nettle called Mala Mujer or Caribe (Cnidoscolus angustidens), a spiny-fruited Buffalo burr (Solanum rostrata) with a big sphinx moth larvae feeding on it, and a small bush of white hibiscus with a pink center. Butterflies were nectering on everything including skippers, Gulf Fritillary, Tiny Checkerspot, Dogface.

Cardon, Queen's Crown and Sea of Cortez

Mala Mujer or Caribe and Buffalo burr

We left for another habitat type. This included Cardon cactus, Senita or old man cactus (Cereus schottii), Organ Pipe Cactus (Cereus thurberi), Buckhorn Cholla (Opuntia acanthocarpa), Pencil Cholla or Junping Cactus (Opuntia lepto-caullis), Turk's Head (Echinocactus horizonthalonius), Prickly Pear, or nopal (Opuntia engelmanii), Century plant or Magay (Agave chrysantha), and Damiana (Turnera diffusa). The Elephant Tree or Cerote (Bursera microphylla) has a peeling aromatic bark and a small aromatic fruit.

Off for the oasis. We drove down hill to a dry riverbed about 100 m wide and drove up the sandy riverbed to a white granite box canyon. Tlaco palms or Palmilla (Erythea Brandegeei) grew at the canyon head where a spring-fed waterfall tumbled about 50 feet to a small creek. A black dragonfly and several black damselflies patrolled the canyon. A small pond contained tadpoles and juvenile toads. A large Diving Beetle swam in the stream just before the stream disappeared into the sand. There was about a dozen ant lion pits (Myrmelean sp.) in the sand. We turned around and drove down the riverbed almost to the highway before turning into the brush and back to the starting place. It was a nice ride and I saw a lot and shot a bunch of pictures. It could have been better a little slower and with more stops. The guide was probably good enough for the normal tourist that wants to ride an ATV but a naturalist he was not.

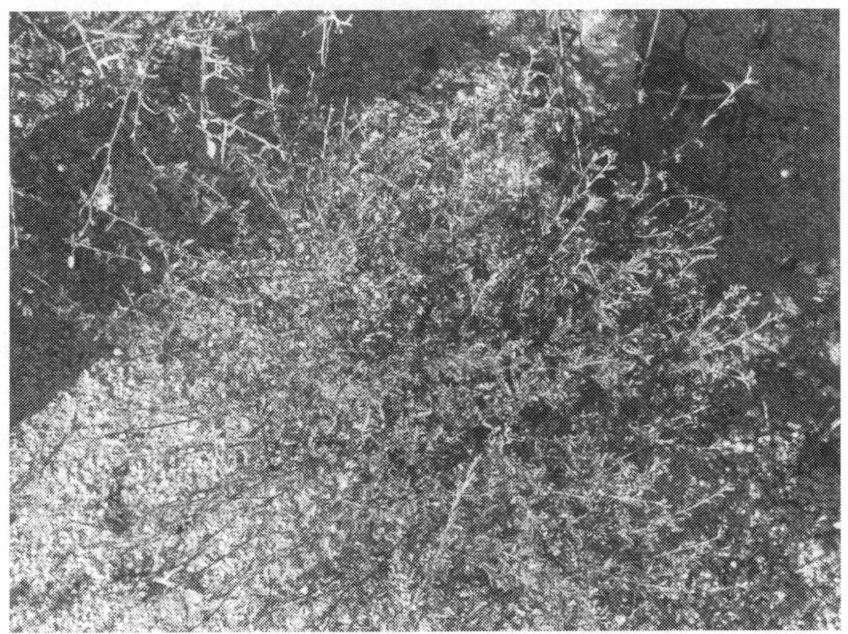

Damiana de California (Turnera diffusa)

Biznaga and Viejilta

Canyon

Waterfall

I got back to the room a walking dust ball. A hot shower felt good.

We went down for the hotel's Mexican fiesta. T'was interesting to see the Baja idea of Mexican food. Large tamales wrapped in banana leaf. Tacittos. Pebil. Rollenos. Salads. Guacamole. Flan. Pound cake. No enchiladas or tacos. Folk songs and dances and fireworks followed this.

Wednesday morning started with the gym and a walk on the beach. This morning I walked roughly north. The beach was steeper and contained less shell fragments. On the way to the beach I came across a patch of a flowering Euphorbia, Golondrina (Euphorbia leucophylla). Its flowers were a quarter inch in diameter and white. There was also Molluga, Crowfootgrass (Dactyloctenium sp.) and what looked like Windmillgrass (Chloris sp.)

A dry river mouth was about a quarter mile north. Nothing of interest but a group of Kildeer. A Dogface butterfly was dead on the beach. Bewick's wren was singing off in the brush.

Several kinds of skippers and a small white butterfly were nectering on the Bougainvillea in pots in front of the hotel.

Golandrina

On the way to town there were Alamanda and Bush Morning Glory (Ipomea leptaphylla). A Caracara (Caracara cheriway) flew over with something hanging from its beak.

We went to *Juanitos*, the place we were supposed to have a free glass bottom boat ride. They said a trip had just left and the next one would be at 1100 but it was booked up. The 1200 trip was empty but since we did not have reservations we could not get on it and we could not make reservations because we were already there.???

We left and went shopping. At *Puerto Pariso* mall we had lunch at *Johnny Rockets*. This was a 1950-style soda fountain complete with jukebox and white caps on the waiters. Just like I looked in high school when I worked jerking sodas. Then we walked along the waterfront looking at the yachts. We stopped at *Art and Sushi* to look at their art. Lots of Boterro bronzes and some local modern art.

Johnny Rockets

Near the *Hotel Melia* were a Gila Woodpecker (Centurus uropygialis) and a bunch of sparrows in a Mesquite tree.

We went back to the condo about 1530. Carol went to the pool and I sat on the patio and typed my notes. About 1700 I went for a run on the beach. A couple of ATVs ran past. One had some guy driving while his dog was running. I thought ATVs were banned from the beaches.

Early Thursday morning I was on the beach again for sunrise. The typical beach morning cool breeze was not present. Burrowing sand worms showed themselves by bundles of tubes of glued sand. We were on the way to La Paz about 100 miles north. Several more people got on after we did then we shot through San Jose del Cabo and San Jose Virjo, past the airport and the water well field, past the bus station at Santa Anita and past the courthouse and prison. The bus traveled to Cabo San Lucas or returns every half hour for 16 pesos. Beats $30.00 US. We proceeded north on Highway 1, also called the Transpeninsular, bypassing small hill country towns of Caduano, Miraflores, Santiago and Las Cuevas. Santiago had 2500 people and the only zoo in the southern Baja.

The road went through the foothills of the Sierra de la Laguna with rolling hills and lots of cactus, Cerote or Elephant Tree, Palo Verde and Palo Blanco. We crossed the Tropic of Cancer. A Caracara was perched on a tall cactus just waiting. A Greater Roadrunner (Geococcyx californianus) dashed across the road. A pair of Golden Eagles (Aquila chrysaetos) was devouring road kill.

Dry River

We crossed the partially demolished highway across the Rio San Jose. A good size stream was flowing out of the mountains. Recent rains had crested at over 20 feet and left six to ten feet of sand piled on the road. We crossed maybe a dozen other intermittent streams along the road with only a couple others showing bad high water damage. Several Crows (Corvus brachyrhynchos) were sitting on a sand bar.

Salt cedar or Tamaris (Tamarix pentandra) was on some of the sandbars and should be gotten under control before it gets to be a real nuisance. Several Turkey vultures were circling overhead.

Blue water appeared ahead as we approached Bahia los Porros. The road passed along a ridge overlooking the anchorages at Buena Vista and Los Barriles. Lots of sail boats and other yachts were anchored along several miles of coast. The communities were full of coconut trees and villas of mostly Canadians. Los Barilles has been the windsurfing center for the Baja. There were plants of Mariola, Oja de Liebre (Solanum hindsianum) and Malva Rosa (Melochia tomentosa).

Bueno Vista

Leaving the coast the road became winding switchbacks passing over and through five major canyons. The road was edged with yellow trumpet flowers. One canyon contained a marble quarry. The towns of San Bartolo, San Antonio and El Triumfo were old mining towns that had been mined out.

We took a break at San Bartolo. Tamales, coke, and leche quemada for me and tamales and Coke Light for Carol.

Trumpet Flowers

We could see Devils Peak in the distance, 6,000 feet with a pine/ oak forest. From the top you might see the Pacific to Gulf, La Paz to Cabo. There are overnight tours to the peak.

San Antonio had been the capitol for a month. The town had had 4000 people mining gold, silver and copper but now has about 300. It looks like an oasis with date palms.

Next was El Triumpho where General Hidalgo, the hero of 17 September fame, was born. We swung by the house where the most famous spy for Pancho Villa had lived. A US mining company had come to town and wrung it dry in seven years. They left in 1912. This was the first town with electricity and telephones on the Baja.

We left El Triumfo and the hills behind. Level ground with more trees and cactus. We passed through San Pedro with 600 people. This had been the site of a revolt of the Pericú Indians against the Jesuits.

We saw a Green Angel truck. This is a driver assistance program sponsored by the tourist industry to help stranded motorists.

La Paz was the site of the first European settlement by Cortès but there was no permanent settlement until 1811. The US occupied the area during the Mexican War in 1846-48. William Walker from Tennessee via Texas tried to set up the Republic of Lower California in 1853. The area was a pearl diving center, but the trade died off until the Japanese Mikamoto began pearl culture in the 1960's. Today La Paz is a tourist destination with resorts and beaches. The Port of Pichilingue is the ferry stop to Topolobampo and Mazatlàn.

La Paz has a refinery, several college level schools, an anthro- pology museum, theatre, blanket factory and light industry.

Malecon

We visited a blanket factory, and I finally figured out how the loom and the spinning wheel work. We drove into the center of town near the malecòn and major banks to the cathedral where we stopped for an hour and 15 minutes shopping opportunity. I walked two blocks to the malecòn to get pictures of the beach and the ferry. Unlike the Cabo area the beach was covered with unbroken shells although some looked like they had been through a dredge.

On the way back to find Carol I stopped at two banks to exchange a worn-out 50 peso bill (about $5 US). The banks refused to change it saying the bill was old money and worth half a peso. What am I supposed to do with it, send it to Presidente Fox?

I found Carol, and we looked through some shops. She had a bruised heel and thought a cane might help so we looked for a *farmacia* (drug store) to buy a *caña* or *bastión* (cane or walking stick). We found one but it did not have a rubber tip. I asked around and found a *ferreteriá* (hardware store) and found just what I wanted – a *tipo de silla* or rubber chair leg tip.

We all gathered for a quick tour of the cathedral, and then headed for lunch at La Fonda at1400.

Lunch offering included Mexican dishes of fish, pork, chicken and beef. I chose pork ribs with *nopal* (cactus) while Carol chose ribs. Beverage was hibiscus or Roselle water much like lemonade. One difference from US restaurants was a sink in the corner for hand washing instead of a trip to the restroom.

About 1600 we left for Todos Santos. Back south to San Pedro, then onto Highway 19 that loops west and south along the Pacific to Cabo San Lucas. It was about a 50 mile straight shot through level ground to the Tropic of Cancer and the farm country around Todos Santos.

The town was founded in 1734 as Misión Santa Rosa de Todos Santos. The mission was pretty much abandoned after the Pericú Indians rose up against the Jesuits and finally abandoned in 1840.

The area around Todos Santos was an oasis with dates and citrus. It had been planted in sugarcane in the late 1800s. The population survived on agriculture and fishing until the springs went dry and the water supply vanished.

Apparently this was a periodic occurrence since a couple hurricanes recharged the aquifer and the area is currently into organic gardening.

During the 1950's and 60's the town became an artist colony with writers and painters. One famous location from the 1930s, Hotel California, recently reopened a room or two. There were also half a dozen galleries and a local museum and a Canadian bar called "Shut up, Frank".

Hotel California

We got the driving tour through town and stopped by the cathedral across from the plaza. After going through the cathedral we got an hour for shopping to meet back at the Tequila Sunrise bar across from the Hotel California. It was almost 5PM and everything was closing. I signed the wall in the Tequila Sunrise bar along with a few thousand more famous personalities and ordered a damiata margarita for the trip home.

The sun was setting as we left town. We drove through the village of Bahia Pescadero with the nearby agricultural research station and arboretum. It was too early for whale migration and too dark anyway.

Great view of the Pacific. Really great sunset. Along the beach were developments and with small lots with no utilities. We got into the foothills with loose cattle and horses roaming the road. Warning signs along the road featured a big bulls head on a round yellow sign.

The bus arrived in Cabo San Lucas a little after 1900 and dropped people off at various hotels. We were home about 2000 and crashed.

Sunset and Mare's Tails

Early Friday morning I was typing on the balcony listening to the ocean roar. I heard a noise and watched a Gila Woodpecker (Centurus uropygialis) inspect coconut trees.

I headed down for the beach and met a Canyon Wren sitting on an agave bloom stalk. He was calling while inspecting the dead agave blooms and ignoring me. I shot several pictures and have some calls on tape.

The sprinkler system had watered some of the sidewalk and several species of butterflies were puddling (drinking) standing water. On the beach the tide had turned and was going out. Rocks were not yet visible. Mixed with the broken shells was a new sea urchin, the White Sea Urchin (Lytechinus anamerus).

Canyon Wren

Several small plovers had a brown cap and back with black legs and beak and the cape ran over the shoulders but not under the chin. They were Snowy Plover (Charadrius nivosus) running amongst the drift at the high-tide line.

On the way back up the beach I heard a flock of Gambel Quail (Lophortyx gambelii) on the other side of the boundary fence. I went over to the fence and saw half a dozen Quail busily feeding before they disappeared into the brush.

Snowy Plover

Gambel Quail

There was a dead mature ghost crab (Ocypoda sp.) in the drift line and a dead half eaten Surgeonfish. There were several pieces of cactus skeleton and gribble-eaten wood.

A dry river mouth about 300 yards wide had a sand plug extending 100 yards up stream. This was where the river lost velocity and dumped its load of sand. The sand pile was about 4 feet deep across the mouth. Upstream was about 100 yards wide and contained a number of ragweed (Ambrosia sp.) shrubs covered with butterflies including Dogface, Gulf Fritillary and Black Swallowtails.

There was also a number of low growing Jimson Weed or Toloache (Datura wrightii).

There were no "sea beans" on the beach. The only plants that might be available were Tropical Almond and mango. Neither of these was found along the beach.

An unidentifiable gecko was running across the beach a couple hundred yards from any usable cover.

We caught the 1000 shuttle into town. About half way to town the police had a roadblock up stopping all vehicles looking for four jail breakers.

First shopping stop was at *Bla Bla Bla*, a silver jewelry specialty chain.

Next was a Pedi cab ride to a restaurant called La Coral. We found it and the food was good. I had fish tacos or maroscos with two Dos XX beers. Carol had ribs and a light Coke.

Next stop was a designer dress shop called Magic of the Moon. Carol bought two dresses. While she was shopping I went to a bookstore called Libros, Libros. They did not have what I wanted. Carol took a pedicab back to *Puerto Pariso* mall while I walked the malecón. I took a lot of pictures of the harbor.

I also shot pictures of pelicans and Sally Lightfoot crabs (Grapus grapus) and the Sea Cockroach (Ligyda occidentalis) on the rocks.

We stopped for a Coke at *Johnny Rockets* and caught the next shuttle back to the condo.

Mare's tail clouds in the evening predicted a weather change. The next day was cloudy with showers. Saturday morning we were up early to see the sunrise. The sun crawled up behind clouds to the horizon and peeked out occasionally.

Sally Lightfoot Crab

Ready for the trip back to Todos Santos, we went down to the lobby to wait for the van. A group was doing a fashion shoot for one of the large Mexican magazines.

About a dozen people were involved with makeup, lights and reflectors, a wind machine, script, cameras and film and the director and model. We saw the crew that evening in a restaurant down town

This trip went reverse of the trip to La Paz. We went to Cabo San Lucas passing the only Costco in Baja. It was doing a big business. Then we turned north up highway 19. I rode shotgun in front and watched for whales. The weather was overcast for the first day of this vacation. The trip started through winding hills past San Cristobal, and Migrino. The road leveled out on the coastal plain along the Pacific past El Cajoncito. We passed the Ag research station at Rancho Nuevo and turned off to see an oasis and beach at Las Palmas. There were a number of kinds of cactus including Old Man Cactus, Garambullo, or Sentia (Cereus acanthocarpa) and several kinds of Cholla. A sidewinder rattlesnake track crossed the dusty trail. Ball Moss or Heno Pequeno (Tillandsia recurvata) grew on several Ocotillo plants. Adám's Tree or Palo Adán (Fouquieria diguetii) supported lichens (Orchilla). We got down to the palm trees and majority decided not to go to the beach because of possible mosquitoes.

A few miles further we passed El Pescadero then into Todos Santo passing the Shut up Frank bar and the only signal light in town.

We again got the driving tour. The Colonels House where the spy for Pancho Villa had lived. The tile factory. Several galleries. The dormitory where high school students from the surrounding area came and stayed for school. The museum was an old school house. The mission with its new addition. Hotel California. We took a walking tour of the museum and then left to see some of the galleries including the artist Gabos and Charles Stewart.

Cardon and Creosote Bush

Old Man Cactus

Interesting little town and delightful weather. Lunch was at the Tequila Sunrise. Lobster rolleno decorated with pomegranate seeds and fresh basil and a damiana margarita. Carol signed her chair and had a Mexican plate with a Coke. The return trip began about 1500 and covered the fifty miles in about an hour.

We changed clothes and took the shuttle to town for supper at Mi Casa. Good food. The photographic group from the hotel came in right behind us.

Sunday morning we were up to see the sunrise.

Sunrise

Another first - there had been a little rain over night.

We took the 0900 shuttle to town for a glass bottom boat ride. A cab took us to the Hotel Melia and we walked down the beach to Juanitos for our 1000 ride. The boat had engine trouble so we got a 20-minute ride instead of an hour. The boat was a wooden 25-foot with an outboard and a glass covered well. They pulled it in to the beach like a pirate long boat. Everyone was expected to wade out and climb in while it beat on the sand. This is dangerous particularly for the pregnant and heavy set. Carol could not get on and fell down. I was afraid the boat would come down on her leg. Carol refused to go and they refused a refund.

The boat headed straight out for the Arch. We got near the rocks and the boat slowed while the driver tossed out fish to attract other fish. There were a lot of fish like Sergeant Major and wrasses and a big puffer fish for maybe a minute then away we went. We saw the Two Ocean falls, the arch, Lovers Beach, and Seal Rock, and then around the point to the Pacific and pirates' cave and Lovers Beach from the Pacific, then back to the beach in less than half an hour. The tide was high and the water was rough so no stopping at Lovers Beach.

We went downtown and had lunch at the Giggling Squid. I had squid and a beer. Then I tried a drink called Sex on the Beach made of vodka and amaretto. Like real sex in the sand once was enough. We shopped a little more then went back to the condo and the pool.

Lover's Beach

Two Ocean Falls

Los Arcos

Giggling Marlin

Monday morning I hit the beach one more time and came back to finish packing. At 1030 we took a taxi for the 45-minute ride out to the airport. We got checked in and the bags checked and had a pizza and coke for lunch. The plane that was supposed to leave at 1305 did not start loading until 1245.

The flight back was over the clouds marking the jet stream. It was hazy as we began letting down into Mexico City. We had a two-hour layover and again played musical gates to find the proper one. We were back in San Antonio by 2000 and home by 2045.

Conclusion. It was altogether a good trip. There were a few minor glitches. If I were going back I would take a direct flight and bypass Mexico City. I would try to visit the experimental farm and arboretum near Todos Santos. I would see Cacti Mundo in downtown San Jose for a visit to the Los Cabos Botanical Garden. I would also plan an overnight in La Paz to visit the archeological museum and art galleries.

Carl Lahser
24 October 2003

Los Arcos, Cabo San Lucas

6

Mata Ortiz

Mata Ortiz

INTRODUCTION. The Southwest School of Art and Craft in San Antonio, Texas, offered a five day trip to Mata Ortiz 24-28 November 2004 through the Darlene Conoly travel agency in Beeville, TX. Itinerary was to fly from San Antonio to El Paso and then drive to Nuevo Casas Grandes with trips to Mata Ortiz, Casas Grandes, the Museo de la Cultura Norte, petroglyphs in Arroyo de los Monos, Hacienda de San Diego, and the Mormon village of Colonia Juárez.

E-mail references the pottery and the town of Mata Ortiz include:
http://mataortizpottery.com/history.htm,
http://store.yahoo.com/southwestjewelry/maorpoisorgr.html,
http://www.mexconnect.com/mex/mwilliams/mlopez.html,
http://www.indiansun.net/MT079.asp,
http://www.mataortiz.com/mataortizpottery.htm.

References to the Casas Grandes archeological site can be found at:
http://www.tourbymexico.com/chihua/cgrandes/cgrandes.htm,
http://savytraveler.publicradio.org/show/features/2000/20000318/casas.shtml.

A plant checklist for the park area is found at: http://dwason.ucnrs.org/documents/flora-dodson.de. I noticed many additional plants around the hotel and in Mata Ortiz not on the list.

About 200km (150 miles) southwest of El Paso is the center of the Casas Grandes culture. The people and the principle city were called Paquíme. Paquíme was a major trading center from A.D. 900-1200 with evidence of influence by the Toltec culture. The ruins of Paquíme include an interior water system and a system of canals that provided water for a corn/bean/pepper agriculture. Pyramids and ball courts were constructed. Adobe structures, some two and three stories high, remain as maze of foundations and scattered walls. The largest structure contained 50 or more rooms.

The Paquíme produced superior pottery of red, brown or black geometric patterns on a cream background. The village of Mata Ortiz with about 2000 people is the modern center for production of pottery using materials, techniques and style after the Paquíme.

Recent History. Around A.D.1340 Paquíme was destroyed possibly a result of civil war, attacks by other tribes or, more likely abandoned because of adverse environmental changes like a prolonged drought. The inhabitants retreated to the Sierras and abandoned this area. The archeological site called Casas Grandes has been partially excavated and is available to the public from Nuevo Casas Grandes.

Beginning in the 17th century the Apaches became the dominant tribe for about 150 years. The Apaches were finally rounded up by General Cook in 1884 and taken to reservation in Arizona and New Mexico.

Hacienda de San Diego

Don Luis Terrazas was given a land grant in the 1890s for his part in the war against France. Terrazas brought in cattle and built his herds to 250,000 plus horses and sheep and built 99 haciendas on his million acres.

Pancho Villa grew up on Terrazas' land. Villa came to power as a bandit he raided the ranches killing personnel and cattle. Villa was not caught and his raids eventually bankrupted Terrazas.

Pearson/Juan Mara Ortiz

In 1885 32 Mormon families, running from the U.S. marshals for their practice of polygamy, crossed into Mexico and settled near Mata Ortiz to the chagrin of Terrazas. They brought tools and livestock and began farming on land near Colonia Juarez. They were joined by other Mormon families and dammed the rivers for water to irrigate peach and apple orchards.

Lumber was harvested beginning in the 1880's. A small mill was running in 1890 in Pacheco. Success of lumber and agriculture brought in the railroad sponsored by Porfirio Diaz. A railroad tent camp was created in 1907 at the rail end.

In 1909, F. S. Pearson from Canada and Enrique Creel, son-in-law of Terrazas, created the Sierra Madre and Pacific Railroad. A sawmill cut the local timbers for railroad ties. The camp was called Pearson. Pearson sold out in 1914 and died when a Germany submarine torpedoed the Lusitania in 1917. The railroad changed hands several times being called the *Noroeste* or Mexican Northwestern Railroad and later called the Chihuahua al Pacifico. In May 1925, Pearson was renamed Juan Mata Ortiz after Juan Mata Ortiz who helped defeat the Apache chief, Victorio.

The lumber company, Bosques de Chihuahua, owned much of the land around Mata Ortiz. In the 1930s President Lazaro Cardenas accelerated land reform by organizing numerous *ejidos* on former haciendas. Mata Ortiz was one of these. The town prospered until the 1960s when the rail yard was moved to Nuevo Casas Grandes. By the 1970s the area was remote and poor.

A young man named Juan Quezada developed current pottery making in the 1970s. The original art and techniques of the Paquíme were reinvented and refined based on pottery shards Quezada found in the area. He located local materials and began to perfect his art. Once the pottery began to sell Quezada taught his family and about 200 local people the potter's skill. There are now about 400 potters working in town.

Abandoned Depot at Mata Ortiz

The Paquíme polychrome clay pots called *ollas* were made by the coil method on a rounded bottom made with a "puka" mold. The contemporary are made by what Quezada calls the "single coil" method. Current *ollas* are decorated with pre-Columbian figures called *Moctezumas*, geometrics called *cuadritos*, incised designs called *calcado*, and more contemporary zoomorphic wildlife designs called *sgraffitto*. Also made are ceramic figures called *monos*.

The Trip. Many of the members of the tour gathered Southwest Airlines gate in San Antonio for the short flight to El Paso. Wheels were in the wells at 1:37pm. The sky was relatively clear with several bands of popcorn clouds. Every stock tank in sight was brim full as a result of recent rains.

I was surprised to see the plane about half full. Usually Southwest is full to standing room.

The route crossed several oil fields with their network of roads leading to the pumping sites.

Further west the hills looked different than around central Texas where the vegetation bands are circular as the layers of different kinds of limestone are exposed. The western hills exposed layers showing long parallel bands. It is a common misconception about our hills that the hilltops and valleys are the same configuration now as when they were formed 70 million years ago. Truth is the original valleys collected more silt/mud and developed thicker and denser layers. These layers were more resistant to erosion and have become the hilltops while the thinner, less dense layers eroded faster and are now the valleys.

Somewhere around Ft Stockton we passed over a big vehicle test track with the oval track about a mile diameter and the shorter tracks inside of the oval.

Near Balmorhea Guadalupe Peak was visible to the northwest covered with snow.

Dust clouds met us just east of El Paso. We were on the ground at 2:55 pm MST. It was clear and windy in the 60s. Three vans met us at the airport. We loaded up and headed for the rental agency to pick up the rest of the group.

We left El Paso about 4 pm heading about 120 miles to the Columbus, New Mexico, and the border crossing to Palomas in the Mexican state of Chihuahua. We arrived at Palomas about sundown. Immigration was no problem but there was a glitch in getting the rental vans through customs. The rules are different every time I cross the border.

By now it was about 8 pm and we decided to eat before getting on the road. We walked about a block south to the "Pink House". The restaurant was essentially out of food. No meat. I had quesadillas, a Tecate beer and a hot chocolate with water.

We drove to Mexico highway 2 in the dark. At Ascensión we crossed Rio Casas Grandes where shrimp was for sale. We continued on to Janos where we intersected Mexico 10. Everyone woke up when we almost ran into an old truck with no lights creeping along the road. We turned south to Nuevo Casas Grandes and arrived at the motel about 10 pm. Missed our welcome margaritas. My roommate was Dennis Smith the ceramics chair at Southwest Crafts Center. We got moved in and shortly crashed. Light began creeping around the drapes a little after 6 am on Thanksgiving Day. Official sunrise was about 6:45 am. The lawn was sparkly with frost with a temperature about 30°.

MANANA TEA

"Cafe, Senior?"
"Hot tea, please."
"Que?"
"Una taza de te caliente, por favor."
"Oh. Si, Senior. Right away."
Hot water arrives but no tea.
Time passes.
"Mozo, por favor."
"Senior?"
"Traigame una taza de te?"
"Si. Si. Right away."
The water is like warm when the tea bag arrives.
"Mozo, por favor."
"Senior?'
"Traigame una taza de aqua caliente?"
"Que?"
"I want hot tea, dammit!"
"Oh. Si, Senior. Right away."
He brings me a cold beer with a sly grin.
"Salud. And to Hell with the tea."

* * *

By the time we had consumed a pretty typical American breakfast and loaded the vans it was getting tolerably warm.

Across from the motel were a Pemex, a bar/liquor store, park and a municipal stadium.

We left for Casas Grandes to visit the archeological site of Paquíme and to have Thanksgiving dinner at the home of Spencer MacCallum. Groves of peaches, apples and pecans lined the highway. We crossed the Rio Casas Grandes lined with cottonwood trees bright yellow from the snow and freezing weather of the previous week.

First stop was at Spencer's to drop off the turkeys for Thanksgiving dinner. He was still in his pajamas. Next stop was a shop on the corner across from the square. This shop was famous for its rattlesnake and sotol pickled in what smelled like tequila. A sip of this stuff is supposed to be good for rheumatism. No one tried it. The shop sold rings of various styles and sizes to set the round bottom pots on along with many other local artifacts.

We drove out to the Paquíme site. The museum, Museo de la Cultura Norte, was half buried so as not to distract from the ruins. Primary landscaping was with native cacti and shrubs. I was surprised and a little disappointed to see two species of Eucalyptus planted on site. These were the same two species presenting a problem in California originally planted to be used for railroad ties. These trees were too soft and flammable for lumber and have become a nuisance.

The museum has a circular floor plan with numerous bilingual interpretive displays from archaic to contemporary. There is a nice gift shop.

Aljibi, Central Plaza, and La Casa de la Noria

The path through the site begins in the Acequia Madre, an abandoned irrigation and water supply structure. The path passes the ball court (Jungo de Polato) with a raised dais for the elite. This structure resembled those in the Southwest more than those in Yucatan. In the distance to the east was a structure built in the shape of a cross, the Monument of the Cross.

The next items of interest were a tomb and the central water system (Aljibi). The Edificio de los Ofrendos is thought to be a tomb but this is not certain. Nearby the Aljibi, with a water inlet, stilling basin, and storage reservoir was located on the west edge of the central plaza.

On the east and south of the central plaza were several multi-room structures. Each had an interior courtyard. The doorways, described as T-shaped, were about 30 inches wide but have sill with a one-foot by one-foot cut in the center. They remind me of the street crossings in Pompeii with slots for chariots wheels. They were probably built for internal defense to slow an intruder.

T-shaped doors

To the south was a second ball court. To the southwest a second Aljibi. In the southwest corner were the House of Serpents and the cages where ceremonial parrots were kept.

We left in time to get to Spencer's hacienda by 1400. After a tour of the hacienda grounds dinner was served. Turkey. Spanish rice. Fruit tamales. Refried beans. Beer. Punch. The Bueno Noche beer was one of the best I ever had in Mexico.

After eating we went to visit two others haciendas Spencer was renovating. One was maybe five acres fenced with adobe. Rooms were built along the inside of the east wall. There was a limekiln built to make lime for stucco to coat the adobe bricks. The second house was more Federal style updated and furnished with period pieces. I asked about owning property in Mexico.

Spencer said there was no problem owning property 100% so long as you were at least 50 miles from the coast and 100 miles from the U.S. border.

Zaguan lives

The plaster was coming off an old adobe wall
An gate became visible
– a zaguan

A large gate and portico
to allow stock and wagons
inside the wall to deliver hay
and other cargo inside the wall
to rooms off the courtyard

The plaster was removed.
The zaguan exposed and restored
A zaguan gate was found
and the zaguan lives.

A grackle was singing in the top branches of a golden cottonwood.

Grackle Love

On the highest branch of a cottonwood
midst leaves turned golden by frost
a gleaming black great-tailed grackle perched
Swaying in the breeze, he sang
sang to challenge any other golden-eyed males
Several grackles strutted about in the a coral
feeding on spilled grain
ignoring but occasionally looking at the singer.

Many small homes are also workshop and gallery. I saw several old men sitting outside their homes in the sun sandpapering green pots in anticipation of decorating these pots.

All the pottery is signed. When Juan Quezada first began to sell his pottery in the late 1960s traders tried to make them look like antique pieces of Casas Grandes ware. A friend told Juan that many artists signed and dated their pottery. Juan tried this and sales dropped. Traders began scrubbing off the painted signatures and still tried to sell them as antiques. Juan began to etch his name into the clay. This was adopted by the whole community. We finished and headed back for the motel just as the near full moon was coming over the mountains. We stopped at the home of Blanca Ponce, a potter. She had moved to the big city for better education for the kids and would accompany us to Mata Ortiz the next day. Blanca took us to another pottery shop with less quality wares and accompanied us to the motel where our margaritas were waiting.

Potter at Work

Friday morning was cold but not freezing. After breakfast we loaded up and picked up Blanca, our guide. First stop was an upscale shop that had really good pottery. Unofficial pottery grades are collector, museum, high quality, commercial, and tourist.

Onwards to Mata Ortiz and many shops. Every time we stopped we drew additional potters out of thin air in the streets. Much good pottery. I bought a total of seven pieces of various styles and sizes. I have pieces from Oaxaca and Arizona signed and dated in the clay back to 1960.

After lunch we the Hacienda de San Diego. Don Luis Terrazas was given a land grant in the 1890s for his part in the war went out to against France. Terrazas brought in cattle and built his herds to 250,000 plus horses and sheep. He built 99 haciendas on his

Pock marked walls

million plus acres. This hacienda was built in 1904. The caretakers are 5th generation on the land.

Poncho Villa grew up on Terrazas' land. Villa came to power as a bandit and raided the ranches killing personnel and cattle and eventually bankrupted Terrazas.

The hacienda has walls pockmarked by bullets from Villa's raids. The rooms are large and airy with high ceilings where bats live in their season. There are many interesting architectural features like the hot water heating system from a boiler in the kitchen fireplace. A lot of money would be needed to renovate and restore the facility. There are iron posts from New Orleans holding up the front porch. Many of the stone slabs show the stonecutters marks made to get paid.

Other structures on the site include the granary where the family hid during Villa's raids, a building containing the offices and stables, and the barracks-like former housing for the workers.

Stonecutters mark

Many of us walked down to the river in anticipation of visiting the petroglyphs in Arroyo de los Monos. The river was up and had to be crossed three times to get to the petroglyphs so this was abandoned. We skipped flat rocks on the river, watched a flock of ravens harass a Red-tailed hawk, saw a Sinaloa wren and a small flock of pigeons, and returned to the hacienda.

The well for Hacienda de San Diego had been long abandoned. The present water supply came from the off-site Mormon village of Colonia Juárez.

Juan Quezada

On the way to Mata Ortiz we stopped at the pottery gallery of Felix Ortiz in an area called Barrio Porvenir. These pots have mostly large geometric or animal scenes painted over the slip. Outstanding pieces.

Saturday we went to the other end of town and visited several more potters. After lunch we visited Juan

Quezada for a demonstration of pot making and firing. The raw products were collected and ground to powder. Minerals for coloring pots include ores of iron (black), manganese (purple), and copper (green). These powders are hydrated (soaked in water) for up to a couple years.

The forming of a pot begins with mixing the clay with sand and volcanic ash to keep the pots from cracking. The use of a rounded bottom also reduces cracking. Forming the pot begins with putting prepared clay into a rounded mold called a "puka". A single thick "tortilla" of clay is attached and worked into a thin-walled pot. Lip, neck, and decoration are added and the pot is air-dried. Slip was added and the pot was decorated and polished before firing. These pots are fired one at a time. The pot is placed under a protective pot and covered with stacked fuel. This is lighted to get a fire all around the pot. This burns down and the pot is moved out to cool.

Firing a pot

Saturday night we had a group dinner followed by a howl at the near-full moon.

We were up early Sunday morning and on the road about 7:30 am. Sunrise began brilliant red and orange but clouded over before the sun appeared. We drove north under an overcast sky. A partial rainbow sprang from the western horizon.

Fields of dry land sorghum, cotton, red peppers, corn and cattle occupied both sides of the highway. A flock of Lincoln sparrows dashed across the road. Roadside mesquites gave way to acacias and creosote bush.

The road went into the hills of the Potrillo Mountains and many of crosses and memorials to crash victims sprouted on many curves

Lincoln Sparrows

A flight of fifty small finches
explode from the ground
avoiding a bouncing tumbleweed
They disappear
into the dry grass a hundred feet away
in the cold and blowing snow.
Lincoln sparrows in the winter scene

We arrived in Palomas and crossed over to Columbus for the drive to El Paso and the airport. I was home in San Antonio by 1700.

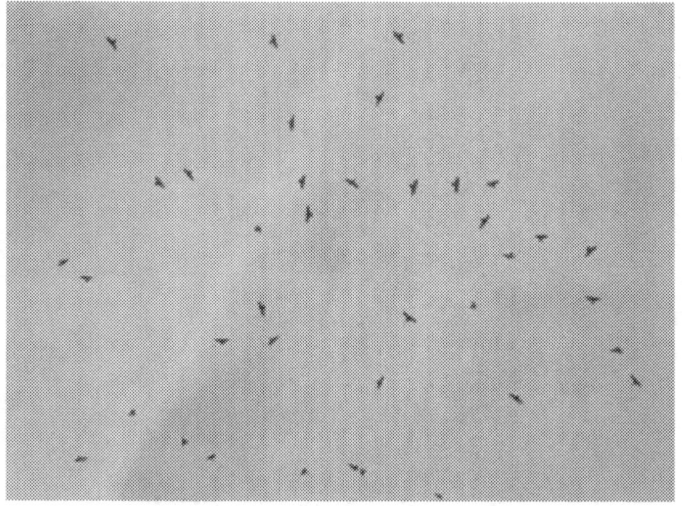

A Kettle of Ravens Harassing a Red-tailed Hawk

Round and around
a kettle of fifty ravens drifting to the south
encircle a red-tailed hawk.

*****

Mata Ortiz Pottery

7

Partners in Flight and Bird Watching

McAllen, Texas to Saltillo, Mexico 15-22 Feb 05

Partners in Flight and Bird Watching McAllen, Texas to Saltillo, Mexico

15-22 Feb 05

For over 40 years my mode of recreational driving has been largely creeping along the shoulder of the road at 15 mph looking at flowers, butterflies, and birds and stopping at new road cuts to look for fossils. I even stopped to skin road kills and tanned many of the hides.

I am retired but have over forty years of experience as a natural resources manager and getting paid for what I like to do. Over the years I have been to a number of professional meetings with field trips attached. Many of them were enlightening and enjoyable but not up to the standard set by the subject the Partners in Flight (PIF) meeting in McAllen, Texas, and bird watching trip to Monterrey and Saltillo, Mexico.

TRIP TO the VALLEY

Registration was to begin on 16 Feb 05 so I drove the roughly 300 miles from San Antonio, TX, to McAllen, TX, on 15 Feb. I left about 0900 on an overcast morning in the mid 50°s. By 1000 the weather was about 60°F. It was clear overhead with no horizon. My route from home was around SE San Antonio to Floresville and then across to Pleasanton on TX 97. Some of the mesquite, oak, and hackberry were budding out and Acacia was blooming golden. There were several dead skunks along the road. Just past the Promised Land Dairy there were a Crested Caracara and several Turkey vultures. A coyote was walking across a pasture. There was about a half-mile fence line planted with Afgan (Mondale) pines. The land was sandy and relatively flat.

The road intersected US 281/I-37. I turned south towards Georgewest and Falfurrias. The highway crosses the Atascosa River at Pleasanton and again near Campbellton and joins the Nueces R. near Three Rivers. The road also crosses several creeks that are usually a mile wide without a drop of water.

Ten more dead skunks and several dead vultures road kills occupied the road shoulders along with a couple of raccoons and a coyote. The grass was still brown with patches of Brassica in bloom. Three Rivers was essentially bypassed by the highway and did not offer much besides a Vallero petroleum processing plant and several oil well supply companies. On to Georgewest.

Georgewest was a smaller town and also bypassed. But it had signs for a small museum, the Grace Armentrout museum and a park called Cactus Park. Speed limit was reduced to 30 mph. This is the kind of place I would look for a speed trap at a road intersection leading to San Antonio, Corpus Christi, McAllen and Brownsville.

A six-foot welded wire fence extended several miles along the highway. It was not tall enough to act as a game fence. There was a dead vulture and a red-tailed hawk that were probably road kills.

Alice was a little larger and also bypassed. The roads to Robstown and Corpus intersected US 281. South of Alice the land was flat and had been cleared. No conspicuous wild flowers.

I stopped at Premont for a Dairy Queen chocolate dipped cone and headed on south. There were several roadside memorials to traffic victims – crosses and flowers.

Next town was Falfurrias. The first fruit stands appeared on the east or northbound side of the road. South of town was a truck weighing station and an immigration office. The road became a divided highway with oak trees in the median. The oaks disappeared after a few miles and then reappeared as a large copse with oaks on both sides as well as down the median. A sign announced the road as the future international corridor. There were quite a few disposable flowers of commerce - plastic bags - decorating roadside trees. Finally, there is a big sign announcing, "Welcome to the Valley" sponsored by a big trailer park.

Oleanders and palm trees began to appear. Freeway construction began a few miles north of Edinburg and extended to US 83 at Pharr. I headed west on 83 to McAllen and found the motel. It was about 3:00 PM and the room was not ready yet. I see the valley still runs on manãna time. The weather is pretty much the same year around and there is no tomorrow.

I walked across to the mall across the street. Same collection of stores you might find in Maine or Singapore.

I finally got moved in and about 6:00 PM I went to happy hour and found several people who were also attending the conference. There was enough to eat at happy hour to not have to go out for supper. About 8PM I went back to the room and crashed.

PIF MEETING

I was up early and hit the breakfast buffet and left about 7:30 for Bentsen-Rio Grande Valley State Park and World Birding Center. Going west on US 83 there is an inconspicuous sign for the park that says to get off on Bentsen Drive. In fact, you need to get off on Bentsen Palm Road at the community of Palmview and go about 3 miles south through the trailer community of Palmview South and cabbage fields. There is a large private trailer park and a small Park parking area. Neither the Park parking area nor the Birding Center entrance was well marked. The park manager says it's the Department of Transportation who controls the signs.

Anyway, I finally arrived in the area and drove past the parking area. The Birding Center and parking lot are outside of the former park entrance. The Park is closed to traffic and had closed the 72 trailer hook-ups in the park. I turned around and found the small sign for the parking lot. Then I found the Birding Center by following some people who looked like birders and knew where they were going. In the reception area I paid the entrance fee as a senior citizen and joined a walking tour group. This tour consisted of riding on a tram between birding sites and walking around several birding sires. Our guides were knowledgeable winter visitor volunteers who had been coming to Bentsen Park for years.

Typical Valley Road

First stop was at a feeding station at the former Park headquarters. The tram stopped and in a couple minutes several Javelinas came out to feed on corn. A flock of Plain Chachalacas flew in. Several Green Jays, a Long-billed Thrasher, several Great Kisskadees, two Clay-Colored Robins, two male Altamira Orioles, a Golden-front Woodpecker, a tree full of Mexican Grackles, and several White-tipped Doves were feeding on sliced oranges, seeds, corn, and a water station.

Kiskidee

The second station included a water site and an open park. There were more **Green Jays** and a **Javalina** near the road. At the dock were **Red-winged Blackbirds**, a **Great Kiskidee**, an **Orange-crowned Warbler**, a **Pie-billed Grebe**, several **Common Moorhens**, a **Green Heron**, a flyby by a **Green Kingfisher**, a **Yellow-rumped Warbler**, a **Ruby-crowned Kinglet**, and a **White-eyed Vireo**. We walked about a half-mile towards where the tram waited. There were **Ladder-backed Woodpeckers**, **Inca Doves**, a **Belted Kingfisher**, a **Ringed Kingfisher**, four **Altamira Orioles** including a yellowish hybrid, and a couple of **American Robins**. The last stop was at the new hawk tower. We saw **White Ibis**, **Snowy Egrets**, and two **Gray Hawks**.

We were back at the gate about 1030. I got off the tour at the former HA building and watched the feeding station for a half-hour. Nothing new arrived and I walked back to the center.

Chachalaca

I left and drove back to US 281 called Military Highway. The road was developed by General Blackjack Pershing while he chased Pancho Villa. I stopped at the library in Alamo to see if they would be interested in a book about my mother's growing up in Alamo 80 years ago

I left and found the Santa Anna refuge hoping for a few more birds and maybe some butterflies. It was a little early in the year for many flowering plants and the snow on Christmas 2004 (first time in history) caused damage to the butterfly populations and the normal flowering plants.

Park tram

On entering the grounds there were Northern Cardinals, Green Jays, Red-winged Blackbirds, Inca Doves, and Great-tailed Grackles. I did see and photograph a Blue Wave Butterfly. I saw a Checkerspot and several Guava Skippers. The weather was about 80 and overcast. Not a leaf was moving. There were small areas of mosquitoes. At the resacca overlook were Snowy Egrets, a Tropical Kingbird, a Moorhen, several Pie-billed Grebes, a White-eyed Vireo, and several Canvasback ducks. There was a Hackberry Snout Butterfly on Eupatorium. An area with Pricklypear (Opuntia) Cactus had a lot of dead crunched snails of the genus Rabdites probably indicating the presence of a Roadrunner. Near the exit were several flowerbeds with Lantana, Eupatorium with Guava Skippers, Sage and Hummingbird flower.

Eupatorium and Guava Skipper

Mexican Blue Wave Butterfly

On leaving the park there was a **Northern Mockingbird**, several **Northern Cardinals** and **Green Jays**, and a bunch of **Red-Winged Blackbirds** making noise like there was a hawk or owl hidden in the branches.

I left the Refuge and went on down Military Highway to La Feria where I grew up. Passing one of the plowed fields I saw a **Long-billed Curlew** walking the furrows.

Downtown La Feria

The water and sewage plants were gone and the reservoir was being dredged and cleaned up for a recreation area and nature center.

I drove through town. All the churches were still there but bigger. The schools had been replaced and the new library built. Along the main street the newspaper had moved. I stopped to see if the paper might be interested in publishing a book on my growing up in La Feria. I had lunch in the building that once housed the Mexican movie house.

I drove past where we once lived and found all the old neighbors gone.

I stopped in Mercedes and found everyone I had known 50 years ago gone. As I drove back to McAllen a **Cooper's Hawk** with black bars on its under wings swooped up across the road and perched on the power line.

I registered at the conference, hit the happy hour, and crashed. Everyone was in the lobby by 0630 to go to the International Birding

Center so I rode along. The route was easier having been there. We all boarded two open trams and were taken to the places I had visited the previous day. It was interesting being with about 50 expert birders.

We were on the trail a little before 7 AM. This was a little early even for early birds. A **Black-crowned Night-heron** was flying down the irrigation canal.

The feeders were being filled at the entrance site and there were no birds. We passed another feeding stations that had not yet been serviced. A few birds and several **Javalinas** were waiting.

Across from the resacca viewing station we could see a dead tree with **Double-crested Cormorants** and **Anhingas** and a **Golden-fronted Woodpecker** perched on a power pole. On this side a **Vermillion Flycatcher** sat in a tree. Calling birds included **Green Jays**, **Northern Cardinals** and **American Robins**. **Red-winged Blackbirds** and **Great-tailed Grackles** flew across the water. It was 7:40 when the first **Kiskakee** and **Altamira Oriole** started calling. A **Snowy Egret** flew over the water. **Ladder-back and Golden-fronted Woodpeckers** flitted between trees and a **Western Screech Owl** was in a hole in an oak tree its plumage matching the bark.

We passed the former trailer site and stopped to try calling with no luck. A **Bobcat** walked across the road. We went to the Hawk Tower and saw one **Gray Hawk**, several **Snowy Egrets** and a couple of **White Ibis**.

Back at the visitor center were several **Savanna and Lincoln Sparrows** hopping amongst the shrubs. The plants in the landscaping were not labeled. I asked but there were no lists of plants or butterflies in the park.

The weather was still cool and overcast with possible rain A cool front was due in the afternoon.

We drove back to the meeting and the presentations began at 10 AM. The presentations were very good. The motel served a sandwich buffet that took most of the lunch break. A poster session and silent auction were held in the evening.

The front passed and then came back from Mexico as a warm wet front. Friday morning it was 59°F and rainy. I slept late but more dedicated birders went back to the Birding Center or to a couple other birding sites.

Again, the presentations were outstanding. Lunch was a Mexican buffet. There was an organization meeting for the trip to Mexico.

BIRDING in MEXICO

By 6 AM I was up and packed. I checked out and headed for breakfast. There were several tours going out to several Valley sites as well as the one to Mexico. I left my pickup in the parking lot. At 6:30 three cars and a van began loading the 24 people going on the Mexico trip. We left about 7:00 and crossed the Rio Grande near Reynosa. Immigration was easy but getting the vehicles across was a minor problem.

While waiting in the immigration parking lot the group spotted a number of birds. I saw Great-tailed Grackles, Pigeons, House Sparrows, Tropical Kingbird, Starlings, White Pelicans, and a Snowy Egret. Some of the members claimed 15 species.

Everything finally pleased officialdom in about an hour. We took the scenic tour of Reynosa and stopped for Pesos for the toll road and finally hit the road. At the first checkpoint we were lucky enough to hit the random selection to have to unload the van.

The weather was foggy with less than a half-mile visibility. Roadside vegetation looked like typical Tamaulipan thornbrush. Birds along the road included Chihuahuan Ravens, Kestrels, and miscellaneous large hawks. A pair of Eastern Meadowlarks leaped up and dropped into the grass. By 10:30 the visibility was over a mile.

Several road cuts showed banding of gravel and clay. As we approached Monterrey the hills became highly bent limestone. We saw a Crested Caracara sitting on a large Joshua Tree. Black willow trees were leafing out along several dry creek beds. We entered Monterrey and found a place to gas up. Then we found a mall and bought groceries for the trip. Several of us tried the local tacos across from the mall.

Papilo victorinus, on a mulberry tree

There was a just hatched butterfly, Papilo victorinus, on a mulberry tree in the parking lot. It was a cool day, and it took some time for it to pump up its wings.

The parking lot had a tower with a security person watching traffic and thievery. Any problems noted in the parking lot were announced by a siren or loud speakers.

We drove out to Parke la Estanzuela for lunch and birding. This was a family park in the mountains and had a number of trails and picnic areas.

The variety of habitats included a creek and moist creek bottom with Polypoid ferns growing from the oaks and black walnuts. The creek bottom had watercress, Ranunculus, chickweed, Galium, Veronia and other cool season or aquatic associates. There were a lot of escaped landscape plants like Crassula, Pittosporum, and citrus. Leaf-cutter ants were hauling dime-size pieces of leaf back to their underground fungus farms.

The upland areas must be calcareous and get dry since there were numerous gelatinous colonies of Nostoc like the Texas hill country. The creek wound through what appeared to be Cretaceous limestone with no obvious fossils. The hills were more like brown flaky shale with bands of gravel.

First bird seen was a kestrel atop a light pole. Other birds seen were Audubon's Orioles, Green Jays, and a Black-headed Grosbeak. The weather was overcast to foggy. Temperature was in the 50s.

Leaf Cutter Ant

About 3:00 PM we were on the road towards Saltillo. There were many steep slopes with lots of switchbacks. The road ran through a relatively narrow canyon. The canyon walls were shale with quartzite inclusions and a stream ran along the road. We made several stops for bird watching. I heard a Canyon Wren and saw a bird that looked similar to one.

Plants included strawberries, anemone, and several ferns and dry grasses and the ornamental Vinca.

About 5:00 PM we arrived at the cabins. We unloaded the vehicles and moved in. Mexican Jays were calling. There was a run back up the canyon for use by bird looking.

Up on the mountainside were several pine trees that looked like they had an infestation of one of the pine beetles probably the Ipps Beetle. Selective cutting might save a lot of trees but no one seemed interested.

Red Tillandia

There was a mountain above the motel that looked like a volcanic plug but it is all limestone. Supper was prepared and served outside under the stars. We cooked Fajitas for 24 for supper with a little beer and other refreshments. There was no hot water because the gas bottle for the water heater was empty. Manāna? At least Mountain the water was drinkable so we washed in cold water and heated water for rinsing. Everyone crashed around 10:00 PM.

I got out my night vision scope. Worked well in both passive and IR modes. It's only a second-generation gadget and they are up to fifth generation equipment for the military.

Sunday morning began in the 50s. It began to get light about 7:00 but the sun did not get into the canyon until about 9:00. Breakfast was Huevos Ranchero with fresh papaya and pineapple.

We cleaned up and headed west down the canyon. Birds spotted included a woodpecker, several Eastern Phoebes, miscellaneous hawks and an American Kestrel.

We stopped along a stream in a deep canyon. There were pretty little waterfalls. Butterflies included a White-banded Skipper and a Tiger Swallowtail. Vegetation was much like early spring in the Texas hill country. Camas Lily. Watercress. Galium. Dandelion. Vinca. Mexican Gold Poppy. Eucalyptus. An Eastern Phoebe landed on a rock in midstream. This area appeared to be a combination of picnic area and outdoor restroom with disposable diapers and such. Algae in the creek indicated an addition of nutrients from sewage, agricultural runoff or the effluent from the trout hatchery up stream. I would recommend treating the water before drinking it. The creek was channelized in places to provide the water supply. There were a couple of trout hatcheries along the stream.

I walked about half a mile further down the road and around the corner to a roadside weekend BBQ stand. They were grilling chicken and selling apple wine and several kinds of pickled fruits. A new pickup pulled up and the driver spoke English. He had grown up in Alice, TX. He retired from AT&T five years before and moved to Mexico. He said the local ranch belonged to a big politician. He also said this area was all limestone with no fossils but that there were fossils west of the mountains near Saltillo.

Mexican Convenience Store

The valley began to widen with lots of nice farms with orchards and cattle and honey production. A few trees were blooming that looked like pears. Apples were not blooming yet.

We stopped at a small village. House Sparrows. On up the mountain we stopped to look. I saw a small lizard like Uta. Western red cedar was in bloom. Pines were beginning to candle out. Madrone. Brassica. Erodium. A yellow butterfly looked like a yellow Dogface. A pair of small golden butterflies was doing their mating ritual circling each other and spiraling higher. Many of the orchards had netting covers that were to protect the fruit from parrots.

Next stop was at an overlook for lunch and more looking. Parrots were supposed to be along the ridge tops. After lunch groups started out in all directions. I started up the hill and ran afoul of a barbed wire fence.

Several pines were marked for cutting. The stripped bark showed Ipps Beetle damage. Several trees had been hollowed out to collect pine tar. There were bunches of red-flowering Tillandia and a cute little round cactus plant. There were a number of madrone trees and several fern plants and patches of mosses. I was getting winded and found the altitude at about 6000 ft. Going down was difficult with slippery pine needles. Back at the road we had a snack and headed home.

Apple Orchard with Parrot Netting

We got back home and a number wanted to make another trip. I stayed home and napped then got out my GPS. It said the motel was at 4394 ft at 25°22'08.9" N and 100°13'06.7" W. Small blue lobelia and burr clover were in the lawn.

Supper was shrimp and corn salad and pork stew with a little mescal.

Monday morning we were up and on the road by about 8:00. Through the canyons we passed through an 8000 ft pass and were out on the Valle de Santiago, to the flat Chihuahuan desert south of Saltillo. This plain was surrounded by mountains in the distance. I saw Crested Cacacara, Lincoln Sparrows, a Peregrine Falcon, a Spotted Towhee, several Eastern Phoebe, a Loggerhead Shrike, some Western Meadowlarks, a Western Bluebird, and several American Robins.

We stopped along the road near what appeared to be a local dump where I saw Lincoln Sparrows and a Roadrunner. Next stop further west found a Long-billed Thrasher, several Long-billed Curlews, a Kestrels, a Horned Lark, and several Mountain Plovers. Burrowing Owls were living in a large Black-tailed Prairie Dog colony. A Prairie Falcon flew over and everything ran for cover.

Joshua Tree and Prickly Pear Fence

A Joshua tree forest was to the south of the road but there were no roads into it. Joshua trees had been along the road occasionally but were much more common and larger west of the mountains.

We turned around at a small town and began the ride back to the border. This village had a synagogue and several satellite dishes and a round blue elevated water tank. There were walls of prickly pear cactus or Joshua trees around some of the homes. There were House Finches and House Sparrows.

One more stop. A couple miles back there was a dirt ranch road that crossed a wide field of Prairie Dogs and entered the thorn brush again. We turned off and parked. I saw no birds. It was snack time and hit the road again. Virga was off to the southwest but disappeared as the clouds covered the sun.

We intersected the main road, Highway 57, between Bautista and Saltillo and turned north. We had just passed an Ostrich farm. We passed many cornfields south of Saltillo. At one of the gas stops I bought some Pan de Pulque. I had never seen this before but it certainly was good. The toll road bypassed Saltillo and Monterrey and were back at the border about 8:30. A wrong turn took us across at Progresso instead of Reynosa. We were back to the motel by 9:30.

FINI

I checked out and was on the road by 7:30. It was cool and misty so I drove straight through and was home by 11:30.

The trip as a whole was outstanding. While I only saw 62 species 15 were new to me. Experienced birders undoubtedly saw many more. The presentations were high quality and many of the discussions were helpful. Might try it again some time.

8

San Miguel de Allende

Dec 2006

Carl Lahser

San Miguel de Allende

Introduction

In November 2006, Carol and I received an e-mail for a potential home exchange in December in San Miguel de Allende, Guanajuato, Mexico. I thought it sounded like a good deal and Carol agreed. We answered and set up a trade 8-20 December 2006. It was a very good exchange.

Checking transportation possibilities, we decided against driving. We found airfare to Leon, the closest airport at 144 km to the west, would be close to a thousand bucks plus 60 bucks each way per person for ground transportation. We looked at surface transportation and found no passenger train. I found that senior tickets on a Americana bus would be $98 each round trip and that the trip would take about 18 hours. The first class buses included movies (in Spanish) and a restroom. We chose the bus. Our son decided to come along for a week, but his bus fare was about the same as both of our senior tickets.

Background

Since you are probably unfamiliar with San Miguel, it is located at an altitude of 7,000 feet in the state of Guanajuato, in the north central portion of Mexico. It is near the transition area between the mountains to the east and the Central Highlands to the west and south about 200 miles north of Mexico City. This is near the geographic center of Mexico. The Central Highlands is relatively flat agricultural land called the Bajío, Mexico's breadbasket. (It is called Bajío or low place relative to the mountains that surround it.) These highlands are Upper Cretaceous limestone with some metamorphic intrusions.

There is a large volcano, the *Hill of Moctezuma*, SE of San Miguel. It last erupted about 12,000 years ago. This must have been a large explosive eruption since it removed much of the volcano's conical top.

San Miguel is an agricultural center and made a reputation as a weaving center. It was on the main silver road between Zacatecas and Guanajuato and on to Mexico City. There were a number of inns in San Miguel that allowed the drovers to shelter and feed their mules. Inns provided security and every Inn was required by law to provide a comb and toothbrush by the well for the drovers. The local farms provided fodder and replacement mules. Each mule carried 300 pounds of silver to Mexico City or Guanajuato and returned with silver coins for pay and with various items for sale or trade. Each mule drover handled 12-15 mules. The drovers banded together and hired their own army for the trips.

A portion of the silver road was flooded and now lies under the San Miguel city water reservoir.

The regional archeological record goes back about 6000 years Irrigated farming began about 200 BC. Modern history begins in the early 1500s, when this was still the home of several indigenous tribes - the Chichimecas, the Otomi, and the Huachichilis.

In 1542 a Franciscan friar, Juan de San Miguel, established a mission to save the Indians. The mission was located where the territory of the three tribes overlapped near a fork in the river. Unfortunately, the river disappeared during the dry season so Friar San Miguel's replacement, Friar Cossin, found a better location. The mission was moved near a permanent spring in 1544. Local legend says the spring, called El Chorro, was located by a couple of hounds looking for a cool place to sleep.

Mission San Miguel was, at the time, the most northerly Spanish settlement and was harassed by local Indians. A Spanish garrison was established in 1555 to protect the town and the silver road. With the garrison came ranchers, farmers, and prospectors. By the end of the 18th century, San Miguel was one of the most prosperous cities in New Spain. The population grew and it had an estimated 40,000 people in the late 1700s when New York City and Philadelphia were still trading posts.

In 1804, Spain passed the *Consolidacion de Valles Reales*. For 300 years the Catholic Church had served as a banker, providing low interest loans. This decree allowed the Crown to call in and collect all loans immediately. It hit most of the landowners hard and bankrupted some. This, and the continued discrimination against everyone not pure Spanish, lead to unrest. The cities of San Miguel, Delores Hidalgo, and Guanajuato were major players in the Mexican War of Independence from Spain that began in 1810. If you are interested you can find information on the Mexican War for Independence in many sources.

In 1826, the town was renamed San Miguel de Allende after war hero, Ignacio Allende born in San Miguel. After independence, in 1821, the silver road was diverted to pass through the town of Celaya. San Miguel declined until 1938 when the Escuela de Belles Artes (School of Fine Arts) was established. The school attracted artists and art students from around the world. San Miguel was home for a time for artists like Frida Kahlo, Diego Rivera, Jose Alfaro Siqueiros, and others. Many had leftist leanings and Siqueiros was a professed Communist. Many of the students and visitors stayed in San Miguel along with many WWII veterans who studied under the GI Bill. It has since become a tourist destination, and has a large expatriate colony of an estimated 12 to 16 thousand Americans and Canadians. Current total population is around 80,000 and growing.

And Away We Go.

Anyway, Carol spent about a week cleaning the house, choosing clothes to take, and getting ready to go. On **Friday, 8 December**, we boarded the bus and left San Antonio around 1500. The weather was chilly and overcast from an El Niño storm, and a cold rain began as we were leaving the station.

The yucky, overcast weather persisted over the brown winter grass and bare trees of the Tamaulipan thorn brush. Clouds had begun to break on the SW horizon as the sun set. We zipped through Laredo. By 1800 we were across the border and on the toll road to Monterrey in the dark.

The bus stopped for fuel and a pit stop at the Pemex station collocated with the tollbooth. The restrooms had a 2 pesos price tag. The restrooms had American Standard fixtures that barely worked. (Contractor friends who had worked in Mexico all pulled their hair about the lack of work schedules and time lines for delivery of material. Also, there was no standardization of brick and lumber sizes, plumbing fixtures and pipes, electrical parts and equipment. Then, when a job was completed, there was no basic routine maintenance.)

About 2130 we drove through the back streets of Monterrey to the central bus station for a passenger stop. After Monterrey, there were short stops in Saltillo, Matehuala, San Luis Potosi, Santa Maria del Rio, San Luis de la Paz, Delores Hidalgo, and, finally, San Miguel de Allende. Lights of villages and houses dotted the darkness.

Dawn broke about 0600 near Santa Maria del Rio, with low stratus *El Niño* clouds and fog clinging to the hills. *El Niño* had dropped unseasonal rain. Water was flowing in normally dry streambeds and standing in roadside puddles and cropland furrows reflecting the breaking dawn like mirrored beads. Silhouettes of prickly pear and buckhorn cholla cactus, and Acacia trees were becoming visible. The sun finally poked through the scud about an hour high around 0700.

There were a couple of places where gullies were heading or eroding into the roadbed. This could cause major road damage since the roads were built on narrow roadbeds without shoulders this could be dangerous and cause major problems for transportation.

Ball moss was growing on the power and telephone lines. This probably caused a lot of line loss in an already inefficient distribution system.

We passed the turnoff to Leon where the airport closest to San Miguel was located. We soon came to an intersection leading to Guanajuato or to Delores Hidalgo and San Miguel. About 0700, we made a brief stop at Delores Hidalgo. The Church of Our Lady of Guadalupe is located in Delores. This was where Father Miguel Hidalgo proclaimed the *Grito de Delores* at 0500 on 16 September 1810 that kickstarted the Mexican War for Independence from Spain.

Ball Moss

Along the highway leaving Dolores were numerous car repair and muffler shops. (This country must be rough on vehicles.) There were numerous shops making and/or selling ceramics, pottery, and colorful double-fired Talavera tiles and antique shops that were selling copies of antique furniture, farm wagons, etc (instant antiques?). There were some of the rattiest-looking Casuarinas or Australian Pines I had ever seen as street and median trees.

Several small villages, each with a prominent church, were visible nestled in the surrounding hills. These were probably old mining towns or farming communities. Several fences of living Old Man Cactus (Myrtillocactus geometricans) looked like so many cedar posts.

Downtown

We arrived in San Miguel about 0800 and were met by our hosts. We took our bags to their house, and then they took us out to buy groceries. We had rare luck in finding a parking spot in front of one of their favorite restaurants and stopped for lunch. (I had fish tacos with jicama salad and roasted prickly pear with a Pacifico beer.)

They returned to the house with our groceries while we took a quick walk around the central area of San Miguel for about an hour. I don't think I have ever seen such a colorful town. Houses and buildings painted yellow, gold, shades of green and blue, pinks of a dozen shades, reds from brick to fire engine. Forty years ago Newfoundland and the Maritime Provinces of Canada had colored houses but salesmen with white vinyl siding took away their color.

House Exterior

When we returned, we read each other's house operating instructions. We got the Cook's tour learning to operate the house. We talked for about an hour, and then they loaded up and left to spend the night with friends before they left for our house in San Antonio, Texas, the next morning.

Here is a brief description of the house. It is located in a gated community called a Colonia east of the central part of town and about 700 feet higher than the central part of town. A 10-foot high wall encloses three patios and a three bedroom 3 1/2 bath two-story house with domed, brick ceilings. Turrets on the roof serve as skylights and for ventilation. Like most homes in the community, it has a large cistern under the house that receives relatively low-pressure water, which is then pumped to a storage tank on the roof from which water is gravity fed to the house. There are 110AC appliances, satellite cable and Internet connections, and electric or gas room heaters in each room.

Homes in San Miguel were listed in the real estate ads from $80,000 to $1.6 million U.S. dollars depending on size and location. Many were sold furnished to some degree. We were told property was evaluated at 300 pesos per square meter. This equated to about $3 per square foot. Shop space downtown rented for about 1600 pesos per square meter per month - about the rental price for commercial spaces in San Antonio.

Almost all buildings had rebar poking up from the roof to prove they were still under construction and eligible for reduced taxes. We also saw this in Greece and Italy for the same reason. Urban myth? Firecrackers were popping about every 15 seconds all evening. Beginning about 0330 until around 0600 the fireworks sounded like the next revolution. This is supposed to be celebrating something – birthdays, feast days. Who knows?

Going Down Town

Charles and Carol were up watching movies on TNT and had eaten breakfast and started the laundry by 0630. They were ready to hit the ground running but nothing was open until at least 1000. We walked downhill to town about 1030, after locking three separate doors, and the front gate to the house. Each door, the front gate, the side door, the dining room door and the door to the second floor, had a separate key and each was also secured with a padlock. It made coming and going from the house a production. This is not only to prevent theft but also to prevent kidnapping for ransom. According to residents petty theft is the major problem in San Miguel, but kidnapping is becoming more common in other parts of Mexico.

There is a small park in the gated community that has a fountain, several benches, and flowering plants. Several orange trees were producing ripe fruit and beginning to bloom at the time we were there. There were a couple of volunteer fennel plants with butterfly larvae stripping them to the stems.

The mile walk into town is not an easy trip given the often-steep grade of the cobblestone streets and lack of decent sidewalks. The drop in elevation was about 700 feet. Some plants had had freeze damage at the top of the hill. We resolved to take a taxi back up. All of the streets in town were either cobblestone or dirt. This helped to maintain the old fashioned appeal of the place and reduced water runoff.

There were few traffic signs and no traffic lights. Toves or speed bumps (also called sleeping policemen) are numerous. Drivers seem to rely on the one by one rule to get from point A to point B safely. Normal speed limit was about 20 kph and the cars pass through intersections alternating directions one at a time. They got all upset if anyone broke the rule. The taxi drivers rented their taxis and paid for their own gas. Standard fee any place in town was 20 pesos and most of their trips were two miles or less.

I stopped many times during the walk to look at local plants and noted about a hundred species, mostly ornamentals or exotics. I also took about 400 pictures. The houses were very colorful and the some of the doors could qualify as works of art in their own right. A book called Doors of San Miguel contains pictures of some of the more striking examples. There are, in fact, businesses that specialize in producing elaborate ironwork, doors and doorknockers.

When we reached a main cross street, we caught a cab to the bus station to make reservations for the return trip. Good thing we did, since there were only five seats left on the bus for San Antonio.

Another taxi took us back to the middle of town for lunch at Harry's Cajun Restaurant that our hosts had recommended. I ordered sweetbreads off the menu but was told they were out so I ordered

Jambalaya. The meal was tolerable for Mexican Cajun cooking especially since it came with a complimentary margarita.

Temperature was about 70 and clear, so we walked and looked and shopped and took pictures until about 1400. We took a taxi back home with our loot. Carol and Charles spent the afternoon dozing, watching DVD movies. I watched birds.

In the courtyard I saw two Dusky Hummingbirds and an Amethyst-throated Hummingbird, several House Finches and House Sparrows, a Loggerhead Shrike, a small flock of Great-tailed Grackles, numerous doves, and a Cactus Wren.

Dusky Hummingbird

On **Monday morning** we had a reservation for a day trip to Guanajuato for 0900. They picked us up on time and we were off. The other passengers they were to pick up bowed out at the last minute so it was just the three of us. The road went south and west around the end of the municipal water reservoir. The Silver Road from San Miguel to Guanajuato had run along the river but had long ago been drowned when the reservoir was constructed. West of the lakes were scattered copses of oaks along with the mesquites, acacias, and cactus. There were some leafless branches of Kapok trees with white flowers. Dry land farming produced corn that was cut and stacked for supplemental cattle feed. New air pollution laws prohibited burning the fields anymore.

We passed through several small towns before entering the suburbs of Guanajuato. The city was built along an intermittent river in a canyon, so the space for expansion was limited. An underground drainage system had been built to eliminate any chance of flooding and many of the main roads were built in the old riverbed running through a system of tunnels. The city was built on the higher ground on top of the tunnel system and up the slopes.

We surfaced, and passed through a contemporary residential area built in the late 1800s and passed the city water reservoir. Housing contained many modern European features such as front gardens. The road wound uphill to a wondrous overlook where our guide pointed out various historical buildings and other features. A funicular took us back to downtown.

We passed the opera house (Theatro Juarez) in the former mint building and a cathedral. Then we crossed over to a plaza of trimmed Breadnut trees (Brosimum alicastrum) that had looked like a bright green lawn from above. (These trees were trimmed several times a year. They had been netted for a couple years to discourage Great-tailed Grackles [*Cassidix mexicanus*] from roosting and pooping on everyone. This netting prevented the birds from roosting in the trees.)

Guanajuato

We were guided to a really good candy store and a local tequila showroom with beautiful stain glass skylights and a large lighted Christmas tree of tequila bottles. We passed through several plazas, passed government offices and the University of Guanajuato, looked in at several of the narrow residential alleys, and, finally, stopped for lunch about 1300. I had Guanajuato style enchiladas that amounted to two enchiladas with a lot of fresh vegetables. One last shopping stop was at a ceramic shop that specialized in Majolica or Talavera pottery featuring examples of museum and collector grade pottery. It was about 1500 when the bus picked us up for the ride back to San Miguel. I had hoped to see the Rivera museum and the mummy museum but since it was Monday, most of the museums were closed even if we had had the time.

This had been a colonial city with mostly single story buildings until the mid 1800s. The international exposure provided by the War and the new President Juarez brought in new European ideas. Many of the new buildings were built in Renaissance, Greek revival, Art Nuevo, Baroque, and other styles or mixes of styles. Buildings were built to as many as three stories, and the Colonial interior courts were replaced with front yards with exotic plants. The university buildings were rebuilt and were spread out over several campuses. Two of the biggest mine entrances were redesigned into modern structures. There were numerous statues adorning the plazas. The city became a mixture of old and new as opposed to the primary Colonial character in San Miguel of Mexican baroque and classic baroque styles.

Tuesday morning, Charles and I walked about a mile over to the San Miguel botanical garden, El Charco del Ingenio, for a tour. We had been told the tour started at 1000 and got there about 0930, only to discover that it had started at 0900. We caught up quickly, though, and joined the tour. This 220-acre park and preserve was located within the city and dedicated to preservation of and education about Mexican native plants and the environment. It includes dry chaparral, canyon, and wetland ecosystems and includes archeological, recreational, and ceremonial spaces used by indigenous peoples. A plaza contained a Christmas display by the indigenous tribes. There was a lake and riverbed that were part of the city water supply. The preserve boasted over a thousand species of vascular, terrestrial, and aquatic plants, ferns, mosses, and lichen.

We returned to the house about noon and decided to walk over to the "Tuesday Market" about a mile away. It was interesting but disappointing. The market was maybe three blocks long and two blocks wide with hundreds of vendors selling a wide variety of food, clothing, and miscellaneous items. I got the impression of poor vendors selling cheap stuff to poorer people.

Tuesday evening, we went out for supper at a barbeque restaurant on a cold outdoor patio. Anyway, my steak was outstanding.

Wednesday morning, we were in front of the Parroquia to begin a walking tour of downtown at 1000. The zocalo, or El Jardin or the Plaza Principal is the main plaza shaded by trimmed breadnut trees. A hundred years ago it was a bare area used as a parade field, market, and impromptu bullring but had been landscaped beginning about 1910.

We began with the Parroquia, which means parish church. This was the Oratorio de San Felipe Neri and Santa Casa de Loreto with its single sugar cake bell tower. Next to it to the north is a private chapel, Templo de Nuestra Senora de la Salud. There were once tunnels from the Parroquia to all the other churches in town. There were about 20 churches and chapels but only one parish church. (A little bit of Church politics?)

On the NW corner of the Parroquia is a statue of Ignacio Allende and the Plaza Civica. Across from Allende's statue is the Allende home and museum, built in Mexican Baroque style. To the left, on the west side of the square, is the home of Allende's brother and called La Casa de las Conspiraciones (House of the Conspirators) where some of the plotting meetings for the War were held.

Next door is the Canal House built by Count Canal in post-Mexican Baroque. The Canal House has arches because town regulations required it to match the building across the plaza that contained arched portales that were rented out to vendors. This also caused his front door to be around the corner. The house was connected by tunnels to their private chapel and their stables so they would not be seen, and they would not be exposed to the dust, noise and horse pollution of the street.

Across the street from the Jardin is the Presidencial Municipal (city hall). Across the street is the Casa de la Princesa, which probably never housed a princess.

Further down the street is the Plaza San Francisco and the Templo del Tercer Orden built by the Franciscan Third Order. Behind the chapel is the Convento de San Antonio.

Around the corner to the left Juarez street runs into the Plaza Civica with a statue of General Allende. The General had prevented the revolutionaries from capturing and killing the Spaniards who had taken refuge in a former boy's school. Beyond the Plaza are the Templo de Nuestra Señora de la Salud Oratoria and the Oritoria de San Felipe Neri and Santa Casa de Loretto. A block along Calle Insurgentes Street is the Santa Ana Church and the Biblioteca Pública, a Spanish-English library operated mostly by volunteer expatriates.

On the corner of Mesones and Hernandez Macias is located a theatre, El Teatro Angela Peralta, built in 1891. It was named for the Mexican soprono, Angela Peralta, who was also called the Mexican nightingale. Since the 1870's there were a number of theatres in Mexico so named where she had performed. The front wall of the theatre was used as the backstop for a firing squad in about 1914 rebellion.

We entered the long yellow building, the Centro Cultural el Nigromante or Insituto Belles Artes, where many WWII veterans studied art. In the former dining hall was an unfinished mural by Siqueiros. Around the corner is a domed chapel for the Convento de la Concepcion run by nuns. They borrow a priest for services. The Insituto Belles Artes occupies part of the original structure. After the tour we had lunch and spent a couple hours shopping. We were home by 1600.

Insituto Belles Arte Garden

Thursday we took a local bus to Dolores Hidalgo to see the sights of the beginning of the Mexican War for Independence. I saw an Agave in bloom in someone's patio and the flower stalk was decorated with Christmas bulbs.

Shopping

First stop was the Hidalgo House museum. This was where the priest lived, and it contained many historical documents. There was also an art exhibit. Father Hidalgo had been well off and was an entrepreneur that introduced vine making and pottery to the area.

We walked a block to the zocalo and the Parroquia de Nuestra Señora de Delores where Hidalgo issued the Grito. There was a grape plant, possibly a descendent of the vineyards that Hidalgo had planted around 1800. The Spanish tried to destroy all the grapes and winemaking equipment during the War.

Church at Dolores

After hitting a couple shops, we ate lunch, and then browsed in some of the shops along the highway that sold Talavera pottery. It was surprising to see the different qualities of the pottery and tile.

On our way back to San Miguel, I saw a Mississippi Kite fly across the highway.

We were back in San Miguel about 1700 and stopped at the Mega superstore for some groceries on the way home.

Friday was the day for Charles to return to San Antonio. After he packed up, we went to town for lunch and last minute shopping. He took a cab to the bus station about 1630 for an 1800 bus. Due to border delays he got to San Antonio about two hours late the next day at 1600.

Saturday Carol and I went to the Biblioteca Publica (public library) for their flea market sale for scholarships. I bought two clay masks and a couple of books on plants. Carol bought some earrings made with laminated pressed flowers.

Gallery

We visited the Belle Arts then the Academy Allende. The Academy had two galleries open. One had well designed jewelry and a couple pieces with fire agate. The other had excellent watercolors.

After browsing in half a dozen other galleries, we went to the Restorante Belle Italia for lunch. We had fillets. I had Bueno Noche, a special holiday beer. We were home by 1600. This restaurant was authentic right to ignoring customers for 15 minutes on arrival followed by typical, interminably slow, Italian-style service.

Sunday morning we went down to the Biblioteca to participate in their home tour for their building fund. For $15 US per person, the city provided city buses to move about a hundred people for a tour of three upscale homes. The money is used to maintain and improve the library. One home had expanded to cover six lots and evolved into a bed and breakfast. Another had been a stable and recently renovated. The third belonged to a retired, entertainment writer from California. The home had a good view, many birds and animals, and entertainment memorabilia covering the walls. Every time you moved there seemed to be a step up or down or a narrow stair due to building on the contour of the land.

After the tour we went to the Café de Parroquia. Carol wanted to take a cab for a two-block trip so we had a 10 block drive around one-way streets and the taxi finally backed up about half a block to our destination. Could hardly believe this. (I had tamales while Carol had a steak. The tamales were different. One of my tamales had cheese and the other looked like it was stuffed with alfalfa sprouts.)

We walked past the Parroquia. They had erected a Christmas tree and decorated it and the plaza. A lot of people were sitting around the square visiting. Kids were chasing the pigeons. The pigeons were strutting around looking for food and watching out for kids. We stopped for ice cream cones and were home about 1600.

Ice Cream Wagon

Monday morning we packed up and got ready to leave. About 1030 we headed downtown to do any last minute shopping and have lunch. This day was the best weather of the trip naturally. We met an Oaxacaneo selling handmade rugs from Oaxaca. We supported Oaxaca and bought a beautiful small rug.

One gallery had paintings and ceramics by Godet. Outstanding modern work. We stopped at one last gallery and saw several outstanding paintings by David Ramos Orosco.

I bought my required T-shirt. We had lunch and headed back to the house.

I called a taxi about 1600 for transportation to the bus station.

A couple of young kids were handling the bags. Some of the bags probably weighed as much as they did. They got tipped for moving them from the taxi inside then again when they loaded them on the bus.

The bus left on time at 1800. An hour later we stopped in Dolores. Next stop was San Louis Potosi in the fog. Along this stretch of highway the road had washed out like I suspected it would and there was a one-lane detour through the brush.

Monterrey was the next stop about 0300 with a cold rain.

We were in Nuevo Laredo about 0730. We off-loaded while they x-rayed our bags and waited some more while the bus was x-rayed. We were finally across the border by 1000. The bus was delayed about an hour while they changed a bad battery so we arrived in San Antonio about 1400 in a cold rain.

Until next time……..

9

Oaxaca Day Dream

22 August 2007

Carl Lahser

Oaxaca Cancelled

by

Carl Lahser

Introduction

This report is a little weird in that it is my first major trip to be cancelled. This time, instead of reading and paraphrasing information, I have decided to copy pertinent references into the document.

I have wanted to visit Oaxaca for years. As you can see from the following (Section 1), it would have been an interesting visit. We scheduled the visit in May 2006.

Unknown to us, the annual teacher's strike had begun and got gradually more involved and interesting (This will be discussed in Section 2). The strike finally turned violent, and in mid August we considered cancelling the trip. We looked at the possible loss of about $1500 in tickets and reservations and thought maybe we could work around the violence. On 29 Aug, the US State Department issued a Public Announcement advising tourists to think twice about visiting Oaxaca and the Mexican government began denying parties permission to visit to the area. Then, like someone was telling us something Hurricane John appeared as a tropical depression off of Punta Angel on 28 Aug. Since I'm not as young or dumb as I was once we cancelled.

Cancelling only cost us about $200, but it might be worth the cost not to get shot at or kidnapped. We lost rental deposit money but got to keep our airline fare to use by next May.

Picture this: You spend the day around Oaxaca looking at the various archeological sites and exploring the public markets. In the evening you relax at a table around the zocalo. It is a cool moon lit evening. You order a cold Corona and a plate of chapulines on tlayuda tortillas with avocado and watch the evening promenade. You finish the evening with a cup of hot chocolate and some pan de yema and stroll home.

In June of 2006, my wife and I were planning to go to Oaxaca. We had airline and hotel reservations made. About this time the teachers in Oaxaca went out on strike when the governor refused their annual pay raise. The teachers set up camp in the zocalo. On 14 June 2006, violence began when the governor sent troops to clear the streets. We cancelled our hotel reservations. Continental Airlines cancelled our reservations but kept the money on account for later reservations.

Sporadic but highly localized violence over the next year resulted in 28 deaths along with jailing several hundred others. Close to a hundred had "disappeared". This was just the latest in a long history of violence, corruption, and human rights abuses in Oaxaca and a violent chapter in the history of the annual teacher strike. I had wanted to speak and read Spanish better. While looking for information on Oaxaca I found several Spanish language courses at schools located in Oaxaca. For curiosity I checked the prices. I found the Solexico language school with room and board for about $300 a week. This was cheaper than many hotels. The schools assured me the violence was localized and they had not personally seen any.

We still had about $500 left on deposit with Continental Airlines from the cancelled tickets to Oaxaca. I decided to go to an immersion Spanish language course in Oaxaca. I would be living with a host family hoping that Spanish would stick this time.

I made reservations from 3–22 August. I got a senior rate for about $400 for a flight from San Antonio with a direct flight from Houston to Oaxaca avoiding going through the hassle of the Mexico City airport. I had checked with the Mexican airlines and found the fares were about $800 for San Antonio-Mexico City-Oaxaca flights.

For a little background Oaxaca is a city and the state. Oaxaca City is 900 miles south of Houston and about 300 miles SE of Mexico City. It is home to 16 indigenous tribes including Zapotec, Mixtec, Amusgo, and Chatino all of Olmec or Mayan roots. Half the population is indigenous and speaks an indigenous language. The other half is non-indigenous Mexican. Most of the entire population speaks at least some Spanish and many speak some English.

Oaxaca is the fifth largest of Mexico's 31 states. Together with the neighboring state of Chiapas this has been one of the poorest areas in Mexico. Literacy is about 75%. The daily wage is less than $5/day for 70% of the workers.

NAFTA has done little to improve Oaxacan lives but has caused economic problems such as the sale of US subsidized and genetically modified corn. Profits from foreign investments in oil, wind power, and gold mining in the state of Oaxaca have not come back to the indigenous people. This area has resources that could make it a world leader.

Physical setting ranges from sea level coastal swamps to high cloud forests reaching up to 12,300 feet. Temperature in Oaxaca City ranges from the 50s to the 80s. There are basically wet and dry seasons with summer being warm and wet and winter a little cooler but dry.

The area has a wealth of archeological sites and ethnic diversity. It is a focal point for biological diversity with 300 species of butterflies, 600 species of birds and possibly 1800 species of plants. This was the tip of North America before the rise of Central America and is the center of dispersion of plants and animals in both directions.

There has been human habitation in the area for 10,000 years and settlements with agriculture about 3000 years with several hundred varieties of corn alone. Primary farming method in the past was the milpa. These were plots where as many as 30 food plants were grown in the same field at the same time. Problem was there was usually only one harvest a year. Dry land farming and cattle are today's agriculture.

This should be an outstanding experience. My presentation may be uneven in places such as using common names instead of the scientific names due to not having necessary references. Spanish terms will be kept to a minimum.

Day 1.

Friday the third of August 2007 finally arrived. About 0445 Carol drove me to the airport to be there two hours early like the airline recommends. I was checked in and through the inspectors by 0515 and sitting in the terminal.

The sky lightened a little as we were boarding the plane. We were off the ground in time to hang the sun up and had a smooth flight to Houston. A fifteen-minute trek from terminal C60 to terminal B63 got me to the gate as they were loading.

The plane was an Argentine Umbrer 145. This was one of those long thin short people planes. We flew about a hundred miles south and were feet wet out over the Gulf of Mexico. Once past Brownsville we began to fly just inland, over coastal marshes and farmland marked by a coastal lagoon and barrier island to the east. The island was cut periodically by rivers emptying into the Gulf.

Fluffy contrails hung in the moist air and thunderheads were getting an early start. There was a layer of stratus clouds at about 10,000 feet. The thunderheads were already higher than our 30,000-foot altitude. A few minutes later rows of thin popcorn clouds speckled the sky below us.

About 500 miles down the line we headed back out to sea to avoid air traffic between Tampico to Veracruz. We turned southwest and were feet dry again a hundred miles north of Oaxaca.

Bare topped mountain ridges framed valleys that were speckled with villages. Soon we crossed over some larger cities and entered the central valley. A lot of farms and even a few greenhouses broke up the savannah. We landed about 1130.

Oaxaca had a small airport with one runway. There was little bird strike potential with no standing water or birds visible. The airfield was nicely mowed. Near the terminal a flock of grackles (Quiscalus mexicana) called some ornamental trees home.

Immigration and customs were finished quickly. I had the opportunity of opening my bags for customs. Out in the waiting area I saw a sign held high with my name, Carlos, on it.

I was met by Carlos Giron and his wife, Concepcion, and some of their extended family. We took my bags out to his pickup and headed for my temporary home at Casa Giron, Matamoros 502, Colonia Centro, Oaxaca City, in the state of Oaxaca, Mexico.

The route passed numerous open-air shops as opposed to the glassed-in, air-conditioned strip malls in San Antonio.

After I got unpacked I got out my GPS and went for a walk marking several waypoints. The house was at N17 03 51.9 and W96 43 43.4 at an altitude of 5,176 feet.

First stop was at a bank to change some currency. The rate was roughly ten pesos per dollar. I looked at shops with jewelry, pottery, clothing, woven goods, and handicrafts for about two hours and headed back for the house. I arrived in time for lunch about 1500. It was chicken with red mole served under a palapa.

There were at least three other students staying in various rooms. One was a schoolteacher. One was a peace activist.

The third one was a PhD archeology student working on a dissertation site. He had come for a refresher course in Spanish. We went out for a beer and I asked some questions about milpas, etc. There appear to be a lot of old records but they were not in Oaxaca and are mostly handwritten in Spanish.

I crashed about 2200. It was in the upper 70s. A couple hours later it was in the lower 70s and a blanket was comfortable.

Day 2.

I was up about 0700. Breakfast was in the palapa at 0830 – rolls, tea and a mix of steamed chayote and tomatoes.

I walked to the Centro Cultural de Santo Domingo that contains the Museum of the Cultures of Oaxaca in the renovated Templo y Exconvento de Santa Domingo. Construction of the church began by the Dominican friars in 1575. The convent was added in 1608. The Dominicans were expelled in 1859. The buildings went downhill as armyArmy barracks finally becoming a stable. Restoration began in 1898 and was finished complete with museum and ethnobotanical park in 1998. The museum in the old convent area covers the historical and cultural aspects of the indigenous tribes to present day.

I asked the archeologist on duty if the indigenous groups used ground corn for a fungicide or deodorant. He said they used perfumes of flowers but to his knowledge they did not use corn meal or cornstarch. Fresh dry corn ground very fine works well for fungal rashes, athlete's foot, black spot on roses, etc. I would bet that since most of the Oaxacanos have changed from loose fitting clothing and sandals that many of them have athlete's foot and associated fungal rashes.

I visited several shops along the way to the zocalo or main plaza. The bookstores had nothing on natural resources.

Along the streets at the building bases were plants like Euphorbia, bluestem, cudweed, clover, Euphorbia (Euphorbia prostrata?), bluestem (Triniochloris stipoides), cudweed (Gnaphalium attenuatum), burrclover (Medicago sativa), straggler daisy (Calyptocarpus viails) and other common weeds.

A caged mockingbird had songs I never heard a mockingbird sing before. There was also a pair of noisy caged budgies. A few house sparrows and pigeons check out the patio for crumbs. A large dark hummingbird dropped in to visit some West Indian lantana (Lantana camara) flower heads. It was quite likely Doubleday's Hummingbird (Cyanthus doubledayi).

Several of us talked about a lot of things such as why learn Spanish until about 2200 when I crashed.

Day 3.

After Sunday breakfast I went down to near the Santa Domingo church to meet a tour driver, a Zapotec named Andres Mendoza Ruiz. We two left about 0930 to see the Tule tree at Santa Maria del Tule nine miles east of Oaxaca. This is a huge Mexican cypress (Taxodium mucronatum) locally Ahuehuete or Sabino. It is said to be over 2000 years and looks like it could be. It measures 14.05 meters (43 ft) around and 42 meters (126 feet) tall and dwarfs the church, Templo y Exconvento de San Jeronimo, beside it.

The Tule Tree

I have seen a zillion trees
Of many species
In many places
But the Tule tree at Santa Maria del Tule
Was impressive
Like Meteor Crater but not Grand Canyon
Huge but small enough to comprehend
This is a huge Mexican cypress
Taxodium mucronatum
Locally called Ahuehuete or Sabino

The claim to be 2000 years old might be a stretch
But it measures
14.05 meters (43 ft) around
And 42 meters (126 feet) tall
Dwarfing the 200 year old church,
Templo y Exconvento de San Jeronimo
That squats beside it.
IT'S BIG!
CARL 6Aug07

Tule Tree

In a large plaza next to it the Tule tree festival is celebrated on 7 October each year.

We continued another four miles to Tlacolula to visit the public market in a street closed for the occasion. I had heard the markets referred to as "tianguis" but not on this trip. I tried fresh pulque (fresh agave nectar just beginning to ferment) and the grasshoppers of the genus *Sphenarium* (called chapulines) fried with sal de gusana and lemon juice. Indigenous people consumed about 30 species of insects. She also had tepache (pineapple beer). Vendors offered fruits and vegetables, clothing, tools, leather goods, and etc. Local crafts were elsewhere. I was surprised to see two vendors with rambutan (Nephekium lappaceum) that spiky-looking red Oriental fruit.

Tlacolula Market

The market at Tlacolula is only on Sunday
Market days rotate amongst several villages
The market occupies three blocks of the main street
Parking is at a premium
Awnings shade the tables and stalls
Varieties of vegetables and fruit
I had never seen before

One lady had big jars of
Fresh pulque (agave wine)
And tapache (pineapple beer)
And a basket of chapurines (grasshoppers)
That I had to try

Clothing, Tools
Toys
Fresh meat
Tacos and local food
Carl 6 Aug 07

Tlacolula Market

Another mile or so further we stopped at a mescal factory. There were piles of huge pineapple-looking objects that were the heart of the agave plant (Agave salmiana). These would be roasted. The roasted plant would be mashed in a horse-powered press. The uice would then be fermented and distilled. I tried the au natural mescal with the salt and worm mix and then several cream variations with fruit, raspberries, coconut, etc. The creams were good and I bought some small sample bottles.

Watching the horse go around the press reminded me of an old farmer. He told me he raised tobacco but did not smoke. He said that after looking that old mule in the ass and seeing it tinkle on the tobacco there was no way he would smoke or chew.

One Reason not to Drink Mescal

Watching the old bony horse
Going round and around the mescal press
Reminded me of a good reason not to drink mescal
Watching the ass end of a horse all day
Without a diaper
Salud!
Carl 060807

It was another 10 km to the village of San Pablo Villa de Mitla and the archeological site. There were fields of agave for mescal and a lot of corn at different stages of growth. Peruvian Pepper Trees (Schinus molle). Wildflowers including two nightshades (*Solanaceae*). Tropical almond trees *Terminalia catappa*. A large yellow-flowered caltrop (*Tribulis grandiflorum*) that looked like evening primrose from the highway. Australian pine. Castor bean. Australian Pine (*Casuarina equisetifolia*). Castor bean (*Ricinus communis*). Fences of *Lemaireocereus*. Plantago major. Paloverde *Parkinsonis microphylla*.(*Parkinsonis microphylla*). *Acacia* sp. Eucalyptus. Phragmites or Common Reed (*Phragmites sp*) and willows (*Salix sp*) along the waterways. Citrus including oranges, tangerines, great fruit, and limes. Triniochloris stipoides and what looked like Bluestem (*Andropogon sp*).

The highway was a new stretch of the Pan American Highway and in good physical condition. There was not exactly a shoulder but like an extra half of a lane like on some Canadian roads that was regularly driven on especially when someone was trying to pass you. This lane was also used by disabled vehicles since off the blacktop were ditches, rocks, etc.

There was a pickup on the roadside with the hood up. Two men were leaning over the fenders working (?) and five kids were watching over the radiator. Looked like a government job.

In Oaxaca the main streets were a new design with crisscrosses, medians and local access roads about a year old. Several past Presidents had promised to change the system and this is the first improvement to overcrowded street infrastructure. We arrived at Mitla and parked.

Near Mitla were shelter caves with human use dating back to 8000 BC. Some evidence of early uses of grain was found in these caves long before the introduction of true agriculture about 750 BC.

I walked to the site through a group of vendors. (Vendors are carefully regulated to prevent mobbing the site. They are selected, permitted, and rotated by the village councils.)

There were five sites at Mitla but only two, the Group of the Columns and the Church Group, had any development. The others were in the village and not easily accessible. Some of the site had minimal restoration but some of it restoration was old and needed repair. The main area of interest was the Columns Group. There were two platform structures with about a 10,000 sf plaza each with a temple base and steps. The first site was the Palace of columns with fretwork panels (called greca) that were strictly for decoration. The second structure had two tombs under the base. The Church Group was partially covered by a modern church built on the site and using stones from the Zapotec temple. Some of the red and white stucco coloration was still visible.

Mitla First Temple

In the ruins were several plants including a Lepidium species, pigweed (*Amaranthus hybridus)*, a small orange composite, lavender composite (*Osteospermum fruticosum)*, puncture vine with large yellowflowers (*Tribulis grandiflorum*), and Bermudagrass (*Poa sp*).) flowers, and Bermudagrass. Some of the rocks had lichens on them. A house finch was parked on the top of a thorny shrub.

A couple of the vendors had masks of carved wood and decorated with armadillo shell or porcupine spines. One was made from armadillo shell.

Returning to Oaxaca the driver pointed out other sites – Yagul, Lambityeco, and Dainzu. Dainzu, about 6 miles from Oaxaca, means Hill of the Candelabra Cactus in Zapotec. One structure had been partially restored. The site had some remarkable bas-relief carvings of ball players. There was also a tomb and a ball field.

Lambityeco was a small site. It was part of the much larger Yagul site with hundreds of unexcavated mounds. This was probably a salt-making center.

Mounds

The Oaxaca Valley is rife with mounds
Unnatural mounds that should raise man's curiosity
Mounds that hide:
Temples and courtyards
Ballparks
Foundations of homes
Forts
Watchtowers
Fields
Water and irrigation systems
Roads and crossroads
To and from the Valley

Mounds covered
With windblown dust
With hillsides eroded by a thousand monsoons
Covering communities abandoned
In hurricanes or droughts
The ravages of war
Kingdoms covered by today's cornfields
Fiefdoms hidden under cacti and Acacias
Villages and churches built from
Carefully cut and carved stones
The palaces of their ancestors abandoned
1200 years ago.

History is waiting.
Carl 6 Aug 07

We returned to near the Santo Domingo Cathedral. I took a walk to find the location of the Solexico language school and then headed home. After lunch of chicken in red mole sauce several of us sat around and talked until the family kids decided to play chess. Pretty lively game. I crashed around 2200.

Day 4.

I was up about 0700. It was cloudy and about 68. After breakfast (OJ and a big chicken taco) I left to arrive at school by 0830 for my Spanish placement test. Since my grammar was almost non-existent I was only a little above beginner's level. I would have two classes per day covering grammar and vocabulary with a break and finishing at noon. After class I walked around and found a new bookstore and bought a little book in Spanish on the ethnobotany of the coastal area. I walked past the zocalo, which was almost empty and then headed back home.

The afternoon meal was at 1500 every day (some of the students had afternoon classes). Today it was chicken in green pepper (pablano) sauce. The big meal was supposed to come around 2000-2200 but I seldom went out to eat at night.

After lunch I went for a walk a couple blocks downhill to the Templo and Convento de San Juan. The convent had been converted into the University of Oaxca School of Fine Arts. It was nice inside and several students with violins or cellos were sitting in the patio. Across the way there was a large plaza in front of the ornate Basicilica de la Solidad. Down the steps was a tree-covered plaza with an abandoned fountain that contained half a dozen ice cream vendors, which I resisted.

Heladodores (Ice Cream Vendors)

In the square by the Basilica
Were several ice cream vendors.
Early in the morning they began making their wares.
Ingredients in ten-liter cans were immersed in cold brine
They periodically stirred the contents scraping the sides
Until the ice cream was set.
The product was sweet and flavorful
But almost crunchy with ice particles.

Exotic flavors like:
Leche Quemada
Besso Oxacano
Zapote

Magenta colored Tuna (Prickly pear)
Mango con/sin chilies
Rosas
Each outstanding but different
So little time for so many flavors
Carl 070807

I worked on my homework assignment on the patio for a couple hours until it began to rain. Moving to my room I continued reading until crash time. Exciting aint it.

Day 5.

I was up about 0700 to go over my homework. After breakfast of rolls and tea I walked eight blocks to school. School was three hours of verbs and vocabulary until noon.

This day the school had a little cooking class at 1400 that I signed up for. I shopped and wandered back to the house and dropped off my books then started back for the cooking class. The dish was "Tingo de Pollo" of shredded chicken cooked with sliced cabbage and onions and topped with a sauce of tomatoes, garlic, and chipotle served on a bun or a crisp tortilla.

Back at the house lunch was a bowl of pozole and a crisp tortilla with avocado topped with white cheese. After lunch I broke down and hit the ice cream vendors for a scoop of Besso (Kiss of) Oaxacano and a magenta colored scoop of Tuna (cactus fruit).

I noticed some of the street gutters were dangerous to pedestrians and cars alike. The streets were blacktop and after several layers had been applied. Some of the gutters were at least six inches deep.

The signal lights were dangerous too. There may be none, two or four and possibly a pedestrian scramble crossing light depending on the amount of traffic. The cars have the right-of-way.

For an old town Oaxaca had less of a tangle of wires crossing the many of the streets than many other old Mexican cities. A lot of the utilities were underground in conduits under the sidewalks with only streetlights and traffic signals obstructing the narrow sidewalks.

What Can I Do

While staying in Oaxaca
I did my best not to be the Ugly American.
I try to leave anyplace in better condition
Than when I arrived.

Suitcase one had my basic requirements
Suitcase two had baby clothes,Soap and shampoo samples
And school supplies
Destined for a small Zapotec village school.

I spoke to potters and weavers and carvers
Praising their craftsmanship and suggesting
New designs for sales to tourist.

I discussed plant uses with ethnobotanists
Trading uses of local plants
For the uses of the same plants elsewhere.

I discussed training for the indigenous people
In integrated pest management and grounds maintenance
But was told this training would encourage them to run off to the US
I think the officials misunderstand their constituents.

The indigenous I spoke to had a good background
In these subjects from farming and living close to the land
They did not want to leave their families and communities
Without cause.

Some of the young indigenous
Look on a trip to the US as a quest and not as a necessity
Their friends have done it and so must they
Go and slay their own dragon

I observe, and record, and discuss, and debate
Botany, history, anthropology, literature,
Social conditions, customs, behavior, and even politics
And write my trip report.
Carl 22 Aug 07

Talking to people who had been to Oaxaca in the past the impression was Oaxaca as a small village in the jungle with a large indigenous market. Wrong.

Oaxaca is a State and Oaxaca City is a relatively modern large city of 600,000 to a million. It has a dozen nice museums, twenty churches, and several libraries and bookstores. It is on a mile high dry plain. There are about 16 indigenous groups some of which, like the Zapotec, have maintained their own language. Everyone speaks Spanish.

There are a few permanent markets. The weekly open markets are primarily for local consumption items like food, clothing, and tools. There may be a few stalls for luxury goods or tourist stuff. Most of the tourist items like woven goods, pottery, fashion clothing, and electronics are in small specialty shops with varying price and quality.

Other than language and a few details the people are much like those in the US. They have local preferences in food and clothing. There are motorbikes, MP3 players, computers, landscaping, and etc. The kids play kids games like tag, monopoly, computer games, chess, and hang out like kids in other places. Local politics, work, car problems, shopping, cooking, and other activities are much the same.

In 2006 the world press and local websites gave the impression that Oaxaca was a war zone. There was some scattered violence and there were human rights violations in the shadows and these had an adverse impact on tourism one of the main industries. Some of the locals had the impression that killing tourism was part of the domination of those disagreeing with the government. A conspiracy theory? Maybe. More likely this was an application of Friedman's shock doctrine.

Time to crash.

Day 6.

It was 0700, clear, and about 72°F. Might be hot today. Might be a hot day. I bought an ethnobotany book and a guidebook to Monte Alban archeological site at the museum bookstore. I found several tours for the weekend to Monte Alban and surroundings.

Today's lesson was in irregular verbs. Great fun. After school I looked at several shops selling rugs. All the rugs had natural material and dyes. Some had better control of the patterns or had better designs and color mixes. Depending on size they ran from $35 to $200 with various discounts.

I also stopped in to see a potter and tried to explain making totem pole type figures for tourists. She had learned her art and style as a child so I doubt any changes.

Lunch was Pasta soup, flank steak and tortillas with papaya juice. After lunch I went through the two big central markets. These were much larger than any I had previously visited and had a lot more vendors. Along the streets were shops with pottery, tin art, clothing, jewelry and such that were not offered inside.

Passing the zocalo I looked at the front page of several local papers and saw that PAN had whipped the PRI party but the final results were not in yet.

On the way home I stopped at the Tomayo Museum. I had expected Tomayo paintings but he had used some of his riches to set up a good museum on pre-Columbian pottery.

I could not resist a detour to buy a dish of ice cream. Rosas and Besso de Angel (Kiss of the Angels).

Day 7.

Breakfast was a large flat omelet with beans, salsa, and tortillas. School was irregular verbs. Returning from school I stopped at the indigenous women's co-op. They had the wooden animals, tin ware, and other arts but no weaving or pottery. These items were well done and had high prices that went to the co-op. You get what you pay for.

I stopped at a shop across the street from the co-op with the blouses or huipils. Really great colors and workmanship but prices were like designer clothes at home. A huipil (blouse) for $50-300 and up to $500 for matching skirt and blouse. Many were hand-woven fabric with designs integrated. Some were extensively embroidered. The shop also sold mescal. I guess this was to keep the men happy while the wives spent money. I sampled the mescal with the salt and caterpillar mix and bought some chapurines (grasshoppers) and three kinds of chocolate.

Time to get some laundry done. $3 a kilo and ready next day.

Lunch was tamales with limeade. They were cooked in banana leaf and served with a red mole sauce.

Day 8.

Friday finally came. There was a little field trip from 11-12 to the Cochote organic market with fresh vegetables and fruit and fast food. I sampled tajate (it was too watery for my taste) and several local dishes. On the way out I bought a variety of candies – Biznaga, leche quemada, coconut, candied pumpkin, squash and figs.

Cochote Organic Market

The Friday Market was a couple blocks
South of Santo Domingo church.
Fresh vegetables and fruits
And Mexican fast food
It was full of people taking their lunch

My favorite was the candy man with
Leche quemada, bisnaga (cactus)
Candied figs and oranges
Candied squash and pumpkin
Coconut and divinity.
My sweet tooth runeth over.
Carl 110807

Tejate is made from roasted and powdered cocoa, sugar, masa, and powdered mamey. I found it a little weak since the solids settled out rapidly. (I tried a package of it after I returned home and the solids settled even using a blender. The commercial product should probably have an emulsifier added to keep everything in suspension.)

On the way home I bought a tour to Monte Alban. I moved into a larger room and found there were no three-prong plugs. I needed to change some money and buy an electrical adaptor so I went out foraging before lunch.

Lunch was fajitas and limeade.

I did my homework and crashed early.

Day 9.

Breakfast was entomoladas similar to ravioli. Very good. It was Saturday and I had a tour at 1000 to Monte Alban. It would also stopped at Arrazoa where the wooden animals called alebrijes were carved and San Bartalo Coyotepec to see a traditional potter of the black pottery. After a final stop at Cuilapan de Guerro to see a 16th century monastery we were scheduled for lunch.

The van picked me up at ten of ten and went to a hotel where we met three other vans to sort out who went where. We were on the road about 1015. A couple minutes later we were in a traffic jam. A cop finally broke up the snarl and we were on our way.

In just a few minutes we pulled onto a one-lane blacktop road leading to the site. After parking we ran the gauntlet of vendors to the museum. Entrance fee of 40 pesos ($4.00) was not included in the tour price. We had about 15 minutes to hit the museum, gift store, cafeteria, and restrooms before beginning the tour.

The site began about 750 BC. It passed through five developmental periods and finally lost executive control during a drought period about 800 AD.

One of the many ways of tracking the age of an element was the eventual use of a framed stairway instead of just steps.

First stop was a residence and tomb 56. This was a middleclass home with only the foundation left. Rooms surrounded a courtyard with the tomb under the center of the courtyard. Many of the middle class homes followed this plan.

The guide pointed out some of the useful plants like kapok tree (*Ceiba pentandra*), which and the aromatic sacred copal tree (*Bursera bipinnata*) that is the tree the alebrijes are carved from.

We followed the trail up two sets of steps. Then we passed the southern platform and the upper-class sunken patio to an overlook of the grand plaza. The guide discussed the history of Monte Alban and pointed out the significant features.

We proceeded along the top of the north platform and down another set of steps into the grand plaza. This large plaza was large enough to hold the whole population so all the classes could be gathered to get the word. The plaza was acoustically engineered so that the high priest or other leader could speak from between the columns on the north platform and everyone in the plaza could hear him (3,000?). The plaza was large and flat and ringed by with series of temples, tombs, an observatory, and a ball court and a set of steps leading up to the south platform.

Words from the High Priest

Imagine a hot dry spring afternoon
The high priest in robes and jewels
Between the center columns
Announcing to the crowd
That the high noon offering had been accepted
And the rains would begin
And nourish the crops

Imagine what happened
When the rains did not come
And there were several
More elaborate offerings
And still no rain
And the mini-ice age of the year 800
Brought a drought
Carl 110907

I climbed the south platform. Hanging on to the handrail I found I was nose-to-nose with a number of species of wild flowers. Lupines (*Lupinus sp*). Gauara (*Gaura coccinia*). Dayflower. Verbena. Salvia.

The guide discussed ball courts explaining variations in the construction and use amongst the various tribes. The "seats" were not seats but the framework to support a smooth plaster wall from which the ball bounced. Some walls were vertical and some sloped. The games were not for entertainment but had religious or political significance in choosing leaders and settling disputes. This one was unique in not having the vertical hoops of some sites, having small circular structures in the corners of the court, and having a stone platform in the center of the field that was possibly the starting place for the game.

An astrological observatory was used to determine the equinox and predict the coming of the rains.

About the year 800 the earth began a mini-ice age that that caused major weather changes in Europe and probably in the New World and the many cultures changed dramatically. One theory of the decline of Monte Alban about 800 AD was the failure of the rains to come as the priests predicted and the end of the theocracy. The military leaders could not keep the society together.

We returned to the entrance and proceeded on the next leg of the trip. A turnoff from the entrance road headed downhill over a rough unpaved road. There were several short sections of paved road over bridges and through several small towns. We passed through a virtual cane tunnel along a creek to the village of Arrazola.

The carving of alebrijes dated back only 25-30 years but had become a big business. The carving was done in an open shed with a machetes and homemade tools. Body pieces were fitted with limbs, etc, and these were nailed in place. The pieces were dried and then painted a base coat of acrylic paint. After the base coat was dry the pieces were taken inside where several women and girls did the detailed painting. Their showroom contained hundreds of creatures waiting new homes.

There were a couple newspaper articles on albrijes stating the carvers were underpaid and cheated by meddle men serving as brokers and that children were exploited to make the albrijes. I thought the workmanship was too good for children.

Albrijes

A new ancient art form – Albrijes
Thirty years old and selling well – Albrijes
Carver let you blade run amok – Albrijes
Painter let you mind run wild –Albrijes
Tourist let your hands be filled with Albrijes
Carl 110807

Next stop was at Culipan de Guerro to see a Dominican monastery. It was destroyed by an earthquake and had been only partially rebuilt when the Dominicans were expelled. The architectural style was different from the Franciscans.

About 1530 it was lunchtime. We stopped in a buffet with a good variety including red, green, and brown molle, rice, mashed potatoes, and grilled steak, chicken, sausage, and cactus. There was a salad bar but too many flies. Desert was braised pears, apricots, and figs, rice pudding and three kinds of cake. Best, there were also tall cold Cokes.

Lunch was followed by a stop at a potter in San Bartalo Coyotepec. He and his family made shiny black pottery. A teen age potter showed us how to make a pot from kneading the clay to initial form to a more finished form using a portable wheel and a rounding tool. Slip was added and the pots air-dried several days. Then they were carved or decorated. Finally, the pots were fired. The secret to the shiny black finish was rubbing with a quartz crystal to finish the work. He had several hundred pots for sale. I left some sketches for totem pole pottery for maybe the next fad in pottery.

We were back to the zocalo by 1700. I stopped in an ATM since I had run out of pesos and the banks were closed.

Back home I typed up my notes and finished my homework.

Day 10.

Sunday breakfast was *tamal de mole*, hot chocolate, and pan de yema.

I left at 0845 to be at the school to catch the bus for a trip to the village of Benito Juarez in the Sierra Madre del Norte. We drove 55 km and up a couple thousand feet from the savannah (matorral) to the pine-oak forest. Wild flowers at last. Lupines. Orange Castellija (*Castellija sp*). Different agave. Mexican Pine (*Pinus ayachuite*) locally called *pinabete* or *ayacahuite*. A large leaf oak locally called *roble*. All the trees were covered with lichens.

The village contained a restaurant, general store, police office, visitor center and school and a basketball court. We parked across from the restaurant for a half hour potty break. The front yard contained yellow clover (*Melilotus indica*), burr clover (*Medicago sativa*), Gnaphalium, evening primrose (*Oenothera rosea*), dandelions (*Sonchus asper*), and oxalis (*Oxalis tetraphylla*). Ornamentals plants included red cedar, vinca, geraniums, hydrangeas, and peach trees.

We began the trek up the two-mile trail to the mountaintop with numerous wildflowers. I shot about 150 pictures so I can try to identify them when I get home. A seep had several flowers along with ferns, mosses and liverworts.

There were several houses and farms along the trail. They had to carry water for drinking from the village. One field contained a quarter acre of calla lilies (*Zantedeschia aethiopica*).

I went at my speed looking and taking pictures. Everyone else would get a quarter mile ahead and stop for a break. We finally reached the top. There was a fire tower at about an altitude of 3300 meters. The fog was rolling in and the temperature dropped to the mid 50s.

We started down in the cool damp fog. The group was way ahead again but so what. I found a small garter snake (*Thamnophis eques*) that had been run over.

Back at the bottom we had lunch of soup, tamal, green tortilla, aqua de melon, with hot chocolate and sweet bread (pan de yema) for desert.

After lunch there was a trip back up the hill to a trigolet or zip line. I rode up in the van and napped while the others took the zip line ride about a half-mile down hill and a walk back up. It was cold and I must be getting old.

On the way back to the main road I saw a falcon and a kettle of vultures. Some small animal poked its head out from under the brush and darted back out of sight.

We were back at the school about 1730. I walked home, took a couple Tylenol, typed up my notes and crashed.

Day 11.

Breakfast was tacos with tea.

The class was on weird irregular irregular verbs. It was getting complicated but over the past weekend I had understood much of what was being said in Spanish.

I stopped at the botanical garden to arrange a tour of the garden in English, got some pesos, and looked for a barber.

Lunch was chicken soup, grasshoppers, peas and rice and lemonade.

Day 12.

Breakfast was tea, a sliced banana, and sautéed mushrooms.

It was cool and overcast but no rain. It had been the same for several days and possibly the end of the rainy season.

School was a review of everything to date. Great fun. The teacher and I took off just before 1100 to visit the ethnobotanical center. I was a little disappointed with the tour. It was in English, but it was designed for tourists and covered maybe 2% of the plants in the garden. The guide was an American retiree who had a set spiel. It was a good tour but not quite what I wanted.

The park covered about 6 acres and contained several hundred plant species. The tour began with the edible plants – corn, beans, peppers, amaranth and gourds. We stopped at a sila, pachote or kapok tree that was sacred to the Aztecs and Mixtec. We discussed a couple other trees like the Bursara family and the agaves. The tour lead back to past the Ficus trees that produced the bark used for bark paintings, yucca, elephant foot, cycads, plumeria, and cactus.

The guide explained the making of cochineal dye from the little white scale insects (Dactylopius coccus Costa) that fed on prickly pear. These bugs had been hybridized over time to produce more cochineal and were even had raised in small bark boxes. This maroon dye was the largest export from Mexico and had been used to color the red coats of the British army.

Back at school I sent another e-mail home and asked the school for assistance in getting a weekend trip to Puerto Escondido. They would check.

There was another cooking class where I learned to make green mole sauce with chicken, potatoes and chayote.

Lunch was stuffed bell pepper with bananas and cream for dessert.

I worked on homework until about 1800 then went out for a couple hours.

Day 13.

Breakfast was sweet rolls, tea and a ham and egg omelet.

More irregular verbs.

Lunch was pasta soup and chicken with green mole sauce.

Street scenes are neat but usually occur when I don't have a camera. I saw a burro with a saddle tied in front of a store. A few of the women carry baskets of stuff on their head. Balloons seem to be a big thing with kids, especially the long thin ones. Lots of cars, trucks, and motorcycles and an occasional pushcart or burro.

There was a shower about 1900 and, later, a couple hours of rain.

Day 14.

Breakfast was enfriolitos and melon juice.

School was more irregular verbs and vocabulary work. One more class day. I had asked the school if they could assist me in a trip to Puerto Escondido for the weekend. I now had a ticket for 1600 Friday and return Saturday evening or early Sunday morning.

I also had an appointment with Sr. Laurencio Lopez Nuñez, a botanist and seller of herbs. He also ran a temazcal or sweat lodge. The taxi made several shots at finding the address before we finally arrived. I rang the bell and was met by a middle-aged man with rampant hair and a full beard. He had been working on his plant collection for 13 years and was working on a book of the plants of Oaxaca state. He said at the rate he was going it might be published in 20 years due to a lack of funding.

Supper was pasta soup, steak and beans with rice pudding. It rained for about an hour about 0200.

Day 15.

Breakfast was tacos and black beans and tea.

This was the last day of class. We began the day with a field trip to the chocolate factory where they ground the beans and mixed in various quantities of sugar and spices. The end products were sold in bulk or in packages. Prominent were mixtures with sugar, with vanilla, or with sugar and dried milk. There were also varieties with

coffee, mocha, and a diabetic low sugar chocolate. Hot chocolate sold by the cup included the special with sugar and cinnamon, Argentine with coffee, Swiss, and chocolate made with water, or with milk.

The Chocolate Hotel

As we headed for the central market
We were engulfed in a cloud
A cloud with the smell of chocolate
The sign read La Soledad
Maker of chocolate and mole
Not to mention the chocolate shop
And my kind of place the Chocolate Hotel

Six kinds of chocolate with milk or water
Pan de Yema, Atole blanco
And a small hotel

Can I move in NOW?
Carl 180807

The shop next door specialized in horchata and atole. Mixing and packaging were similar to chocolate.

We went through the market looking at fruit, breads and cheeses. An ice cream vendor had cheese-flavored ice cream along

with the standard flavors. One of the vendors was selling the fresh tunas of the cactus, (Escontria chiotilla), locally called *Chiotilla or Xixuega* in Zapotec. I thought it tasted better than the prickly pear tunas. *Chiotilla* was also sold dried.

We passed several five star hotels and walked through the lobby of one in a renovated convent to see the former convent laundry. We stopped in several specialty shops on the way back to school.

At school we practiced dialog until the bell rang. I sent an e-mail to Carol, and got a call finalizing a tour of the archeological sites arranged for Monday.

This was an interesting and profitable two weeks of school. I learned some new vocabulary, corrected some bad Spanish, and was exposed to Spanish grammar. Now I need to practice. I can understand much more than I did in the past but I'll never make it as an interpreter. I cannot remember the words so speech is limited.

My instructor said I had a heavy accent. I asked if it was my English or Spanish and she said both.

Lunch was at 1500 and I headed for the pickup point for the trip to Puerto Escondido.

About 1500 it began to rain. I asked the van driver if it was raining at Puerto Escondido. He suggested I go to the nude beach and I would not have to worry.

We departed right on time and about an hour later we were entering the Sierra Madre del Sur Mountains. Approaching every village corporate limit there was a series of signs warning about "topes" or speed bumps or commonly called sleeping policemen. These were in conjunction with the "reductor" sign that means slow down. Some of the speed limits are strange. Printed on the highway like 23 or 31 kph. In villages were pedicabs with foot power or pulled with a motorcycle. There appear to be a couple in every village.

There were occasional individual Inca Doves (*Scardafella inca*). I had heard the Mourning Dove (*Zenaidura macroura*) calling around Oaxaca.

There was a sign that said 305 km to Puerto Escondido. Once we began to climb the roads were very curvy with no more than a couple hundred yards of straight away for passing, which the driver did frequently. Some people had said they got seasick with the constant changing direction.

We passed over or through several mountains from 7,000 to 10,000 feet. This was primarily seasonal deciduous forest. There were several areas of pine-oak forest but mostly tropical evergreen forest. Vines were trying to take over the world. Much of the forest had been clear-cut and a variety of plants had invaded.

Down at the bottom of a valley we were near a stream. There were areas with fan palms and coconut palms. We stopped for a break at San Pedro, a small town that had a flock of mid size parrots (*Aratinga canicularis*). It was just after sunset and I could hear them and see dark silhouettes.

Depending on altitude the roadside markets had sugarcane and pineapples and coconuts as well as citrus and other fruit. There were many small plots of nursery stock of young cactus or agave plants for replanting. Several greenhouses sat on one hill. Some of the tropical trees seemed to think it was spring with new leaves and flowers but then it is the end of summer and some tropical trees bloom and fruit over our northern winter.

There were signs that said to keep our highways clean. However, near many villages and at pull offs along the road there were piles of trash.

It rained or was foggy most of the way. Twice visibility dropped to a couple hundred feet. When the sun peeked through I could see we were headed south.

The rain caused occasional rockslides. Local crews were strategically stationed with loaders and trucks to keep the road clear. Some of the hills were made of white or green limestone. The higher formations were of a red or purple conglomerate. Volcanic origin?

We came down from the pine and through an area of red cedars. There were also Cecropia trees (*Cecropia peltata*) and castor bean plants (*Ricinus communis*) and fan palms. Most of the farms had banana trees and chickens. Cattle, horses, and donkeys roamed loose. It was after dark and we rounded on curve to find a large white cross. A little startling but we had seen hundred of crosses or memorials along the road.

The road was of asphalt with center and side markings but generally no shoulders. Sort of a minimal road but well maintained.

A mouse darted across the dark wet road. A bat (*Lasiurus cinereus?*) flipped across the headlight beams. I could hear a bunch of tree frogs (*Hyla baudini*) calling. In the background was the occasional sound of small frogs like Acris (*Acris gryllus*) and occasional toad calls. The air was clear and the vegetation was as bright green as I had ever seen.

We arrived about 2330. I caught a cab to the Hotel Ines that had been recommended. It had the look of typical tropical disrepair. The room had two built-in platform beds and a shower. I opened the metal-sash windows after checking the screens and turned on the ceiling fan.

Down the street a hundred yards was an all night restaurant. I had a late supper of octopus Mexican style served with fries and tortillas and a Pacifico beer. The place had several tables filled with couples. There was also a group of surfers by their appearance.

I took a walk over to the beach. The beach faced roughly south. Big waves were crashing but without the luminescence. The tide was coming in.

There was a lot of traffic along the beach at 1 AM. Couples strolling. A bunch of kids playing volleyball. Dogs.

I took a hot shower and crashed about 0130 to the sound of scuttling geckos, the tweet of tree frogs, and the hum of the ceiling fan.

Day 16.

I was up about 0700 because the sun was up and my room faced roughly east. The tree frogs were winding down and a rooster had just begun crowing. My room was called the Bamboo and there was a big clump of bamboo growing in front of the door. I could see the hammock I got tangled with in the dark getting to my room.

I looked at the room - concrete brick with a corrugated metal roof and metal window and doorframes and a sheetmetal door. This was quite functional in a hurricane prone area. The shower and kitchenette walls had mildew like every place else in the tropics. The hot water was really hot probably 150°F and came out spitting and steaming. The bathroom sink had only cold water and the faucet was on the end of a copper pipe not attached to the sink.

The hotel probably had about 60 rooms on two levels with a sauna, pool, and bar. There were several more small hotels just like it along this strip of beach with $40-50 rooms. Several nice cars with Mexico City license plates filled the parking lot. When I returned after breakfast there were a lot of kids playing in the pool.

The landscaping was a tropical accident of several kinds of palms, bougainvillea, hibiscus, croton, philodendron, etc, with no obvious planning.

I went out for a beach walk about 0800. Clean tan sand. No shells. I was told that Bahia Blanca nearby to the east was a sheller's beach. The drift line had assorted debris and lots of Styrofoam beads but not much trash.

Right in front of the hotel big waves came up over a bar a quarter mile out. These 20-foot swells were covered with surfers waiting for just the right wave. The beach was lined with spectators most of whom had cameras. Lots of bikinis. A few were topless.

Surfers and Real Surfers

Darkly tanned young men paraded
Along the beach mid morning
With new surfboards and fins

Real surfers arrived at daybreak
In old rattletrap VWs
With faded cut offs and old long boards
They headed for the surf
And were quickly out on the giant swell
Looking for just the right wave
Carl 190807

I walked about a mile east down the beach past all development and walked back along the back beach looking at vegetation and whatever the storm tides might have deposited. Railroad vine. Tribilus. Tridescancia. There was a high bluff with some nice looking homes and a military base along the ridge. Along the roadway were nut sedge and a Poa of some kind. A lizard (*Cnemodophorus sacki*) was skittering along the road.

I walked out to the surf again and walked to the rocky point at the west end of the beach. There was a statue of a pair of hands on a big rock just off the beach. I looked around the rocks and found no rock dwelling shells. On the way back to the hotel I found two Triqui women that had a few beach worn shells and bought a few.

Along the street were little shops selling CDs, surfing stuff, and T-shirts. There were several hotels and a number of places to eat and drink. Back at the hotel I checked out and headed west along the beach.

It was almost noon so I stopped at one of the places out on the sand that served food and drink and rented umbrellas. I had octopus for lunch and occupied their table for over an hour watching the waves and people then headed up the beach again.

A Brown Pelican (*Pelecanus occidentalis*) passed heading east as did a Franklin Gull (*Larus pipixcan*) and a Royal Tern (*Sterna maxima*). Further out a Brown Booby (*Sula leucogaster*) was heading west. Grackles (*Quiscalus mexicana*) and sparrows (*Passer domesticus*) foraged in the drift lines.

I walked around the rocky point and then continued west towards the harbormasters office and the anchored tour and fishing boats. About 1400 I reached the end of the beach and found another place overlooking the beach and bought a couple Cokes. Several Magnificent Frigatebirds (*Fregata magnificens*) cruised the beach and circled over the fishing boats. Pelicans were perched on some of the moored fishing boats. I watched the Frigatebirds and the bikinis, and the families at the beach and the approaching rain clouds.

A little after 1500 it began to rain. The beach umbrellas and tables and chairs had been stowed and some of the fishing boats were being beached. I went up to the street and caught a cab to the van pickup area.

The van was supposed to leave at 2000 but when one came by at 1700 I took it. It was cool and overcast and would be light for another three hours.

The driver drove like he was practicing for the Grand Prix and passing everything on the road. The road lead through some really neat mountains but the wild ride and the dark tinted windows prevented picture taking. It had taken 7.5 hours to go but only 6.5 hours to return. I was home in bed by midnight.

The views are outstanding and the waves rock. After this short trip I would not recommend Puerto Escondido for more than a day unless you are a surfer or just want to sleep in the sun for a while and watch bikinis.

Day 17.

Sunday morning. After breakfast of a sweet roll and tea at 0730, I walked to the Hotel Chocolate for Atole and hot chocolate about 1100. I walked back through the markets looking at the produce and fresh fish. There were several piles of fresh tilapia, shrimp, and snappers. I found a big basket of Jamaica flowers (*Hibiscus sabdariffa*) that is the ingredient in Aqua de Jamaica.

Day 18.

Breakfast was scrambled eggs, tortillas, and tea.

I had a 0900 pickup for a trip to the archeological sites of Dainzu, Lambityeco, and Yagul. These were near Mitla.

Dainzu was about a mile from the Pan American Highway. The entrance fee was 27 pesos. The site was a raised platform with central stairs that were added on about 700 AD. A few upper class houses had been uncovered. Several tombs had been found. The ball field was partially reconstructed. A series of bas-relief panels had been uncovered and were on display showing ball players in action. The site had been mapped but would not be excavated.

Dainzu

Lambityeco was a small but important site. The entrance fee was also 27 pesos. This was the first site to have a temazcal or sweat

Lambityeco

lodge. The small pyramid had unenclo sed steps and a small patio in front with an altar in the center. This site had shale pads incorporated in the design. Behind the pyramid were a house foundation, an altar and a double tomb with a male and female portraits and an important carved frieze. Another temple contained carvings of the rain god Cocijo and a female companion to demonstrate the duality of life. The site was the first site to use a yellow plaster instead of the red and white of other sites.

The **Yagul** site was much larger and had some unique features. There was a frog-like figure with a bowl on its back to receive offerings. It looked much the Chocmul figure at Chichinitza. No evidence had shown that there had been human sacrifice.

There was a triple tomb similar to the cruciform tomb at Mitla. This was different in that each tomb wing was separate with a body chamber and its own chamber for offerings. The entrance had nichos for offerings.

The ball field had the walls covered with flagstones instead of stucco.

One of the more important structures was the six-chambered maze built to allow the king or priest time to escape out the back and up the hill where he had a tomb-like underground hiding place.

We went up the fortress to see the hiding place. I tried to keep up with the guide and found myself getting light headed. No wonder – the guide was in her twenties and we were over 7000 feet.

We returned about 1400 and I spent the afternoon working on pictures in the computer.

Day 19.

This is a day to see whatever I might have missed and to maybe buy a few presents. Tomorrow is go home day.

Breakfast was tortillas, eggs and tea.

About 1000 I went too see some shops I had visited before for something for Carol. Jewelry? Clothes? I decided on pillow covers. At the market I decided to try a couple new ice cream flavors – cheese and mamey zapote. I also bought the obligatory T-shirts.

There was an art display at the public library. I found two other small exhibits but nothing spectacular.

I was back at the room about 1400. Lunch was boiled shrimp and rice with a sliced apple in yogurt for desert. One of the new students was a Lutheran minister. Another was a young student from Zurich. We discussed the world situation for a couple hours.

A little after 2000 I went out for chocolate.

The Zocalo

A quiet pleasant evening in Oaxaca
A half moon hangs over the zocalo
An empty table beckons me to sit
And watch the promenade
I order a Corona and watch the activity

Kids chase long colorful balloons
A little girl comes by selling gum
Families out for their promenade
Stroll by with their kids
I order a plate of chapulines with avocado
And tortillas and another Corona

Police of several kinds
Walk through the crowd in pairs
Ignored by almost everyone
An old lady comes by selling shawls
A young boy shows the diners
Bracelets clear up to his elbows

Quecha musicians play Inca music
Of tall snow covered mountains
Of glacier lakes and deep blue skies
Of ice cold fast running streams
Racing and tumbling
To the Amazon and the far Atlantic

I order a cup of hot chocolate
And pan de yema
A couple passes walking a small dog
Couples sit on benches
Choosing the shadows
Lost to this world

A pair of police passes walking slowly
One comments quietly on a blond in a short skirt

A shoeshine boy stops and cocks his head
I shake my head and ask for the bill

Its time to stroll home and leave the magic
Carl 210807

There was a hurricane due to hit Veracruz about the time we were to leave in the morning. We shall see if there is any problem tomorrow.

Day 20.

We were going to leave but the flight was cancelled due to Hurricane Dean running over Veracruz. Sonny, the archeologist, called the airline and was told the next available flight from Oaxaca to Houston was a week away. Continental booked us on a flight from Mexico City to Houston at 0900 on Day 21. We went to the bus station for tickets to Puebla. We could spend the afternoon sightseeing and go on to the Mexico City airport later in the evening.

The first class bus left at 1100. The highway led through savannah and up into Sierra Madre del Norte Mountains with pines and oaks. We descended into the lush Tlaxcala Valley with farms and then back into the barren hills supporting a forest of tall cactus of Pachycereus columna-trajani with P. chrysomallus and Lemaireocereus Treleasei, multiple-trunked yucca trees (Yucca elephantipes), and prickly pears and various acacias and other shrubby and probably thorny trees. We arrived at Puebla about 1600 through intermittent rain and fog.

Since heavy rain was not prime sightseeing weather we decided to go on to the Mexico City airport on the 1700 airport special bus. The bus was on time until it hit a traffic jam caused by a three-inch rain that flooded Mexico City. It took four hours more to reach the airport. Streets were running water and trucks and busses were up to the floorboards. There were people in waist deep water and hundreds were waiting on the sidewalks for the water to recede.

In the airport all the hotels were full so we got a late supper and spent the night on the lobby floor near the Continental counter.

The hurricane had passed and the weather cleared. The plane was arrived in Mexican time and I was home in San Antonio in mid afternoon.

10

Copper Canyon

Carl Lahser

Background

Copper Canyon or Branca del Cobre consists of 20 canyons that total over four times the length of the Grand Canyon. This complex is located about 200 miles south of El Paso in the Sierra Madre (Sierra Tarahumara) Mountains. Its name came from the greenish tint of lichens growing on the canyon walls that looked like stains resulting from copper nails used in ship construction.

Northwestern Mexico was home to maybe 15 major tribes including the Mayo, Yaqui, Tehueco, and Tarahumara (Rarámuri) Native American groups and the temporary home to the Apache.

The canyon area is famous for the native Tarahumara (Rarámuri) men who dressed in *tagora* (breechcloth) held in place with a belt, *napacaka* (collarless blouse), cereal bowl haircuts, *koyera* (head bands) and huaraches (sandals), and for the long distance races called *rarajipari* that has covered as much as 230 miles from Chihuahua to El Paso. Currently the women dress in the full skirts, full blouses and headscarves while the men wear jeans, boots and straw cowboy hats. Only dance groups and old men wear the traditional clothing.

The Spanish contacted Indians in Northern Mexico and called them Tarahumara. This Native American group called themselves Raramuri. Over the years the Spanish and Mexican people took tribal land and enslaved or hired many of them to work the mines. The Jesuits tried to settle the groups and introduced orchard culture, goats, and sheep. Rebellion against the government lasted over a hundred years.

Another group of indigenous people are the Mayo. This tribe belongs to the Pima group and occupies 15 towns along the Mayo and El Fuerte Rivers. They are mostly farmers and artisans. There are about 40,000 Mayo. They all speak Spanish but retain their native Cahita, which is a variation of the basic Uta-Aztecan Pima language. Their history begins with Spanish contact in 1599. They joined with the Yaqui tribe to fight the government in 1684 and were finally defeated in 1887

Major cities along the canyon are Chihuahua, Creel, Divisadero, El Fuerte, and Los Mochis. There are numerous small towns and villages scattered through the mountains that may include shelter caves.

Chihuahua, the capitol of the State of Chihuahua, was founded in 1709. It is a colonial city of a million people. There are several historical points of interest including the cathedral, the aqueduct, the Art Noveau city museum, Pancho Villa's home and his unused mausoleum, the dungeon where Father Hidalgo was kept, and the state capitol building where Hidalgo was executed. The capitol building contains a number of murals by Piña Moro of incidents in the state history.

Creel, 300 km west of Chihuahua, is relatively new. It was established in 1906 by Governor Enrique Creel as a social experiment to civilize and socialize the Rarámuri. With the coming of the railroad, Creel changed from a sleepy native outpost to a Mexican logging town. It has grown rapidly with hotels and tours. Tourists began arriving in 1961. It has become part artist colony, part commercial center and mostly a tourist center.

Diversadero is 50 km further west and overlooks Urique Canyon, one of the major branches of Copper Canyon. It is a major tourist stop.

El Fuerte was a Spanish fort built on the El Fuerte River in 1564. The town was in a fertile valley and became a major stopping place on the Camino Real between Guadalajara and the northern silver mines. It is the home of the Mayo Indians.

Albert K. Owen began the commercial and financial center of Los Mochis in the late 19th century. It was built on the principles of Utopian socialism, and finally failed after surviving some 30 years. The city proper was first settled in 1893 by a businessman named Benjamin Johnston, who built a sugar refinery around which the city developed. The Fuerte River — with the same name as the valley — irrigates an extensive region whose main crops are vegetables, corn, beans and sugarcane. Los Mochis is the terminus of the railroad. The regional airport is the starting point for many visitors to Copper Canyon.

The port of Topolobampo is 20 km west of Los Mochis down the Rio Fuerte. It is one of the best natural deep-water ports in Mexico and one of the most important in the Mexican Pacific. It is a ferry terminal to La Paz, Baja California and is famous for its fish and shrimp. A water desalination plant provides much of the domestic water. Topolobampo was the site of a "utopia" colony from roughly 1884 to 1894, influenced by the urban planning ideas of Ebenezer Howard. The colony failed because of malaria and other environmental factors. The colony moved inland to Los Mochis.

Albert K. Owens and President Porfirio Diaz began the Ferrocarril de Chihuahua al Pacifico. The intent was to connect the cattle and produce markets in Kansas City to the port of Tompolobompo on the

Gulf of California. Arthur Stillwell began construction of the railroad in 1900. By 1914, tracks were laid between Ojinaga/Presidio on the US/Chihuahua border. The railroad moldered until 1943, when the Mexican government pushed it through the mountains to Los Mochis and the port of Topolobampo. It was completed a hundred million dollars and 90 years later in 1961.

I first heard of Copper Canyon in 1963, while I was attending Texas A&M College as a wildlife biology major. The railroad had been completed on 23 November 1961 but had been partially operational since the late 1940s. Several of the graduate students had been summer employees during the biological survey of Mexico. These trips were contracted by Mexico and led by The Wildlife Department head, Dr. W. B. Davis. Each summer, they headed to a different state in Mexico with several trucks of supplies. The students said Dr Davis would tear the labels off all the cans and they would eat several random cans per meal. This reduced squabbling over who ate what but generated other comments when several meals consisted of four cans of, for example, peaches. They had stories of winching a truck down the canyon wall at Posada Barrancas between Creel and Divirsadero to scout the Rio Urique canyon.

I had also read the book, "In the Sierra Madre" by Jeff Biggers. It was one of the best books on the area and discussed living in a Tarahumara village for a year.

Since the railroad construction took several years, climbing the mountains proved to be a cactus collectors dream. I was told that when the train came to a steep grade the collectors would go to the front of the train and get off. Then they would grab any cactus in sight and jump back on the caboose as it passed. Surveyors, construction crews and cactus collectors stripped any archeological sites that might have existed along the railroad right of way.

This is my personal observations of a week in canyonland.

Getting There

Darlene Conoly, a travel agent who had led a trip to the pottery center at Mata Ortiz that I had taken, had a trip to Copper Canyon planned for March of 2008. My wife said it sounded interesting, so we signed up. The trip left San Antonio to Houston to Chihuahua on 10 March returning on 17 March.

The San Antonio and Houston airports were green with clover and highlighted with patches of evening primrose and Indian paintbrush. These flowers were a few weeks early, but we did not have much winter and don't forget global warming.

We flew Continental on a 40-minute flight to Houston then took a direct 2-hour flight on an Embraja ERJ (short people airplane) to Chihuahua bypassing the hassle of going through the Mexico City airport. The route was roughly Houston to Del Rio then south to Chihuahua. About an hour out of Houston we crossed the Rio Grande. The location was near two big oil fields. I remember flying over this country at night 50 years ago when this part of Texas looked like a field of fireflies at night from the "sour gas" flares.

The area between the border and Chihuahua was barren Chihuahua thorn brush with very little hint of people. Few roads. No water. We found civilization a few minutes north of town with irrigated farms, a lake called Laguna de Bustillos, and some apple orchards and dry land farms. Chihuahua in the Tarahumara language means "dry and sandy place".

Chihuahua City

Chihuahua City sits in a big dry valley with the Sierra Madre Mountains to the west. The airport was large and modern. There were no birds or much vegetation. We landed and ran the full length of the runway before turning around and taxiing back up the runway to operations.

Darlene and our local guide, Reynaldo, met us at the airport with a bus. We loaded up and were whisked to the hotel in the center of downtown Chihuahua City.

The city appeared pretty clean at first glance. Population is about 1.5 million and growing like every other Mexican city. There were several large industrial complexes.

On the way to the hotel we passed the Creel house. Creel was a German immigrant who made it big and became mayor. Henrique Creel was famous for being penurious. There was one story about him having a life-sized bust made for a visit by President Juarez. Everyone thought he was being too cheap so he sent to El Paso for a bronze statue of Lincoln and replaced Lincoln's head with the head from his bust of Juarez. The statue looks a bit strange with the head not proportional to the body.

After we checked in at the Quality Inn San Francisco and had lunch, Carol and I had 15 minutes until the downtown tour began. We took a quick walk around the block and saw about two dozen boot shops. Chihuahua is a ranching center and every cowboy needs a pair of fancy boots and a straw western hat. The popular boot-of-the-day was pastel ostrich leather. There were boots in pink, pale blue, chartreuse, and wild stripes running from $75 up.

Back at the hotel we boarded the bus for a city tour to see the parks, prominent buildings and the Pancho Villa museum. The museum was in Villa's house. He lived pretty well for a country boy. The outer hallways are covered in murals and the rooms contained various artifacts including the car in which he was assassinated. We also passed Villa's mausoleum that he never used.

We drove along the remaining section of the aqueduct then toured the cathedral and the capitol building. The capitol was built in 1892 and partially destroyed by fire in 1941. The rebuilt capitol contains a group of murals by Piña Mora depicting local history from the first Spaniards to the revolution in 1910. This was the site of the execution of Father Miguel

Hidalgo y Costilla whose "Grito de Dolores" or Cry for Independence on 16 September 1810 began the movement for Mexican Independence.

Back at the hotel we had a welcome supper with a margarita. We crashed about 9 PM since we had lost an hour and were at 4500 feet and had to get the bags out by 4 AM to catch a bus to the train by 5 AM. Since the automated wakeup button on the phone did not work I decided to show off and ask the operator for a wake up in Spanish. I asked for a "despertarse" and the operator replied in English asking if I wanted a wakeup.

Tuesday morning we got a bus ride through the dark to the train station. Almost none of the stores had security lights or advertising lights. No one was on the streets. Only the Pemex gas station and a couple of small convenience stores were open.

Father Miguel Hidalgo y Costilla

Train trip

At the train station we waited in the cold while the train cars were shuffled and finally boarded. The train pulled out right on time about the same time as the sun rose. We passed the waking city with houses painted pink or green or blue as if you could sleep next to the train track. The railroad right of way was fenced with chain link or stone.

Ferrocarril de Chihuahua al Pacifico

The train crept up hill through farm and ranch land through the villages of Santa Isabel, San Andres, Bustillos, and Anahuac. We made a short stop at Cuauhtemoc at almost 6000 feet. Then we chugged uphill through the Mennonite apple orchards and oat fields and flew downhill to La Junta and Miñaca. Uphill again we peaked out over the continental divide at about 7800 feet at San Juanito. There was a short stop at Creel and Divisadero then downhill for a hundred kilometers to our stop at Cerocahui.

The Mennonite farms primarily raise Red Delicious apples for local sale. The trees were netted to keep the birds out. Great-tailed Grackles were the biggest problem.

We had a 15-minute stop at Divisadero to shop or look at the canyon. The canyon was impressive being longer and deeper than the Grand Canyon but this canyon is softer and greener. Native vendors were there to greet the train selling lunch, baskets and other indigenous art.

Along the way I saw three Mallard ducks, possibly domestic, in a drainage ditch, several Red-tailed Hawks, a Peregrine falcon, a zone-tailed Hawk, a lot of Inca Doves, flocks of Lincoln Sparrows, several American Crows, Great-tailed Grackles, and a few lonesome Black Vultures. I also saw one Jackrabbit. There was some prickly pear and buckhorn cactus and a lot of a dry grass that looked like grama grass. There were acacias, Palo Verde, and scrubby Mexican oak that were replaced by red cedar, larger oaks and white and Mexican pine trees as the altitude increased. Black willow, cottonwood, hackberry, and Arizona walnut lined the few dry waterways. There were a couple stretches of creosote bush and ocotillo that was leafless. The soil was red like Precambrian but this was Cretaceous or volcanic.

We had lunch on the train. About 4 PM we finally stopped and got off the train at Bahuichivo.

Hotel Paraiso del Oso

Everyone was stuffed into two vans and we were off on twenty miles of rough dusty mining road to the hotel Paraiso del Oso about half way to Cerocahui The hotel specialized in hunting and camping trips. It was built on an ejito or farming co-op established by the revolution. It was a picturesque site under some towering volcanic plugs. The facility had been built in the hacienda style with no AC and a wood stove for heat.

After moving in we went for a walk up a nearby dry canyon. This was Tarahumara land, and they had built a dam to store water for irrigation. There were two major shelter caves of archeological interest. One had been a dwelling site and the other had become a sacred site since Catholic priests had buried 53 Tarahumara Indians killed elsewhere. Archeologist had found a few bones and artifacts still buried but animals had probably dug up the rest. There were several other smaller caves that had the entrance stoned in we did not visit.

There were several seeps with ferns like Cliff Brake, Spiny Cliff Brake, and Bracken. There was a moss and plants like Oxalis and Canada Violet. Three pines and four species of oak are found locally. I also saw vetch and Mountain Lobelia. I saw an Acorn Woodpecker, Curve-billed thrasher, and a White-winged Dove. A Black Swallowtail and a white Cabbage Butterfly were seen in the hotel courtyard.

That evening there was a margarita welcome and dinner. After dinner the walk back to the room was under a night sky that was as pretty as I had ever seen. Fantastic clear black sky with no light pollution. Bright stars and even a couple satellites zipping southeast. I got a fire lit in the wood stove, and the room was tolerably warm until the fire went out in the middle of the night.

A group of high school students were staying overnight and several slept in sleeping bags in the patio. Brrr. I feel like I'm getting too old for that kind of stuff.

Next morning I woke to a rooster at 4 AM then to a mockingbird about 5:30. It was cold until I found the can with the bags of fire starter. After breakfast we took a ride to Cerocahui and visited the square, the chapel, and the orphanage. Next, was a trip up in the mountains to a Tarahumara shelter cave where baskets were sold.

he road was narrow and dusty. A mining company maintained it. I photographed a number of plants before we continued up the mountain to a scenic overlook. Wavy Cloak Fern. Black Grammagrass. Beargrass. Hedgehog Cactus. Rock Cress. Ground Cherry. Desert Broom. Beebrush. Ageratina. Agave. Wooly leaf. Wooly Paintbrush. Mala Mujer. Whispering Bells. Checkermallow. Scarlet Bugler Penstemon. Goldenrod.

Tarahumara shelter cave where baskets were sold

El Fuerte

Back at the lodge we had lunch and loaded up for the ride to the train and headed for El Fuerte for the night. We departed about 3 PM.

At higher elevations were ponderosa and Pinyon pines, sotol, beargrass, and agave. On some of the cuts there were plants the looked like the Puya of Peru except these were Schott Agave instead of a Bromeliad. There were sunflowers growing almost six feet tall.

It was only a couple hours to El Fuerte and downhill all the way. We went through several tunnels and descended about 3000 feet. As we exited a long horseshoe tunnel the dedication plaque for the railroad completion and a high waterfall were visible. We passed Temoris Station with sidings to allow trains to pass then crossed the Santa Barbara Bridge across the Rio Mina Plata. Here the Septentrion and Chinipas rivers join to become the Rio Fuerte. Forty km further we crossed the Chinipas Bridge, the highest bridge on the line. Another forty km and we crossed the longest bridge across the Rio Fuerte. Fifty-eight km more and we offloaded at EL Fuerte.

Along the route from Temoris Station the vegetation changed to Slender Sunflower or Girasol, Prickly Poppy or Chicalote, White Morning trees, kapok tree, Honey Mesquite, mesquite mistletoe, castor beans, several oaks, Palo Blanco, and Rock Daisy. It was difficult shooting pictures or identifying plants from the train. However some plants were outstanding and easy to identify.

Sunset was pretty with the bright orange subtropical jet stream roaring northwest. New Mexico and Arizona should catch some weather tomorrow. Overhead the sky was cloudless.

The train progressed slowly through the outskirts of town. A bus met us at the train for the trip to the Hotel El Fuerte. The hotel had been a hacienda. It had been modified into a hotel. The interior and the rooms were decorated with colonial style and antiques. It had a homier feeling than the one in Chihuahua

Hotel El Fuerte

We moved in and came to supper about 8:30. The dining room was small and had seating in shifts. The menu offered shrimp, crayfish, fish and steak. I ordered the crawfish that was actually Macrobrachium or river shrimp and not the Louisiana crawfish. This was the first time for this dish.

Next morning the rooster went off at 5 AM followed by a junkyard dog and captive

Osprey and Snowy Egret

parrots in the patio. A group left the hotel at 7 AM for a bird watch along the El Fuerte River - Osprey, Snowy Egret, Great Blue Heron, Coot, Lesser Scaup, Cormorant, Sparrows, Gilded Flicker, Black-throated Magpie-Jay, and Rough - winged Swallow. There were possibly other ducks in the distance.

Local flowers included Poinsettia, Bougainvillea, verbena, plus some I did not recognize.

Mayo Country

After breakfast we took a ride to the village of Tehueco in Sinaloa state to see an indigenous town and some folk dances of the Mayo Indians. I could not find it on the map. Estimated population was 300. Primary crops produced were beans and tomatillos and some cattle. Tehueco was one of 15 Mayo communities. Other villages are similar but the crops and crafts were different.

Entering town we passed the old mission that was badly damaged in the revolution. We had a windshield tour of the school and co-op, and homes lined up on a *resaca*. Then we walked to a community building where the dance demonstration would take place.

The dancers, called *matachines*, do the Easter season presentations and traditional dances. This dance is common in Northwest Mexico and in Arizona and New Mexico on the reservations. The Deer dancer, called *maso,* has a deer mask and a rattle in each hand. The *Pascolas* (*pahkolam*) or spirit dancers have an oval carved mask with tufts of hair. The dance is a story of trying to convince the deer to sacrifice himself for the hunters and can last all night. The *Pascolas* wear cocoon rattles on their legs to distract

Matachines

the viewers and try to capture the deer. A group of men played flute, guitar, fiddle, water drums and a rasp-like instrument. There were two dances demonstrated parts of the Deer Dance. The costumes were a mask, and white pants and shirt, and a belt and leggings of rattles (*jacannachins*?) made of dried moth cocoons and pebbles and huaraches.

After the dance there was a demonstration of tortilla making.

We visited the church and a local home to see how they lived. It was not much different from where I grew up. Outhouse. Sleeping on the porch. Wood cook stove and electricity. They had running water instead of my old hand pump. Dooryard garden. Citrus trees. Mangoes. Avocados. Bananas.

A pair of house finches was twittering and skipping through the trees. A black swallowtail and a white cabbage butterfly were flitting among the flowers.

Returning to El Fuerte we went to the museum and the zocolo. We went out for supper had a Bananas Foster and crashed.

After breakfast we went to the train station. The train was maybe an hour late or on time in Mexican minutes. A man drove up in a donkey cart and a group of kids with costumes did dances for change. Buskers everywhere.

Divisadero

The trip to Divisadero began through tropical thorn brush. Several leguminous trees. Poppy trees. Kapok. As we went higher there were organ pipe cactus and purple Amapa rosa.

The train pulled into a siding near Cerocahui to allow a freight train to pass. Although this was unscheduled and no one got off, the vendors arrived,

Canyon Overlook

We arrived at Divisadero and checked in at the Divisadero Barranchas Hotel. Although our rooms did not overlook the canyon the bar and dining room did.

We took a walk to look at some shelter caves and a Tarahumara violinmaker. Taking it easy since we were above 7000 feet we stopped several times to discuss various topics – vegetation, history, etc. A barefooted-young man accompanied us. We passed a native home and workshop with the laundry spread out on a rock shelf. We passed two women sitting in the shade weaving baskets. Along the trail were an abandoned adobe house, a well, and a partially enclosed cave. We saw several people up on the canyon rim.

The shelter caves are not too hard to spot since there was a smear of soot on the wall above the cave. The caves are used in the summer and the winter is spent on the canyon floor. There are small fields of potatoes, corn and beans and orchards of apples and peaches.

Tarahumara shelter caves

Baskets are of two major kinds. One is small baskets made Aztec pine needles. The pine needle baskets are more common at elevation. The other kind is made of sotol or beargrass. The sotol baskets are commonly used at home since the floor is dirt and the baskets keep thing clean and organized. The most common sotol baskets are the *guari* type. This type is usually a single weave basket with a round top and a four-corner square at the bottom. These may be made in graduated sizes and can be nested. Another type is the petaca. It is round with a lid and may be double woven.

Other crafts include weaving belts, scarves, blankets, *huaraches*, and carving pine bark figures. The women also string bracelets and necklaces with coral beans, castor beans, and other material including glass beads. Men formerly carved dough bowls used in Tortilla making.

Corn has been very important in Tarahumara society. It is used to make *masa* for tortillas and a corn-based beer called *tesquino. Tesquino* is used as a substitute for currency to pay for labor and to meet social debts. I was hoping to try *tesquino* and possibly have a *tesquinaria* for my wife's birthday. It was funny to hear the bartender say *tesquino* was dangerously strong while he was mixing Margaritas and setting up shots of tequila. *Tesqunio* usually contains 1%-3% alcohol compared to 40% for tequila.

We were discussing strange beverages when the subject of *Chicha* came up. *Chicha* is fermented corn or manioc beer. One Peace Corps acquaintance described it as the Indian women would chew manioc root and spit the saliva into a collection pot. This was diluted with boiled water and let set for a couple days. He said it tasted ok but it reminded him of French kissing all the ugly female inhabitants of the village.

Not all *Chicha* is so exotic. *Tesquino* is made by germinating the corn, diluting the mash with boiled water and let set for a couple days for fermentation. A similar drink on the coast if *tepache* or pineapple beer where pineapples are crushed and covered with boiled water and allowed to ferment a couple days. The water must be boiled to remove oxygen or the fermentation produces vinegar instead of alcohol. I accidentally made a gallon of pineapple vinegar once.

We stopped to visit with a violinmaker on the way back to the hotel. He had modern glue and clamps but original designs. He answered some questions and demonstrated his playing ability with a couple of songs.

Magnificent Hummingbird

Back at the bar was our welcome Margarita, and we watched several Magnificent Hummingbirds at feeders. The sun was setting and the sun line was creeping up the canyon wall and the sky fading to dark. The stars were coming out in the stark black sky.

Supper was shredded beef and creamed peppers with beans and wieners.

About 0630 I went out to hang up the sun and do bird looking. Dickey Jays checking out the garbage cans. Finches. Mexican Blue-mockingbird was singing. Acorn Woodpecker. Sinaloa Crow. Canyon Wren. A Black Vulture was drifting down the canyon rim looking for thermals. A bird that had the shape of a Robin hopped around inside an Oak tree.

The Tarahumara women and children were coming to work. I asked how the particular vendors were chosen. The elders assign locations and times of arrival to prevent overcrowding of the market spaces.

Children are sometimes cute but many of these kids had a runny nose and hair that looked like it had never been washed. Respiratory problems were the leading cause of childhood mortality.

Time for breakfast. My idea of a Mexican breakfast is corn tortillas, *atole*, and a pitcher of fresh *pulque* but this is not available in most restaurants in Mexico. Mescal was not even available in Northern Mexico.

Coming to Work

After breakfast we set out the bags and went for another walk. We saw several overlooks and crossed a suspension bridge. I found a Cretaceous sea urchin in the gravel along the road.

Setting up for the Day

Tarahumara runner

We had an outdoor demonstration of Tarahumara dances about a horse and a fighting bull. Then there was a demonstration of a race and kicking the ball. They have a wooden ball and a stick and kick the ball along the trail. The stick is used to dig the ball out of the brush. The kicker can be barefoot or wear huaraches. The race is discussed in several references if you want more details.

Creel

After lunch we walked down to the train station and waited for the train. A private train stopped for a visit. The train was from Los Angeles and ran about $8000 per person. Our train arrived about two hours late so we arrived in Creel at sunset about 5:30.

After moving in and getting the heater started, we took a walk the length of the main street to the cathedral and the *zocolo*. There was part of a *quinceanera* being held at the church with the following party outside of town. Lots of young males and females dressed to kill. This is the 15th birthday coming out party of a young woman to introduce her to "polite" society at a cost of several thousand pesos.

By the time we reached the church it was almost 7:00 and the shops were closing. We looked in a few shops on the way home for possible return in the morning.

Next morning I was up early to see if the birds were up. I saw only house sparrows and a few domestic pigeons.

When we went to breakfast, I asked the manager if they had *atole*. "Oh yes. We have oatmeal." I said *atole* was made with *masa* and got the reply, "Oh. You know how to make *atole*? No. We only have oatmeal." Where should you look for traditional Mexican dishes if not Mexico? I make *atole* and other dishes at home.

We got our bags out and loaded up on a couple of vans to visit a Tarahumara village of San Ignacio. We bounced along a primitive road to a site with several cabins and a large shelter cave. The young people lived in the cabins leaving the cave for the old folks.

Tarahumara Cave Home

The front of the cave was partially walled in and had an entrance gate. The interior of the cave was divided into sleeping, eating, storage, and room to move the livestock inside in bad weather. This community had its own specialties of carving and weaving.

We left this community to the next tour bus and went to the valley of the mushrooms with a number of wind-carved monuments commonly called hoodoos. This was followed by a visit to the valley of the toads with larger hoodoos. Another mile along was a Catholic cemetery and church. The church had antique art. The church was a primitive structure surrounded by a wall.

We left the church and passed the Tarahumara cemetery and another mile to the highway. We turned south to Lago Arareco for a stop. There were several tourist busses and several cars of picnickers. Several vendors' were spread out on blankets. Besides the baskets and jewelry, there were some small pottery pieces such as cups and spoons and sugar bowls. These were made by the coil method without a kiln but baked like the pottery in Mata Ortiz covered with a bucket with manure for heat. They make a few large *ollas* for cooking and storage and *tesquino* fermentation pots.

Back in town we had the opportunity to do a little shopping. Back at the motel we were ready to go but the bus was an hour late. We started back to Chihuahua with a stop planned for Cuauhtemoc for lunch. The wind began to blow. We had a 45 mph tail wind with gusts to 70 mph and blowing dust with visibility down to a quarter mile. After lunch we got on a toll road into Chihuahua.

The wind stopped about the time we arrived in Chihuahua. Sunset showed the bright orange subtropical jet stream taking the dust to Texas.

We were back at the Quality Inn San Francisco hotel about 6:30 with our final dinner scheduled for 7:00. There was a cake for the 40th birthday of our guide and my wife (ageless).

Next morning.

Breakfast was good. This was the first time to see sliced guava served on a buffet. We packed up and went out to the airport.

One interesting item was two gas stations that were new to me. They were named K-19 and Autogas. This was in addition to national Pemex stations.

I slept all the way to Houston and then to San Antonio. We arrived home about 6:00. That night the dust we left behind in the mountains fell out as a muddy rain in San Antonio.

Carol came down with bronchitis thanks to the dust.

Wrap up

In general this was a good trip. Copper Canyon is more than just a train ride. As my military intelligence friends say "a sweet recon". Next time I would like to go into the canyons probably at a different time of year to find different birds, butterflies and plants. I still look forward to trying *tesquino* and getting local Mexican and indigenous food standards and specialties.

11

Todos Santos Eco Adventure

February 2009

By

Carl Lahser

Introduction.

My part-time handyman work over the past couple years added up to enough for an environmental trip to somewhere. My wife said, "Charge on" so I picked an ecological tour, Todos Santos Eco Adventures located at Todos Santos about an hour north of Cabo San Lucas. Departure from San Antonio was 6 Feb to Phoenix and San Jose Cabo. I stayed at the Cabo Inn Hotel Friday and Saturday nights and was picked up by the tour Sunday morning and returned the following Saturday to fly home. Itinerary included surfing and historical hikes, astronomy, sea lions at Los Islotes near La Paz, a desert ranch, and hikes and snorkeling at local beaches.

Natural setting.

The southern tip of the Baja California peninsula is the State of Baja California Sur mostly south of the Tropic of Cancer. The state covers about 30,000 square miles including several islands in the Pacific and the Gulf of California. The population is about 500,000 people. The Sea of Cortez, also called the Gulf of California, is on the east side of the peninsula and the Pacific Ocean is on the west and south.

From a biologist point of view it could not be much better. There are Pacific and Gulf beaches and marine life, the San Jose River Estuary, oasis, and the Sierra de la Laguna Mountains that rise to 6,000 feet. These mountains catch the clouds and accumulate over 30" of rainfall that support a pine/oak ecosystem. The desert is an extension of the Sonoran Desert across the Gulf in northern Mexico.

This desert is broken into four distinct sub-regions: the San Filipe Desert to the north and east averaging 2" of rainfall a year; the Gulf Coast Desert on the Gulf side, the Vizcaino Desert on the Pacific; and the Magdalena Plains or Central Desert. The climate ranges from desert to sub-alpine. There are also interesting geologic features such as gabbros, ultramafic rock, and lava. There are Miocene era salty alkaline dry lakes, fossils, and a number of shelter caves.

Archeological sites include shelter caves and rock art. Clovis points date habitation back at least 11,000 years. More recent prehistory include the Las Palmas complex in the Cape Region and nearby island in the

Gulf; the Comandú Complex in the central part of the peninsula dating from A.D. 500 to about 1700; and rock shelters containing big painting of people and animals in the Sierra de Guadalupe and Sierra de San Francisco mountains. Some of the paintings are up to 45 feet tall. There were four distinct ethnolinguistic groups: the Pericú between Cabo San Lucas and La Paz; Guaycura from La Paz to Loreto; Monqui around Loreto; and Cochimi through the middle of the Peninsula.

There are about 500 species of native plants including 110 species of cactus and succulents. Rzedowsky listed 23 percent of the plants as endemic. Ecoregions include halophytic, microphyll desert matorral, sarcocaulous matorral, crasicaulous matorral, sarco-crasicaulous matorral, spiny matorral and desert vegetation, plus agricultural regions. There are also various ferns, fungi and slime molds.

There are about 600 species of birds listed for the entire peninsula, 4 amphibians, 43 reptiles and about fifty mammals. There are maybe 1200 species of butterflies and moths, numerous other insects and a number of species of endemic bees and ants.

One of the day trips was to the sea lion rookery at Los Islotes. This is a rocky point and bay in the Sea of Cortez off the tip of Espiritu Santa Island.

Something for practically everyone.

The lists at the end of this narrative are by no means comprehensive but include what I saw during the trip.

References for the trip included:

Radamaker, Kurt and Cindy. 2008. Field Checklist of the Birds of Baja California.

Rodriguez-Estrella, Ricardo. 2005. Terrestial Birds and Conservation Priorites in Baja California Peninsula.

Brown, John W., H. G. Real, D.K. Faulkner. 1992. Butterflies of Baja California: Faunal Survey, Natural History, Conservation Biology.

Roberts, Norman. 1989. Baja California Plant Field Guide.

Epple, A.O. 1995. *Plants of Arizona*.

Martinez, Maximino. 1987. *Plantas Mexicanas*.

Rzedowski, J. 1978. Vegetación de México.

Davis, L.I.1972. Birds of Mexico and Central America.

Keen, A.M. 1960. Sea Shells of Tropical West America.

Johnson, M.E & H.J.Snook, 1955, Seashore Animals of the Pacific Coast.

Historical Setting.

Baja was discovered in 1553 by Fortún Ximénez, a mutineer. Hernán Cortes led a failed expedition to the "Island of California" 1535. Both coasts were explored by Francisco de Ulloa and Juan Rodriguez Cabrillo in 1539-1542. Other explorers and pearl hunters visited Baja over the next 150 years. Between 1683 and 1685 the Jesuit Eusebio Francisco Kino and Admiral Isidero de Atonodo y Antillón tried to establish colonies at La Paz and at San Bruno north of Loreto.

The first colony, Misión de Nuestra Señora de Loreto was established in 1697 by the Jesuit missionary Juan Maria de Salvatierra. Over the next fifty years the Jesuits expanded their influence over most of the peninsula while limiting the civilian settlers.

A mission at San José del Cabo was established about 1730 near watering place at the mouth of the Rio San Jose. San José del Cabo was burned in 1734.

A fort had been established at Cabo San Lucas in the late 1500s to halt piracy and a mission was established about 1730. Cabo San Lucas was reduced to a small fishing village of a couple hundred people until the 1930's when aircraft spotted large shoals of fish. The community grew with the building of hotels and timeshares and sport fishing.

In 1768 the Jesuits were expelled and replaced by the Franciscans under Junipero Serra. In 1773 the Franciscans turned control over to the Dominicans. The indigenous population diminished under the Church due to disease and virtual enslavement for work around the missions.

Todos Santos began around the Misión Santa Rosa de Todos Los Santos in 1734. The patron who provided money for the church did so with the provision that the church would be named for her – Rose.

Much of the town was destroyed during the Pericú rebellion between 1734 and 1737 when the Pericú and Guayacura tribes attacked four missions. According to Father Sigismundo Taraval at Todos Santos the rebellion began when Father Nicolas Tamaral baptized a shamans' wife and refused to let her return to her husband. The mission was abandoned in 1840. About 50 years later it was revived as a sugar town in conjunction with being a handy supply point for the 49ers headed for the gold fields. Sugar was abandoned when an earthquake destroyed the aquifer. Over the past 40 years it has become a tourist destination and artist colony.

All of the sugar mills paid their laborers in script good only at their company store. One of the prominent sugar cane families was the Dominquez family. A young Chinese man named Wong came down from California and married a Dominguez daughter. He opened a general store with the innovation that he took all script. He soon opened two other stores including the one that is now the Hotel California. The original building had a store on the first floor and the first hotel in town on the second floor called the Hotel Rosa about 1928. He also built the first gas station where the Hotel gift shop is located. The property was bought by Canadians who renovated the building as the Hotel California and the gift shop about 2005. So much for the myth.

In 1804 the peninsula was divided into two political bodies with the capitol of the Baha California Sur (south) established at Loreto.

6 Feb.

The magic day finally arrived. My wife drove me to the airport arriving at 0700**.** The US Airways flight numbers and times had changed but I had a widow seat all the way. They charged$15 to check my bag. Cokes and water were $2 and beer was $7.

The aircraft was full and cramped. We were in Phoenix about two hours later. There was an hour and a half layover and then a big A320 took us on an hour's flight across Mexico east of Hermosillo to the farmland near Guaymas and then 20-minutes across the Sea of Cortez straight in to the San Jose Cabo airport. The weather was hazy most of the way

The airport had doubled in size in the past five years when Alaska Airlines built a new terminal which was then appropriated by the airport. The old terminal has been modernized. Immigration and customs lines were upgraded so that I was in a $15 van shuttle to my hotel in about twenty minutes. It took about a half-hour to drive the new rerouted modernized highway to downtown Cabo.

Shills in the airport were trying to sell timeshares and other schemes. I found that the age range was 18 to 70 so I was no longer qualified. Tough.

Cabo area had grown. The highway was much improved. More condos were under construction. A big Sam's Club was next door to Cosco.

The Cabo Inn was painted bright yellow with three floors and twenty rooms. There was a small pool on the roof and a library and lounge. My room was about 12X12 including the small bath. (You got into the shower by shimmying around the sink and climbing over the toilet.) There was an AC unit and a refrigerator that I did not need.

After I was checked-in and somewhat unpacked I put some batteries for the cameras on charge and went to the Moriscos Mazatlan for supper. I had octopus in garlic sauce with a beer. It was mostly tentacles grilled with garlic, onions, and celery served with rice and steamed achote squash. The bill was 130 pesos or about $11. I did not know the rate of exchange had changed but varied from 13-14 pesos to $1 US.

I walked two blocks to the Puerto Paradiso mall and looked in a numerous shops. There were still some high-class shops but now there were a few like Dollar General. A few shops I recognized from last trip. There were more restaurants, including a Hard Rock Cafe and Starbucks. I finally found Johnny Rocket and stopped for malt.

I returned about to the room about 9PM and crashed. People sat in the common area talking until almost midnight.

7 Feb.

I was up and about a little after 0900. I checked out the top floor deck and pool. The pool was about twice the size of a big hot tub. The library contained a few popular paperbacks and several abandoned textbooks.

About a block away I found the El Dengue fruit stand and bought a big fresh papaya drink for breakfast.

Across the street from El Dengue was a bus stop where many different local busses called collectivos and an occasional interurban bus and even a few first class busses stopped. Lots of people waiting. Don't know the fare.

Almost nothing was open until 1000. I walked along window shopping and watching the town wake up. A 24-hour pharmacy. Mr. Frog. The Zoo. TatooTatoo. Burgerking. BlingBling. I found just the thing for Valentines in one of the windows and would be back later. People inside the shops arranging things. There was the squawk of protective blinds being raised. Bags of trash were being removed. Dollies of merchandise were being delivered. More and more traffic. I walked to the end of the road to the Navy barracks and the cruise ship landing.

A Black Swallowtail caterpillar was charging across the sidewalk. I couldn't see either a food source or a site for pupating.

On the way back I went up the road to Solmar hotel and Terrasol Beach hotel. Going through the hotel lobby I went down to the beach. About every hundred yards was a warning sign – Rip tide; No swimming; No wading; No surfing. Big waves rose quickly and tripped over the beach. Returning water tripped some of the waves making white water. Bad surf. You could see big rocks through the waves as they rose.

There we a few small shell like half-inch Venus clams, a half inch long olive and juvenile mussels, and three species of limpets. This population was an indicator of rock and sand bottom and even depth of near shore water. The size of the juveniles indicated winter because spawning is in the fall.

Sand crab burrows punctured the beach. Tan granite sand.

According to my GPS I was at N22.31.3.4 and W107.40.8.2

Leaving the beach the backbeach supported Golandrina, Distichlis (saltgrass), and Devil's Claw (*Espuela del Diablo*). Further back were a yellow composite, Ambrosia, and windmillgrass. A skipper and black swallowtail were nectering on the Ambrosia.

An occasional Brown Pelican or Tropicbird cruised by and there were a few House Sparrows in the hotel bar.

Along the road back to the harbor was a Damiana bush. No one was selling Damiana tea as an aphrodisiac so far this trip. Damiana liquor was available to make outstanding Margaritas.

A Cactus Wren was calling. I found it sitting on a corrugated roof at a construction site.

Lunch was at the Stop Light. Shrimp Quesadeas and a Coke.

Back at the room I showered and napped then typed up the day's notes. I went out to find a bottle of tonic water to stop leg cramps generated by the day's walk.

8 Feb.

It was Sunday morning. The overnight cool was in the low 60s. I checked the pictures from the last trip to Cabo to see if I had missed shooting anything. Only the new places needed a picture. I was up and out for breakfast about 0800.

The Café Matzlan was just opening and let me in. Mexican omelet. Tea. Fresh pineapple juice. I asked if anyone served atole. The manager said this was Mexican home cooking and not usually served outside the house. I asked about tesqueno and tepache and was told I might find them from street vendors but not in any bars.

The route to the beach took me past the police station and firehouse. The firehouse had a Company Store that sold firehouse coffee, T-shirts, and calendars. Good for PR and as a moneymaker to buy gym equipment.

There were several undeveloped pieces of land along the street that led down to the beach. On the beach men were sifting the sand for trash or smoothing out walkways in the sand. The waveskimmers and tour boats were getting set up for the day. A few gulls and pigeons were cruising the beach ahead of the cleaning crew. Beach dining tables were being set. About half an hour later I went back to the hotel to pack and check out.

A sound truck roamed the streets condemning drugs on Sunday. The driver must be deaf.

The hotel lobby had numerous plants. It was open to the sky but covered by shade cloth. Tropical almond and Shefflera leaves fell into the lobby missing the shade cloth. Pothos trailed from the second floor. There was a grill and microwave and a communal refrigerator. Coffee was on all the time. The TV had mostly Mexican stations but also had CNN and BBC.

My tour guides showed up about 1330. One of their vehicles had broken down. We took a taxi to San Jose to pick up a couple that was flying in. After they arrived we waited while they had a bite and left for Todos Santos about 1530. It was a rolling twisting road through tall cardon cactus and elephant trees.

A Common Raven glided across the road and a roadrunner ran/flew across the highway.

I checked in to the Hotel California. Really nice. Room No. 1 on the front corner of the second floor. About 20X24 with a large modern bath. King-size bed. Private balcony. Price was listed at $200/night. Pool. Several sundecks. Lots of art. A bar and dining room. A large gift shop where the first gas station in town once stood. The bar across the street had been demolished and replaced by a shopping mall and a future hotel was being built.

At 7PM we went to supper at an Italian restaurant. The food was OK but not what I expected. Gnocchi were dime-size.

9 Feb.

Temperature in the room was in the lower 70s. I checked the metal balcony railing and some metal outside and found a temperature of 46° F. Pretty chilly.

I went for a little walk and heard a woodpecker calling. There was a pair of Gilla Woodpeckers on a utility pole. A small House Wren disappeared into some shrubbery. A Cactus Wren was calling somewhere across the street.

Beside the hotel was a large empty lot where an art festival had been held. Next to this was the Mission de Santa Rosa de las Palmas. Below the church was a big palm thicket where sugar cane had been raised and native palms had reestablished themselves in the abandoned fields.

Back at the hotel breakfast was a waffle with blue agave syrup. About 0730 the town was waking up. People with backpacks and jackets were heading to work in the morning cool.

Our group headed down a dusty road to Cerratos Beach for a surfing lesson. The beach was a good sandy surfing beach with moderate waves that had a long fetch. There was a shanty village of mostly squatter trailers and sheds. A new resort was being built. The beach had a beach club with fast-food and beer.

The surfing instructor was waiting for us. We slipped on our wetsuits and practiced his four-step method for getting up - 1. Grab the rail and pushup; 2. Move the back knee up; 3. Move the front foot up; 4. Stand and pivot and move the back foot up staying in fighting crouch. My knees would not cooperate but I got up on hands and knees. I was cold in the 66 degree water and I was really short of breath.

Surfing

We got out of the water, stripped off our wet suits and warmed up in the sun before going to lunch.

Back at the ranch we made a walk up la Poza Hill through the desert vegetation to the beach and then back home long the breach. There were elephant trees (*Torote Colorado*), Adam trees, jojoba, and several cacti (*Vejita* in fruit, sour *pitaya*, jumping *cholla, nopal, cardon*). The lichen, Ramalina reticulata called Spanish moss, *Rocella*, or *Orchilla*), was thick on some of the *Torote*. There were a few yellow Brittlebush (*Incense*) along the graded road.

A Hooded Oriole flew over and a Northern Mockingbird was perched on a tall cactus. A small House Wren as flitting through the brush. We found a couple of hummingbird nests.

Supper was at the Coronela Restaurant at the Hotel California. It was a sampling of quesadillas with chicken, beef, fish and cheese followed by a sampling of marlin, crab coquettes, brisket and chicken strips with several dipping sauces

I got a call from my wife about 9PM that my credit card had been cancelled. I called Visa and they said to call my bank, which said to call Visa. Nothing for $30 in phone calls from Mexico.

10 Feb.

I had a night of diarheria probably from the tap water to brush my teeth in the Cabo Inn. I was packed and ready to move to the Villas Lamar. I chickened out on the days hike to the three waterfalls and slept about four hours.

I woke up feeling much better and unpacked. My room was a suite of about 1200 square feet with a separate bedroom, a full kitchen, and big outside patio.

Freshwater Lagoon

My room overlooked the beach and a freshwater lagoon. Frigatebirds and pelicans frequented both. Giant cane surrounded the lagoon and coots and a few grebes paddled around.

I looked down the beach and saw a cloud from a whale's blow. Over a few minutes there were several whales spouting followed by a black streak of the whale's back. Two were close to the beach and three more were further off shore. Neat.

The group returned from the waterfalls trip about 2PM. About 4PM we went to downtown for a historical overview. The Dominguez house. Todos Santos first theatre. Wong's stores. The church.

Super was a learning experience. The chef at the Brown Coffee House demonstrated peeling and preparing pablano peppers and making rellenos. He made the stuffing from shredded smoked marlin. Very good. He also demonstrated handmade Margaritas using Damiana liquor and fresh fruit. This beat machine-made Margaritas ten to one.

When we returned I had received a call from Carol that my credit card was working again. I did not plan on using it but it was nice to know it was available.

11 Feb.

We left about 0700 on an overcast day to drive to La Paz to catch a boat to visit the sea lions on Los Islotes Island. (I often talk in run-on sentences.) There are a couple good web sites with pictures from a similar trip.

Construction of a four-laned highway was underway to within a couple miles of Todos Santos. It will bypass Todos Santos. Like most highway construction it was scheduled to be finished early last year.

When we arrived at the hotel to pick up the boat and equipment we were told the harbor was closed for small boats because of eight-foot swells outside of the Bay of La Paz in the Sea of Cortez. This was unusual but then this was winter and there could be storms to the north.

As an alternate we drove several miles north and east to a series of beaches and ridges overlooking the mouth of the Bay of La Paz. The objective was to walk the ridgeline for a couple miles then descend to the beach and return along the water.

We parked overlooking a picture perfect beach with tan sand and palapas and bright blue water. That would be saved for later after the ridge walk.

Stone Mushroom - Symbol of La Paz

Beach vegetation included Setaria (Bristlegrass), Trichloris (?), Golandrina, a milkweed called Jumete. There was a tidal a bay with Black Mangrove.

Up! Up! And away! About an hour's walk we could see the island cluster where the sea lions lived. The island was about 15 miles long.

The rocks were littered with broken shells from birds dropping them to eat the clams. Along the trail grew stunted *Torte Prieto*, small Mammalaria and a few Chollas. There were several Strawberry cacti. There was also a small plant that looked like Silene or Houstonia.

Then it was down hill to the beach. On the beach was the symbol of La Paz tourism, a mushroom rock. We looked at it and then followed the sea caves and beaches to the van. There were no large or complete shells of any species.

We stopped in La Paz for lunch. We also stopped in an ice cream shop for a scoop of rose petal and a scoop of mango and went across the street to the malacon to sit in the sun. I looked along the water but no shells. We returned to the hotel by about 4PM

There were five whales working the beach.

Supper was at a restaurant run by a Swiss couple. The scallops were very good.

12 Feb.

This was the day for the cliff walk. The walk was about 2 miles from the beach along a mid-1850s wagon road to the gold rush port of Todos Santos. Rocky. Dusty. Steep in places. Sour Pitaya. Coffeeberry. Elephant trees. Lichens. Dried Coral Vine. A Cardinal. An American Kestrel. A clump of wild Barbados Aloe with yellow flowers.

Minerals in the hills included andesite, granite, and quartz

We finally made the top of the cliff and what a view. About 600 feet down was a beautiful rocky cove with breaking waves. A large rock or small island at the base of the cliff had sour Pitaya covering its top. Further along were another cove and the old port. Clear blue sky. The humid breeze had a bit of a chill. Several whales were spouting in the distance.

We came back down the same road to the beach for a picnic and Pelican watching. Flights of the big birds came in just barely off the ground over the dunes.

The beach was a fisherman's beach. Boats were pulled up above high tide. Scrap netting and trash was everywhere. A large flock of Pelicans and vultures sat on the sand waiting for the fishermen.

We returned to the hotel in mid afternoon for a nap and whale watching. Dinner was at the Los Adobes restaurant. We were back in time for sunset and stargazing. Pointing out constellations. Stories about stars. Looking through a telescope. Looking at the stars through my night vision scope. Neat.

A Rough-winged Swallow passed over head and a hummingbird moth fed on bougainvilleas after sundown

13 Feb.

Friday. We drove out to the San Vincente ranch maybe 10 miles into the center of the peninsula. The vegetation was thicker and more varied as we gained altitude. Hofmeisteria, Brittlebush. Esperanza. Real broadleaf trees. A hilly, dusty road.

There were several ranches in the area settled by the original Spanish settlers who refused to leave then the Church was expelled. Small, rather primitive houses. A satellite school with no children. Free-ranging cattle, goats and pigs. The ranch also had several ostriches.

The potter was Doña Ramona. She was about 60 and crippled with a knee needing replacement. She and her family had been doing pottery for several generations collecting the clay on the ranch. Pottery had been a necessity for dishes and pots but she had gone the extra step and embellished the mundane turning the pottery into art. She gave us a demonstration of her techniques.

This was followed by a demonstration of tortilla making by her daughter and a home cooked lunch of tacos. Make the dough. Place a small ball in the tortilla press. Operate the press and remove the tortilla. Pat and spin the tortilla before placing it on the grill. Turn the tortilla and press out the air bubbles. I almost caught my sleeve on fire. The old wood stove was one of the first things built when the newlyweds moved in 40 years before. It was built much like a Chinese kung.

A big bougainvillea bush had a bunch of long-tailed skippers and several small sulfurs and tiny whites.

Back on the highway was a field of strawberries beside the road and a field of Calla Lilies in the distance. Mango trees were coming into bloom.

We returned to the hotel in mid afternoon. I returned to town about 4PM to look in shops and galleries. I took some pictures of historic structures and street scenes.

Three Belding Yellowthroat were in a tree just over my head.

I met the group at 6PM for supper at the Café Santa Fe. I had lobster ravioli.

Back at the room I packed most things and did some typing and crashed.

14 Feb.

It was go home morning. The temperature was about 70 over night, finally warm enough to just use a sheet without a blanket. I was up about 0600 and saw several vehicles driving the beach in the dark. One stopped to fish until it was good light.

I finished packing and did some more typing.

There was a trawler working off the beach. A whale was spouting far off shore. Gulls were swimming off the beach for the first time. The bird on the beach included pelicans, herring gulls and two Black-necked Stilts. Several Snowy Egrets waded in the lagoon margin. Coots and a couple of Grebes paddled on the pond. Several swallows cruised over the cane. House Wrens and a hummingbird played in the landscape flowers.

I heard a Cactus Wren and a Gilla Woodpecker. Sounded like the Terminator, "Hasta la vista, Baby." "See you next trip."

PS

Time arrived to get the bags loaded and head for the airport. The ride took two hours. Another two hours to 2:30PM loading time. I was back in San Antonio by 10:30 Valentines night.

Plantas de Mexico

Plants around Veracruz

Bananas	Coscomatepec
Coffee	Coscomatepec
sugar cane	Coscomatepec
fishtail palm (Caryota)	Fortine
Royal palm (Roystonea)	Fortine
Oranges	Mx 150 libre

Plants of Mexico City, Teotihuacan, and el Risario Butterfly Preserve

Agavadae

Agave	Agave Americana

Pinaceae

Oyamel	Abies religiosa

Plants of the Baja trip

Names in italics are introduced or ornamental plants.

Lichens	
Orchilla, Rocella (on Adám's tree)	Ramalina reticulata
Bracket Fungi	possibly Fistulina on coconut
Flamecap?	possibly Gymnopilus on coconut
17 Cattail family (Typhaceae)	
Cattail	Typha domingensis
27 Grasses (Graminae)	
Crowfootgrass	Dactyloctenium sp.
Windmillgrass	Chloris sp.
29 Palm family (Palmae)	
Tlaco palms or Palmilla	Erythea Brandegeei
Coconut Palm	*Cocos nutifera*
Date Palm, Dátil	*Phoenix dactylifera*
35 Air Plants (Bromeliaceae)	
Ball Moss, Gallito or Heno Pequeno	Tillandsia recurvata
40 Amaryllis family (Amaryllidaceae)	
Centuary Plant or Magay	Agave chrysantha
Maguey	Agave americana
Spider Lilies	*Hymenocallis caroliniana*
48 Willow family (Salicaceae)	
Yew leaf Willow	Salix taxifolia
62 Buckwheat family (Polyonaceae)	
Coralvine, San Miguel, Queen's Crown, Queen's Wreath, Coralitto, or Flor de SanDiego	Antigonon leptopus
65 Four O'clock family (Nyctaginaceae)	
Bougainvillea, Bugambilla	*Bougainvillea glabra*
Four O'Clock, Maravilla	Mirabilis Wrightii

69 Aizoaceae

Carpetweed	Mollugo sp.
96 Pea family (Leguminosae)	
Huisache or Mesquite	Prosopis sp.
Vinorama	Acacia Smallii
Paloverde	Parkinsonia microphylla
Paloblanco	Acacia Willardiana
101 Zygophyllaceae	
Creosote bush, Gobernadora, Hediondilla	Larrea tridentat
104 Torchwood family (Burseraceae)	
Elephant trees or Cerote	Bursera microphylla
107 Spurge family	
Castor bean	*Ricans communis*
Croton	*Croton sp.*
Mallow family (Malvaceae)	
Hibiscus	*Hibiscus rosa-sinensis*
Alterculia family (Sterculiaceae)	
Malva Rosa	*Melochia tomentosa*
Tamarix family	
Saltcedar or Tamarix	*Tamarix pentandea*
Ocotillo family (Fouquieraceae)	
Ocotillo	Fouquieria splendens
Adam's Tree or Palo Adan	Fouquieria diguetii
132 Turneraceas	
Damiata	Tunera diffusa
135 Cactus family (Cactaceae)	
Biznaga	Ferrocactus gracillis
Biznaga, Viejilta	Mammillaria brandegeei
Biznaga, fishhook cactus	Mammillaria dioica
Biznagita, Cochemia	Cochemia poselgeri
Cardon cactus	Pachycereus pringlei

Old Man Cactus, Garambullo, Sentia	Cereus acanthocarpa
Organ Pipe Cactus	Lemaireocereus thurberi
Pencil Cholla or Jumping Cactus	Opuntia leptocaullis
Chain Link Cholla	Opuntia cholla
Turk's Head	Echinocactus horizonthalonius
Prickly Pear, tuna or nopal	Opuntia engelmanii
Combretaceae	
Tropical Almond	Terminalia catappa

156 Morning Glory family (Convolvulaceae)

Bush Morning Glory	Ipomea leptaphylla
Woodrose	?
Moonflower	Calonyction aculeatum

166 Bignonia family (Bignoniaceae)

Yellow Trumpet flower, Palo de Arco Tecoma stans

164 Nightshade family (Solanaceae)

Jimson Weed or Toloache	Datura wrightii
Mariola, Oja de Liebre	Solanum hindsianum
Buffalo burr	Solanum rostrata

173 Madder family (Rubiaceae)

Ixoria	*Ixora coccinea*

180 Composite family (Asteraceae)

Ragweed	*Ambrosia sp.*

PLANTS of the Rio Grande Valley and Saltillo.

Unusual or new. Excludes exotic or landscape plants

Polypoid fern on oaks
Bracken Fern with pines
Ponderosa or Chihuahua Pine
Western Red Cedar in bloom
Camas lily
Joshua Tree
Black Willow
Black Walnut
Hackberry
Mexican Mulberry
Purslane
Chickweed
Ranunculus (Heart-leaf Buttercup)
Watercress
Mexican Gold Poppy
Brassica
Mesquite
Burr clover
Acacia
Opuntia
Madrone
Lobelia
Galium
Eupatorium
Veronia

Plants of San Miguel

Family and Genus	Common Name	Spanish Name
Graminae		
Chloris	Windmillgrass	
	Foxtail	
Pinaceae		
Pinus murrayana	Lodgepole Pine	*Pino*
P. alepo	Alepo Pine	
Agavaceae		
Agave Americana	Century Plant	*Maguey*
A. salmiana	Blue Agave	
Amaranthaceae		
Amaranthus hybridus	Pigweed	*Quintonil*
Anacardiaceae		
Schinus molle	Peruvian Pepper Tree	*Pirul*
Asclepiadaceae		
Asclepas sp.	Milkweed vine	
Asteraceae/ Compositae	Adenophyllum cancellatum	Dogweed
Bidens odorata	Beggar's Tick	*Aceitilla*
Calyptocarpus vialis	Straggler Daisy	
Galinsoga parviflora	Gallant Soldier	*Estrellita*
Gnaphthaliun sp.	Cud Weed	*Hierba de la almorrana*
Parthenium bipinnatifidum	Feverfew	
Sanvitalia procumbus	Eye of the Cock	Ojo de gallo
Sonchus oleraceus	Sowthistle	*Muela de caballo*
Tagetes lucida	Sweet Scented Marigold *Flor de Santa Maria*	

Tagetes lunulata	Mexican Marigold	*Cinco Llagas, Pexto*
Taraxacum officinale	Dandelion	*Diente de Leon*
Tithonia rotundifolia	red sunflower	*Xotol*
Tithonia tubiformis	Tithonia	*Girsol, Xotol*
Xanthium strumarium	Cocklebur	*Abrojo*
Aizoaceae		
Glinus sp.	Carpet weed	
Brassicaceae		
Lepidium virginicum	Peppergrass	*Lentejilla*
Bromeliaceae		
Tilandia recurvata	Ball Moss	*Gallito. Heno Pequeno*
Cactaceae		
Lemaireocerreus marginatus	Organ cactus	*Organo*
Myrtillocactus geometricans	Old Man Cactus	*Bastó*
Opuntia cholla	Cholla	*Cholla Pelona*
O. ficus-indica	Prickly Pear	*Tuna*
O. imbricata	Cholla	*Cardón*
O. microdasys	Teddybear Cactus	*Nopal real*
O. robusta	Prickly Pear	*Tuna camusa*
Convolvulaceae		
Ipomoea purpurea	Common Morning Glory	*Manto*
I. longifolia	Pink Throat Morning Glory	*Cola de Caballo*
Euphorbiaceae		
Euohorbia cyathophora	wild poinsettia	*Catalina*
Euphorbia radians	spurge	*Flor de tierra*
Jatropha dioica	Leather stem	*Sangre de Drago*
Ricinus communis	Castor Bean	*Ricino, Palma Christi*

Fabaceae		
Prosopis laevigata	Mesquite	*Mezquite*
Fagaceae		
Quercus reticulata	White Oak	*Encino Blanco*
Fouquieriaceae		
Fouquieria formosa	Fouquiera	*Palo santo*
Juglandaceae		
Carya illinoinenses	Pecan	*Nogal Pecanero*
Labiatae/_Mimosoidae		
Acacia schaffneri	Twisted Acacia	*Huizache Chino*
Acacia farnesiana	Sweet Acacia	*Huizache hediondo*
Acacia brandegeana	Acacia	*Vinorama. Teso*
Hyptis sp.		
Pithecellobium undulatum	Ebony	*Palo Eba*
Salvia columbariae	Chia	*Salvia*
S. eremostachya		
S. regal	Salvia	*Salvia*
Senna septetrionalis	Senna	*Bricho*
Lamiaceae		
Leonotis nepetaefolia	Christmas candlestick	*Baston de sanFrancisco*
Liliaceae		
Aloe vera	Aloe	*Zábila*
Loranthraceae		
Phoradendron califoricum	Desert mistletoe	*Toji. Guhoja.*
Malvaceae		
Malacotharmnus fasciculatus	Bush Mallow	*Malvia*
Moraceae		
Morus celtidifolia	Mulberry	*Mora Blanco*
Myrtaceae		
Eucalyptus sp	Gum Tree	*Eucalipto*

Nyctiginaceae		
Boerhaavia sp.		
Nyctiginia sp.		
Oleaceae		
Fraxinus uhdei	Ash	*Fresno*
Onagraceae		
Oenothera rosea	rose evening primrose	*hierba del golpe*
Oxalidaceae		
Oxalis decaphylla	Wood Sorrel	*Agritos*
O. corniculata	Creeping Lady's Sorrel	*Agritos*
Papaverceae		
Argemone ochroleuca	Pricklypoppy	*Chicalote*
Salicaceae		
Salix bonplandiana	Willow	*Sauce*
Populus sp.	Cottonwood	*Alamo*
Scrophulariaceae		
Castilleja tenuiflora	Catilina Indian Paintbrush	*Hierba del Cancer*
Solanaceae		
Physalis philadelphica	Groundcherry	*Tomatillo Cimarron*
Verbenaceae		
Glandularia bipinnatifida	Mock Verain	*Alfombrilla*

Ornamental/Exotic Plants of San Miguel

Arecaceae		
Phoenix dactylifera	*Date Palm*	
Veitchia merrillii	*Minilla Palm*	
Acanthaceae		
Justica brandegeana	*Shrimp Plant*	
Ruellia sp.	*Mexican Petunia*	*muhuj*
Thumbergia alata	*Blackeye Susan vine*	*ojo de pajaro*
Apocynaceae		
Nerium Oleander	*Oleander*	*Laurel rosa*
Araliaceae		
Schefflera octophylla	*Schefflera*	
Bignoniaceae		
Jacaranda mimosoefolia	*Jacaranda*	*Jacaranda*
Pyrostegia venusta	*Orange trumpet vine*	*Liamarada*
Buddlejaceae		
Buddleia cordata	*Butterfly bush*	*Tezopán blanco*
Casuarinaceae		
Casuarina equisetifolia	*Casuarina, Australian pine*	*Casurina*
Cupressaceae		
Cupressus lindleyi	*Lindley's cypress*	*Cedro*
Cupressus sempervirens	*Italian cypress*	*Ciprées*
Platycladus orientalis	*Arborvitae*	
Euphorbiaceae		
Euphorbia pulcherrina	*Poinsettia*	*Flor de nochebueno*
Fabaceae		
Cassia tomentosa	*Cassia, Senna*	*Retama*
Erythrina flabelliformis	*Coral Tree, Tiger's Claw*	*Colorín, chilicote*
Delonix regia	*Flamboyant*	*Arbol del fuego*
Lauraceae		
Persea Americana	*Avocado*	*Aguacate*

Meliaceae		
Melia azedarach	*Chinaberry*	*Lila*
Moraceae		
Borsimum alicastrum	*Breadnut Tree*	*Ramon*
Morus alba	*Mulberry*	*Mora blanca*
Nyctaginaceae		
Bougainvillea glabra	*Bougainvillea*	*Bugambilia*
Oleaceae		
Gelsemium sempervirens	*Carolina jasmine*	*Jasmin amarillo*
Jasminium mesnyi	*Jasmine*	*Jasmin italiano*
Ligustrum lucidum	*Privet*	*Troeno*
Ligustrum japonicum	*Wax-leaf Ligustrum*	
Trachelospermum jasminiodes	*Confederate Jasmine*	*Jazmin*
Plumbaginaceae		
Plumbago pulchella	*Plumbago,*	*Plumbego, Tiricua*
Rosaceae		
Eriobotrya japonica	*Loquat*	*Níspero*
Pyracantha angustifolia	*Pyracanthus*	
Rosa sp	*Roses*	
Solanaceae		
Datura sp.	*Locoweed*	*Floripondio*
Umbelliferae		
Ferula communis	*Fennel*	
Verbenaceae		
Lantana camera	*Lantana*	*Alantana*
L. montividensis	*Trailing Lantana*	
Vitaceae		
Parthenocissus quiniquefolia	*Virginia Creeper*	*Guau*
Vitus sp.	*Grape*	*Uva*

Copper Canyon Plant list

Plants listed were from the railroad right-of-way and immediate environs during the week of 10-17 March 2008 and certainly not a complete list. Some plants were left from last year. Some were in bloom. Some were in vegetative stages. Some were recognized on site but many were identified from photos taken during the trip.

References:

Baja California Plant Field Guide. Norman Roberts.
Field Guide to the Plants of Arizona. A. Epple.
Plantas Mexicanas. Maximo Martinez.
Flora of the Dawson- Los Monos Canyon Reserve

Polypodiaceae		
Wavy Cloak Fern	Notholaena sinuate	Bahuichivo
Spiny Cliff Brake	**Pellaea truncate**	
Bahuichivo		
Bracken	Pteridium aquilinum	Bahuichivo
Gramminae		
Black Grammagrass	Bouteloua eriopoda	all
(*Navajita negra)*		
Beard grass	Andropogon sp	all
Cupressaceae		
Red cedar	Juniperus sp.	all Mountain
Pinaceae		
Ponderosa	Pinus ponderosa	all mountain
White pine	Pinus strobiformis	all mountain
Mexican Pinyon pine	Pinus cembroides	all mountain
Pinyon	Pinus edulis	all mountain
Apache Pine	Pinus engelmanii	all mountain
Agave		
Schott Agave	Agave schottii	Bahuichivo
Sotol	Dasylirion wheeleri	all mountain
Beargrass	Nolina microcarpa	all mountain

Lechuguilla	Agave lechuguilla	Bahuichivo
Bignoniaceae		
Amapa rosa	Tubebuia pentaphylla	El Fuerte
Bombacaceae		
Kapok tree/*Ceiba*	Ceiba acuminata	El Fuerte
Cactus		
Hedgehog Cactus	Echinocereus engelmanni	Bahuichivo
Prickly pear	Opuntia sp	all
Buckhorn cholla	Opuntia acanthocarpa	El Fuerte
Organ pipe cactus		El Fuerte
Campanulaceae		
Mountain lobelia	Lobelia anatine	Bahuichivo
Compositae		
Haplopappus	Haplopappus sonorensis	Bahuichivo
Brittlebush/*Inciensol*	Enelia farinosa	Bahuichivo
Woolyleaf	Eriophyllum sp	Bahuichivo
Desert Broom	Baccharis amulosasp	Bahuichivo
Ageratina	Ageratina herbacea	Bahuichivo
Emory's Rock Daisy	Perityle emoryii	Bahuichivo
Convolvulaceae		
Morningglory tree	Convolvulus coeorum	El Fuerte
Cruciferae		
Rock Cress	Arabis perennans	El Fuerte
Brasica	Brassica nigra	El Fuerte
Euphorbiaceae		
Mala Mujer	Cnidoscolus angustidens	El Fuerte
Ericaceae		
Madrone	Arbutus sp	Divisadero
Fabaceae		
Palo Blanco	Lysiloma canida	Creel
Mauto	Lysiloma divaricata	Creel
Honey Mesquite	Prosopis juliflora	Creel

Fagaceae		
Netleaf or white oak	Quercus rugosa	Divisadero
Mexican oak	Quercus oblongifolia	Divisadero
Fouquieriaceae		
Ocotillo	Fouquieria MacDougallii	Creel
Hydrophyllaceae		
Whispering Bells	Emmenanthe penduliflora	Bahuichivo
Juglandaceae		
Arizona walnut/*Nogal*	Juglans major	Creel
Loranthaceae		
Mesquite mistletoe/*Toj*	Phoradendron californicum	El Fuerte
Malvaceae		
Checkermallow	Sidalcea neomexicana	
Divisadero		
Oxadaceae		
Wood Sorrel/*Agaritos*	Oxlis corniculata	Bahuichivo
Papveraceae		
Tree poppy	Dendromecon rigida	El Fuerte
Prickly Poppy/*Chicalote*	Argemone pleiacantha	El Fuerte
Salicaceae		
Arroyo Willow	Salix lasiolepis	Creel
Black Willow	Salix gooddingii.	Creel
Cottonwood	Populus migra	Creel
Scrophulariaceae		
Wooly Paintbrush	Castilleja lanata	Bahuichivo
Porch Penstemon	Penstemon sp	Bahuichivo
Solanaceae		
Ground Cherry	Physalis sp	El Fuerte
Ulmaceae		
Netleaf Hackberry	Celtis reticulata.	Creel

Verbenaceae		
Beebrush	Aloysia sp	Bahuichivo
Violaeae		
Mountain Violet	Viola flagelliformis	Bahuichivo
Zygophyllaxeae		
Creosote bush	Larrea tridentata	El Fuerte

Plants of Oaxaca

Family and Genus	Common Name	Local Oaxacan Name
Agavaceae		
Agave Americana	Century Plant	*Maguey*
Ornamental and escaped from culture		
A. salmiana	Blue Agave	
Grown in fields and used as a base for Mescal		
Amaranthaceae		
Amaranthus Palmeri	**Amaranth**	***Bledo***
Herb raised for seed used as food supplement		
Amaranthus hybridus	Pigweed	*Quintonil*
Invasive weed. Oaxaca, Mitla		
Anacardiaceae		
Mangifera indica	Mango	*Mango*
Cultivated fruit		
Schinus molle	Peruvian Pepper Tree	*Pirul*
Aromatic and invasive shrub or tree.		
Spondias purpurea	Spanish Plum	*uela criolla*
Cultivated fruit		
Annonaceae		
Annona cherimola	Chermoya	*cherimoya o cherimoya*
Cultivated fruit		
Apiaceae/Umbellifere		
Coriandrum sativum	Cilantro	*Cilantro* Coriander
Cultivated herb used in cooking		
Eryngium beecheyanum	Cilentro	*Cilantro Cimarron o*
Cultivated herb		
Apocyanaceae		

Plumeria rubra.	Plumeria	Jacalosúchil o Cacaloxóchitl
Introduced ornamental		Cacalosúchi o *Cacalosuche*
Thevetia peruviana	Yellow Oleander, "Be Still Flower"	
Ornamental tree. POISONOUS		
Vinca minor	Periwinkle	*Flor de paraguito*
Ornamental ground cover		
	hierba del sapo	
Araceae		
Zantedeschia aethiopica	Calla Lily	*Cartucho*
Ornamental flower commercially farmed. Benito Juarez Park		
Asclepiadaceae		
Asclepas curassavica	Vientiunilla	*Flor de culebra*
Wild. Butterfly food. Mitla		
Asteraceae/ Compositae		
Small orange composite yellow center		*yerba de conejo*
Culinary herb.		
Small orange composite dark center		*oprombo*?
Ambrosia sp.		
Common wildflower		
Artemisia ludovisiana mexicana		*Ajenjo, Quije-tes*
Common weed. Central plateau. Medicinal.		
Calyptocarpus viails	Straggler Daisy	*Hierba de caballo*
Cosmos bipinnatus	Cosmos	*Meriso*l
Common ground cover probably introduced		
Gnaphalium attenuatum	Cudweed	*Gordolobo*
Common weed of poor disturbed areas		
Osteospermum fruticosum	Freeway daisy	*Elia*
Introduced wild flower		
Parthenium heterophorus	False Ragweed	*Altamisa*
Common weed. Hayfever.		
Sonchus asper	Dandelion	Cerraja

Common introduced weed		
Tagetes lunulata	Mexican Marigold	*Cinco Llagas, Pexto*
Common weed. Flowers edible.		
Tagetes micrantha	Anis	*Anis*
Not true Aniae. Medicinal.		
Verbesina crocata?		
Escaped ornamental		
Bignoniaceae		
Paramentiera edulis		*Cuajilote, cuailote*
Tecoma stans	Desert Willow	*Cando dulce*
Parmentiera edulis		*Cuajilote o cuailote*
Bixaceae		
Bixa orellana	Lipstick plant	*Achote*
Ornamental grown for spice		
Bombacaceae		
Ceiba pentandra	Kapok tree	*Pochotl (en* náhuatl)
Sacred tree to Zapotec and Mayans. Produces kapok used as insulation and in life preservers.		
Brassicaceae (Cruciferae)		
Lepidium virginicum	Peppergrass	*Lentejilla*
Common summer weed		
Brassica *negra*	Black Brassica	*Xaa-guina-castilla*
Common spring weed		
Bromeliaceae		
Ananas cocmosus	Pineapple	Pina, Hu, Mho-mo, Mustaijcy, Toba-guel, Xiicho
cultivated fruit.		
Tilandia recurvata	Ball Moss	G*allito. Heno Pequeno*
Common epiphyte on oaks and pines		
Burseraceae		
Bursera bipinnata		*Copal*
Used as incense and carving albrijes		
B. gracillis		*Copal santo*

Used as incense		
B. simaruba		*Songolica*, Zongolica
Protium copal		
Cactaceae		
Cephalocereus Chrysacanthus		*Pitayo Viejo*
C. collinsi		*uo-she-ka-ka*
Escontria chiotilla		*Chiotilla*
Ferrocactus robustus		Pinitas
Lemaireocerreus chende		*Chende*
L. chichipe		*Chichipe, Chituna*, Dichitune
L. griseus		*Pitayo de mayo*
L. Hollianus		*Baboso*
L. marginatus		*Chilayo*
L. pruinosus		*Al-ca-uo-she, Pitayo de mayo*
L. stellatus		*Pitayo*
L. Treleasei		*Nutillo*
Myrtillocactus schenkii		Xi-xobai
Nyctocereus oaxacensis		*Lamish-que*
Opuntia ficus-indica	Prickly Pear	*Tuna*
Pachycereus columna-trajani		*Teteza*
P. chrysomallus		
Caricaceae		
Carica papaya	Papaya	Papayo
Herbaceous tree. Edible fruit.		
Casuarinaceae		
Casuarina equisetifolia	Casuarina, Australian pine	*Casurina*
Street tree and escaped		
Caesalpinaceae		
Tamarindus indicus	Tamarind	*Tamarindo*
Produces edible seeds		

Chenopodiaceae		
Chenopodium ambrosioides	Wormseed	*Epazote*
Combretaceae		
Terminalia catapa	Tropical almond	*Almendro*
Landscape plant and tropical nut crop		
Comelinaceae		
Commelina coelestis	Widows tears	*Herba de pollo*
Tradescantia geniculata	Day flower	
T. dracoaenoides	hirsute purple sage	
Convolvulaceae		
Convolvulus coeorum	White tree morning glory	*Camote de Palo*
Ipomoea batatas		*Camote morado*
I. leptophylla		
I. pes-caprae	railroad vine	*Hierba de la raya*
Crassulaceae		
Dudleya sp.	Stonecrop	
Cruciferae		
Brassica negra		*Xaa-guina-castilla*
Cucurbitaceae		
Cucurbita pepo	Squash	*Calabaza*
C. maxima	Squash	*Calabaza pipiana*
Melothira pendula	Speckled gourd	*Sandia silvestre*
Sechium edule	Squash	*Chayote*
Cupressaceae		
Taxodium mucronatum	Mexican cypress	*Ahuehueteor or Sabino*
Juniperus deppeana	red cedar	*Cedro chino*
Equisetaceae		
Equisetum giganteum	Horsetail	*Cola de Caballo*
Wetland plant		

Euphorbiaceae		
Euphorbia prostrata?	carpet weed	
E. Romeriana?		
E. Romeriana?		
Phyllanthus acidus	*Ciruela costena*	
Ricinus communis	Castor Bean	*Ricino, Palma Christi*
Fabaceae		
Acacia angustissima	Acacia	*Palo de pulque*
Acacia spp	Acacia	
Crotalaria pumila	bean	*Chipile, chipil*
Desmodium sp.		
Lupinus sp		
Benito Juarez Park		
Melilotus alba	white clover	*Trebol dulce*
Benito Juarez Park		
M. indica	annual yellow sweetclover	*Alfalfilla*
Benito Juarez Park		
M. officinalis	yellow sweetclover	*Canacua*
Benito Juarez Park		
Medicago sativa	burr clover	*Coba-picinaxi-Cas*tilla
Benito Juarez Park		
Parkinsonis microphylla	*Paloverde*	
Prosopis juliflora	Mesquite	*Inda-a, Yaga-bu*
P. laevigata	Mesquite	*Mezquite*
Fagaceae		
Quercus sp	Oak	*Roble*
Common forest tree above 7000 feet. Some lumber		
Geraniaceae		
Pelargonium sp	Geranium	*Geranio*
Graminae		

Andropogon sp	Bluegrass	
Chloris sp	Windmillgrass	*Escobetilla*
Invasive weed		
Dactyloctenium aegyptium	Crowfootgrass	*Pato de pollo*
Invasive weed		
Orysa sativa	Rice	*Arroz*
Commercial grain crop		
Phragmites communis	Common Reed	*Canoto*
Invasive wetland plant		
Poa pratensis	Bluegrass	*Zacate azul*
Poa spp	Bermudagrass	*Carrizo de milpa*
Ornamental cool season grass		
Poa spp	Bermudagrass	*Carrizo de milpa*
Ornamental		
Saccharum offininarum	Sugar Cane	*Cana*
Commercial crop		
Triniochloris stipoides	Indian Corn	
Zia mays	corn	*Maiz*
Hydrophalaceae		
Phacelia congesta	Spike Phacelia	*Tomasita*
Juglandaceae		
Juglans sp	Walnut	*Nuez, Nogal*
Labitae		
Salvia sp	Salvia	
S. cocinnea?		
Lamiaceae		
Moluccella laevis	Belles of Ireland	
Benito Juarez Park		
Lauraceae		
Laurus nobilis	Laurel	*Laurel de poeta*
Persea Americana	Avacado	*Aguacate*
Liliaceae		

Agapanthus umbellatus	Nile Lily	*Agapando*
Allium sativum	garlic	*Ajo*
Aloe vera	Aloe	*Sabila*
Anthericum Torreyi	Crag Lily	*Coyamol*
Kniphofia uvaria (Tritoma unaria)	Red-hot poker *Flor de Maiz, Flor de Mazorca*	
Yucca elephantipes	yucca	*Izote*
Flowers are eaten		
Y. filifera	Yucca	*Palma de San Pedro*
Malvaceae		
Hibiscus sabdariffa	Hibiscus	*Jamaica*
White mallow		
Yagul		
Mimosoideae		
Pithecollobium dulce	Tamarind	*Guamuche*
Moraceae		
Dorstenia contrajerva	*Contrayerba*	
Cecropia peltata	Snakewood tree, Cecropia	*Guarumbo*
Musaceae		
Musa nana	Dwarf Banana	*Bitua, Bituhua*
M. paradisiaca	Plantain	*playano*
M. sapientum	Banana	*Au-e, Pi-tohua-castilla*
Tiaca, Tsa'am		
Myrtaceae		
Eucalyptus sp	Gum Tree	*Eucaliptoi*
Psidium guajava	Guava	*Guayabo criollo*
Nyctaginaceae		
Bougainvillea glabra	Bougainvilla	*Bugambilia*
Boerhaavia diffusa	Scarlet Spiderling	
Onagraceae		

Oenothera rosea	evening primrose	*Herba de golpe*
Benito Juarez Park		
Gaura coccinia	scarlet gaura	*Aretitos, Linda tarde*
Monte Alban		
Oxalidaceae		
Oxalis tetraphylla	Oxalis	
Palmaceae		
Cocos nucifera	Coconut	*Palma cocotera*
Fan palms		
Papaveraceae		
Argemone mexicana var ochroleuca	Prickly poppy	Quechi-nijchi
Phytolaccacae		
Phytolacca rivinoides	Poke weed	Jabonera
Toxic but can be prepared for eating, Benito Juarez Park		
Pinaceae		
Pinus ayachuite	Mexican Pine	*pinabete* or *ayacahuite*
Above 7000 feet. lumber		
Plantago		
Plantago major	Plantago	Lante
Common summer weed		
Polygonaceae		
Erigonum sp (annum)	buckwheat	
Benito Juarez Park		
E. sp	(effusum?)	buckwheat
Benito Juarez Park		
Ranunculaceae		
Clematis dioica	Old Man's Beard	*Barba de Chivo*
Fences		*o Barba de Viejo*
Ranunculus pediolaris	Buttercup	*Estamasuchil*
Rosaceae		

Potentilla sp	cinquefoil	Tormentillai
Prunus persica	Peach	Durazno
Commercial fruit crop		
Rubiaceae		
Coffea arabica	Coffee	Café Cimarron
Commercial crop		
Rutaceae		
Citrus sinensisi	Oranges	Hi-hin, Ma-hing Yaga-naraxo,Tuzan
C. reticulata	Tangerines	
C. paradisi	Greatfruit	Pamplemusa,
Pe-hui-ina-Castilla, Pomela		
C. aurantifolia	Limes.	Limonero
Rubiaceae		
Galium mexicanum	Bedstraw	Herba de la pulga
Salicaceae		
Salix sp	willow	La-ua-zil
Wetland and stream indicator		
Sapindaceae		
Nephekium lappaceum	rambutan	
Commercial fruit crop		
Sapotaceae		
Calocarpum sapota	*Sapote*	*Zapote mamey*
Edible fruit		
Saxifragaceae		
Hydrangea hortensisi	Hydrangea	*Hortensia*
Scrophulariaceae		
Castilleja sp.		
Benito Juarez Park		
Mimulus guttatus	Monkey-flower	*Lama, Tocasoiahui*
Benito Juarez Park		
Penstemon barbatus	Penstemon	*Jarritos*
P. imberbis	Penstemon	*Chilpantlacol*

Benito Juarez Park		
P. sp		
Benito Juarez Park		
Solanaceae		
Capsicum spp.	Pepper	*chile*
Physalis sp (fenderli?)	Groundcherry	
Benito Juarez Park		
Solanum diversifolium		*Mariola, Oja de Liebre*
Food crop. Some escaped plants		
Solanum diversifolium		
Stinging weed seen at Benito Juarez Park		
S. Donnell-Smithii	Tomatillo	
Food crop		
S. Hernandesii		Huitztomatzin
S. hindsianum		Mariola o Oja de Liebre
Stinging weed seen at Yagul		
S. jasminoides		
S. laurifolium		
S. melongena	Berenjena	
Medicinal. Var escullentum is common eggplant		
S. nigrum	Vishatei	
Leaves eaten as greens		
S. tuberosum	Potato	Nyami-tecuinti
Cultivated		
S. verbascifolium		Hoja de manteca
Potato tree		
Sterculiaceae		
Theobroma cacao	Coco	Cacao
Verbenaceae		
Lantana camara		
Verbena ciliata		

Zygophyllaceae

Tribulus cistoides	goat head	*Cabeza de arriero*
T. grandiflorum	goat head	*Vaivurin*

Vegetation of Todo Santos Baja

Lichen

Ramalina reticulata (Spanish moss or Rocella or Orchilla) on Torote.

Asclepiadaceae		
Asclepias subulata	Milkweed	***Jumete***
Avicenniaceae		
Avicennia germinnans	Black mangrove	***Mangle Negro***
Burerceae		
Bursera odorata	Elephant tree	***Torote Blanco***
Bursera microphylla		***Torote Colorado***
Bursera hindsiana		***Torote Prieto***
Buxaceae		
Simmondsia chinensis	Goatnut	***Jojoba***
Cactaceae		
Ferrocactus gracillis		*Biznaga*
Mammillaria brandegeei		***Biznaga, Viejilta***
Mammillaria dioica	fishhook cactus	***Biznaga**,*
Cochemia poselgeri	Cochemia	***Biznagita**,*
Pachycereus pringlei		***Cardon***
Cereus acanthocarpa	Old Man Cactus,	***Garambullo, Sentia***
Lemaireocereus thurberi	Organ Pipe Cactus	***Pitaya Dulce*** Opuntia
leptocaullis	Pencil Cholla or Jumping Cactus	
Opuntia cholla	Chain Link Cholla	***Cholla Pelona***
Echinocactus horizonthalonius	Turk's Head	
Opuntia engelmanii	Prickly Pear	***tuna*, nopal**
Capparidaceae		
Forchamneria	watsonii	***Palo San Juan***
Composite		
Ambrosia chenopodifolia	Burbush	***Huizapol***
Encelia farinose	Brittlebush	***Incienso***
Eupatorieae		

Hofmeisteria fasciculate		
Euphorbiaceae		
Euphorbia leucophya	Golandrina,	
Euphorbia misera	Cliff Spurge	***Liga, Tacora, Jumetón***
Fouquieriaceae		
Fouquieria diguetii	Adam tres	***Palo Adán***
Graminaceae		
Arundinaria gigantea	Giant cane	
Distichlis spicata	saltgrass	
Setaria	Bristlegrass	
Trichloris (?)	windmillgrass	
Krameriaceae		
Krameria grayi		***Mesquitillo***
Leguminosae		
Lysiloma divaricata		***Mauto***
Liliaceae		
Aloe barbadensis (exotic)	Barbados Aloe	***Aloe***
Martyniaceae		
Proboscidea altheaefolia	Devil'sClaw,	***Espuela del Diablo***
Moraceae		
Ficus brandegeel	Wild fig	***Higuara, Zaluta, Armata***
Polygonaceae		
Antigonon leptopus	Coralvine, Queen's Crown/ Wreath,	***Coralitto, or Flor de SanDiego***
Rhamnaceae		
Karwinskia califórnica	Coffeeberry	***Yerba de Oso, Cacabila***
Saururaceae		
Anemopsis californic	Lizard's tail	***Yerba Mansa, Hierba del Mansa***
Turneraceae		
Turnera diffusa	Damiana	***Damiana***

Birds of Mexico

Yucatan Birds
11-18 Dec 1993

Beaches, Bay and Mangroves on Cancun (CA); state park and shoreline on Isla Mujeres (IM); Chankanaab Park on Cozumel (CZ); Puerto Morales (PM); Dr Alfredo Barrera Mari'n Botanical Garden to Pto Morales (BG); Playa del Carmen (PDC) in Quintanaroo state and Chitzen Itza (CI) and Valladolid (VA) in Yucatan state, Mexico

Family
Common name
Specific name — Location/notes

***Phaethontidae*: Tropicbirds**
White-tailed Tropicbird
Phaethon aethereus — CA Beach, IM,CZ

***Pelicanidae*: Pelicans**
Brown Pelican
Pelicanus occidentalis — CA Bch/Bay

***Anhingidae*: Anhingas**
American Anhinga
Anhinga anhinga — CA Bay, PM

***Ardeidae*: Herons**
Great Blue Heron
Ardea herodias — PM

Cattle EgretPM	
American Egret	
Egreta egreta	CA Bay, IM, PM
***Threskiornithidae*: Ibises**	
White Ibis	
Eudocimus albus	CA Mangrove
***Laridae*: Gulls**	
Caspian Tern	
Hydroprogne caspia	CA Beach
Ringed-billed Gull (immature)	
Larus delawarensis	CA Beach
***Cracidae*: Curassows**	
Central American Curassow	
Crax rubra	BG
***Cuculidae*: Cuckoos**	
Groove-billed Ani	
Crotophaga sulcirostris	VA
***Picidae*: Woodpeckers**	
Guatemalan Ivorybill	
Campephilus guatemalensis	BG
***Tyrannidae*: Flycatchers**	
Giraud's Flycatcher	
Myiozetetes texensis	CA Hotels, PM,PDC
***Hirundinidae*: Swallows**	
Cave Swallow	Tulum
Petrochelidon fulva	
***Corvidae*: Crows and Jays**	
Yucatan Jay	
Cissilopha yucatanica	BG
***Mimidae*: Mockingbirds**	
Graceful Mockingbird	
Mimus gilvus	CA Hotels
***Turdidae*: Thrushes**	

Gray's Robin
Turdus grayi BG

***Vireonidae*: Vireos**

Yucatan Vireo
Vireo magister CZ

***Icteridae*: Blackbirds**

Great-tailed Grackle
Cassidix mexicanus CA Hotels, CZ
Sumichrast's Blackbird
Dives dives CI, CZ
Orange Oriole
Icterus auratus BG
Altamira Oriole PDC
Icterus gularis

***Coerebidae*: Honeycreepers**

Cozumel Bananaquit
Coereba caboti CZ

Birds of Veracruz/Fortine de las Flores

***Ardeidae*: Herons**	
Snowy Egret	Mx 150 libre
Egreta [Leucophoyx] thula	
***Cathartidae*: American Vultures**	
zopilotes (Black Vultures)	Veracruz airport
Cathartes atratus	Mx 150 libre
***Acciptridae* : Hawks**	
Black Crab-Hawk	Mx 150 libre
Buteogallus anthracinus	
Falconidae: Falcons	
Pigeon Hawk or Merlin	Mx 150 libre
Falco columbarius	
***Hirundinidae* : Swallows**	
Tree Swallows	Mx 150 libre
Iridoprocne bicolor	
***Sternidae* :Starlings**	
Common Starling	Veracruz airport
Sturnus vulgaris	
***Icteridae* :Blackbirds**	
Great-tailed Grackles	Veracruz airport
Cssidix mexicanus	
***Parulidae* :Wood -warblers**	
Orizaba yellowthroat	Mx 150 libre
Geothlypis speciosa	

Birds of Mexico City, Teotihuacan, and el Rosario Refuge

***Thraupidae* :Tanagers**

Scarlet Tanager — Teotihuacan

Piranga olivacea

Birds of Los Cabos

***Pelicanidae* : Pelicans**

Brown pelican — Cabo

Pelicanus occidentalis

***Phalacrocoracidae:* Cormorants**

Brandt Cormorant — Cabo

Phalacrocorax penicillatus

***Anhingidae* : Anhingas**

Anhinga — Cabo

Anhinga anhinga

***Frigatidae* : Frigatebirds**

Magnificent Frigatebird — Cabo

Fregata magnificens

***Cathartidae* : Vultures**

Turkey Vulture — Baja, Todo

Cathartes aura

***Accipitridae* : Hawks**

Golden Eagle — Baja

Aquila chrysaetos

***Pandionidae* : Ospreys**

Osprey — Baja

Pandion haliaftus

***Falconidae* – Falcons**

Prairie Falcon — Baja

Falco mexicanus	
Crested Caracara	Baja
Caracara cheriway	
***Phasianidae* : Partridges**	
Gambel Quail	Cabo
Lophortyx gambelii	
***Charadriidae* : Plovers**	
Kildeer	Cabo
Charadrius vociferus	
Snowy Plover	Cabo
Charadrius nivosus	
***Cuculidae* : Cuckoos**	
Greater Roadrunner	Baja
Geococcyx californianus	
***Trochilidae* : Hummingbirds**	
Xantus hummingbird	Cabo
Hylocharis xantusii	
***Picidae* : Woodpeckers**	
Gila Woodpecker	Cabo
Centurus uropygialis	
***Corvidae* : Crows**	
Crow	Baja
Corvus brachyrhynchos	
***Troglodytidae* : Wrens**	
Cañon Wren	Cabo
Catherpes mexicanus	

Birds Todo Santos

***Podicipedidae* : Grebes**

Pied-billed Grebe	Pond
Podilymbus podiceps	*Zampullin Picogrueso*

***Pelecanidae* : Pelicans**

Brown Pelican	Beach
Pelecanus occidentalis	*Peliano Prado*

***Fregatidae* : Frigate birds**

Magnificent Frigatebird	surf
Fregata agnificens	*Rabihorcado Magnifico*

***Ardeidae* : Egrets**

Snowy Egret	Pond
Egretta thula	*Gaceta Nivea*

***Anatidae* : Ducks**

Lesser Scaup	Pond
Aythya affinis	*Porrón Bola*

***Cathartidae* : Vultures**

Turkey Vulture	Desert
Cathartes aura	*Aura Gallipavo*

***Accipitridae* : Hawks**

Red-tailed Hawk	Desert
Buteo jamaicensis	*Bustardo Colirrojo*

***Falconidae* : Falcons**

Crested Caracara	Desert
Caracara cheriway	*Carancho Norteño*
American Kestrel	Desert
Falco sparverius	*Cernicalo Americano*

***Rallidae* : Rails**

American Coot	Pond
Fulica Americana	*Focha Americana*

***Recurvirostridae* : Stilts**

Black-necked Stilt	Beach

Himantopus mexicanus	*Ciguenuela de CuelloNegro*
Laridae : Gulls	
Herring Gull	Beach
Larus agentatus	*Gaviota*
Columbidae : Doves	
White-winged Dove	Town
Zenaida asiatica	*Zenaida Aliblanca*
Common Ground-Dove	Town
Columbina passerine	*Columbina Común*
Domestic Pigeon	Town
Columba livia	*Columbina*
***Cuculidae* : Cookoos**	
Greater Roadrunner	Desert
Geococcyx californianus	*Correcaminos Grande*
***Trochillidae :* Hummingbirds**	
Xantus Hummingbird	Desert
Hylocharis xantusii	*Colibri de Xantus*
Picidae : Woodpeckers	
Gila Woodpecker	Town
Melanerpes uropygialis	*Carpintero del Gila*
***Hirundinidae* : Swallows**	
Rough-winged Swallow	Town
Steigidopteryx serripennis	*Golondrina Aserrada*
***Troglodytidae* : House Wrens**	
House Wren	Town
Troglodytes aedon	*Ratona Común*
Cactus Wren	Desert
Campylorrhynchus brunneicapillus	*Ratona Desértica*
***Mimidae* : Mockingbirds**	
Northern Mockingbird	Town
Mimus polyglottos	*Sinsonte Común*

Corvidae **: Crows**	
Common Raven	Desert
Corvus corax	*Cuervo Común*
Parulidae **:**	
Belding's Yellowthroat	Town
Geothlypis beldingi	*Chipe Peninsular*
Cardinalidae **: Cardinal**	
Northern Cardinal	Town
Cardinalis cardinalis	*Cardenal Norteño*
Icteridae : Orioles	
Hooded Oriole	Desert
Icterus cucullatus	*Turpial Zapotero*
Fringillidae **: Finches**	
House Finch	Town
Carpodacus mexicanus	*Capodaco Común*
Passeridae : **Sparrows**	
House Sparrow	Town
Passer domesticus	*Gorrión Doméstico*

Mata Ortiz Birds 24-28 Nov 04

Cathartidae : American Vulture
Turkey Vulture
Cathartes aura
Accipitridae : Hawks
Red-tailed Hawk
Buteo jamaicensis
Corvidae : Crows
American Raven
Corvus sinuatus
Ploceidae :
House Sparrow
Passer domesticus
Icteridae : Blackbirds
Great-tailed Grackle
Cassidix mexicanus
Troglodytidae : Wrens
Southern House Wren
Troglodytes musculus
Sinaloa Wren
Thryothorus sinaloa
Fringillidae : Sparrows
Lincoln Sparrow
Melospiza lincolnii

Birds of San Miguel

Family/species	Spanish Name
Anhingidae : Anhinga	
Anhinga	*mérgulo antiguo*
Anhinga anhinga	
Accipitridae : Kites	
Mississippi Kite	*Milano de Misisipi*
Ictinia mississippiensis	
Ardeidae : Egrets	
Snowy Egret	*garceta pie-dorado*
Egretta thula	
Anatidae **: Ducks**	
Redhead Duck	*pato cabeza roja*
Aythya Americana	
Rallidae **: Rails**	
American Coot	*gallareta americana*
Fulica Americana	
Columbidae**: Doves**	
Mourning Dove	*paloma huilota*
Zenaidura macroura	
Trochilidae : **Hummingbirds**	
Dusky Hummingbird	*colibrí oscuro*
Cyanthus sordidus	
Amethyst-throated Hummingbird	*colibrí garganta amatista*
Lampornis amethystinus	
Troglodytidae :Wrens	
Cactus Wren	*matraca del desierto*
Campylorhynchus brunneicapillus	
Fringillidae : **Finches**	
House Finch	*pinzón mexicano*
Carpodacus Mexicanus	

***Ploceidae:* Sparrows**

House Sparrow *gorrión casero*

Passer domesticus

***Laniidae:* Shrikes**

Loggerhead Shrike *alcaudón verdugo*

Lanius ludovicianus

***Icteridae:* Blackbirds**

Great-tailed Grackle *zanate mexicano*

Cassidix mexicanus

Birds of Oaxaca August 2007

Oax = Oaxaca
PE= Puerto Escondido
SP=San Pedro Juchatengo in Sierra Madre del Sur

Podicipedidae : Grebes	
Pie-billed Grebe	PE
***Phalacrocoracidae* : Cormorant**	
Double-crested Cormorant	PE
***Anhingidae* : Anhinga**	
Anhinga	PE
Pelican – Pelecanidae	
Brown Pelican	
Pelecanus occidentalis	PE
Frigatebirds	
Magnificent Frigatebird	
Fregata magnificens	PE
Gannets – Sulidae	
Brown Booby	
Sula leucogaster	PE
Amercan Vultures – Catharidae	
Turkey Vulture	
Cathartes aura	Mitla
***Ardeidae* : Egret**	
Snowy Egret	PE
Green Heron	PE
Black-crowned Night-Heron	PE
***Threskiormithidae* : Ibis**	
White Ibis	PE
***Anatidae* : Ducks**	
Canvasback	PE

***Acciptridae* : Hawks**	
Red-tailed hawk	SP
Gray Hawk	SP
Cooper's Hawk	SP
***Falconidae* : Falcons**	
Crested Caracara	Desert
American Kestrel	Desert
Peregrine Falcon	Desert
Prairie falcon	
Falco mexicanus	Mitla
Cracidae	
Plain Chachalaca	Mountain
***Rallidae* : Rails**	
Common Moorhen	PE
***Scolopacidae* : Curlew**	
Long-billed Curlew	PE
Gulls – Laeidae	
Franklin Gull	
Larus pipixcan	PE
Royal Tern	
Sterna maxima	PE
Pigeons – Columbidae	
White-tipped Dove	OaX
Pigeon	
Columba livia	Oax, PE
Inca dove	
Scardafella inca	Oax
Mourning dove	
Zenaidura macroura	Oax
Parrots – Psittacidae	
Orange-fronted Parakeet	
Aratinga canicularis	Mountain

Cuckoos – Cuculidae	
Lesser Roadrunner	
Geococcyx viaticus	Yagul
Hummingbirds – Trochilidae	
Doubleday's Hummingbird	
Cyanthus doubledayi	Oax
Swallows – Hirundinidae	
Barn Swallow	
Hirundo rustica	Mitla, PE
***Strigidae* : Owls**	
Eastern Screech-Owl	Oax
Burrowing Owl	Desert
***Alcidinidae* : King Fishers**	
Ringed Kingfisher	PE
Belted Kingfisher	PE
***Picidae* : Woodpeckers**	
Golden-fronted Woodpecker	SP
Ladder-backed Woodpecker	SP
***Tyrannidae* :Flycatchers**	
Vermillion Flycatcher	Mountain
Great Kiskadee	Mountain
Tropical Kingbird	Mountain
Eastern Phoebe	Mountain
***Laniidae* : Shrikes**	
Loggerhead Shrike	Desert
***Alaudidae* : Larks**	
Horned Lark	Desert
Corvidae : Crows	
Green Jay	Mountain
Tamaulipas Crow	Oa
Chihuahuan Raven	Desert
American Raven	
Corvus sinuatus	Puebla

Finches – Fringillidae	
House Wren	
Troglodytes musculus	Mitla
Mockingbirds – Mimidae	
Northern Mockingbird	
Mimus polyglottos	Oax
Weavers – Ploceidae	
House Sparrow	
Passer domesticus	Oax, PE
Blackbirds – Icteridae	
Great-tailed Grackle	
Quiscalus mexicana	Oax

Birds of Copper Canyon

These birds were seen and many were photographed during the week of 10-17 March 2008. The area of was along the CEPE rail line between Chihuahua and El Fuerte.

References:
Birds of Mexico and Central America. L.I.Davis.
Audubon Field Guide to North American Birds – Western Region
Internet references.

Phalacrocoracidae: Cormorants

Brandt Cormorant

Phalacrocorax penicillatus — El Fuerte

Ardeidae : Egret

Snowy Egret

Egrteea thula — El Fuerte

Great Blue Heron

Ardea herodias — El Fuerte

A*natidae* : Ducks

Lesser Scaup

Aythya affinis — El Fuerte

Mallard ducks

Anas platyrhynchos — San Andres

***Cathartidae* : American Vulture**

Black Vulture

Coragyps atratus — all

***Acciptridae* : Hawks**

Red-tailed Hawk

Buteo jamacensis — all

***Pandionidae* : Ospreys**

Osprey

Pandion haliaetus	El Fuerte
***Falconidae* : Falcons**	
Peregrine Falcon	
Falco peregrinus	Anahuac
Caracara	
Caracara cheriway	San Migue
***Rallidae* : Rails**	
American Coot	
Fulica Americana	El Fuerte
Columbidae : Pigeons	
Domestic Pigeon	
Columba livia	Anahuac
Morning Dove	
Zenaidura macroura	Anahuac
Inca Dove	
Scardafella inca	San Miguel
White-winged Dove	
Zenaida asiatica	San Miguel
***Trochilidae* : Hummingbirds**	
Magnificent Hummingbird	
Eugenes fulgens	Divisadero
***Picidae* : Woodpeckers**	
Acorn Woodpecker	
Melanerpes formicivorus	Divisadero
Gilded Flicker	
Colaptes chrysoides	El Fuerte
***Hirundinidae* : Swallows**	
Rough-winged swallow	
Stelgidopteryx serripennis	El Fuerte
***Icteridae* : Blackbirds**	
Black-throated Magpie-Jay	
Calocitta colliei	El Fuerte
American Crow	

Corvus brachyrhynchos		Cuauhtémoc
Sinaloa Crows		
Corvus sinaloae		San Miguel
Dickey Jay		
Cyanocorax dickeyi		Divisadero
***Mimidae* : Mockingbirds**		
Mexican Blue Mockingbird		
Melnotis caerulescens		Bahuichivo
Curved-bill Thrasher		
Toxoxtoma curvirostre		Bahuichivo
***Turdidae* : Thrushes**		
Robin?	?	Divisadero
Weavers		
House sparrow		
Passer domesticus		El Fuerte
Blackbirds		
Great-tailed Grackle		
Cassidix mexicanus		Cuauhtémoc
Finches		
Lincoln Sparrows		
Melospiziz lincolnii		Anahuac
Wrens		
Canyon Wren		
Catherpes mexicanus		Divisadero

Animals of Mexico

Butterflies near Veracruz

Purple Emperor butterfly (Doxocopa pavon)	Veracruz airport
Orange Long Wing (Dryas iulia)	Veracruz VFR 95
Monarch (Danus plexippus)	Veracruz VFR 95
Whites (subfamily Pierinae)	Veracruz VFR 95
yellow Sulfurs (subfamily Coliadinae)	Veracruz VFR 95
white Morpho	

Butterflies of Mexico City, Teotuhuacan and el Rosario Butterfly refuge February

Monarch	Danus plexippus
Black Swallowtail	Papilio polyxenes
White Sulfur	subfamily Pierinae
Gulf Frittillary	Dione vanillae
Blue Wave Butterfly	
Tiger Swallowtail	

INVERTEBRATES of the Rio Grande Valley and Saltillo February

Guava Skipper
Checkerspot
Hackberry Snout Butterfly
White-Banded Skipper
Dogface
Rabdites land snail
Leaf-cutter ants

Animals of the Baja

Butterflies and Moths	
Black Witch moth	Ascalapha ordorata
Clavipes Sphinx moth	Aellopos clavipes
Whitelined Sphinx Moth	Hyles lineata
Queen	Daucus gilippus
Black Swallowtail	Papilio polyxenes
Gulf Fritillary	Dione vanillae
Dogface	Colias cesonia
Tiny Checkerspot	Dymasia dymas
Long-Tailed Skipper	Urbanus proteus
Beach Skipper	Panoquina panoquinoides
Moth	Ethmia arctostaphylella
Insecta	
Ant Lion	Myrmelean sp.
Predaceous Diving Beetle	
Echinoidea	
Purple Sea Urchin	Strongylocentrotus purpuratus
White Sea Urchin	Lytechinus anamerus
Isopoda	
Sea Cockroach	Ligyda occidentalis

Crustacea	
Barnacle	Balanus tintinnabulum
Sandcrabs	Uca crenulata
Ghost crabs	Ocypoda sp.
Sally Lightfoot Crab	Grapus grapus

Butterflies of Todos Santos

Black Swallowtail caterpillar		
Black Swallowtail	Papilio polyxenes	
Long-Tailed Skipper	on Bougainvilla	Urbanus proteus
Beach Skipper	on Ambrosia	Panoquina panoquinoides
small sulfur	on Bougainvilla	
tiny white	on Bougainvilla	
Clavipes Sphinx moth	on Bougainvilla	Aellopos clavipes
Sandcrab		Uca crenulata

Butterfly list for Copper Canyon

Few butterflies were seen during the week 10-17 March 2008. These were around El Fuerte with the fields of Brassica.

Black Swallowtail
White Cabbage Butterfly
Yellow dog butterfly

Animals of Oaxaca

BJ = Benito Juarez mountain park
Oax = Oaxaca
PE = Puerto Escondido
SP=San Pedro Juchatengo in Sierra Madre del Sur

Insects		
Cochineal	Dactylopius coccus Costa	Oax
Butterflies		
Yellow dog		Oax
White		Oax, BJ
Animals		
Hoary Bat	Lasiurus cinereus	SP
Squirrel	?	Oax
Mouse	?	SP
Prairie dog	Pachycereus columna-trajani	BJ
Desert Cottontail	Sylvilagus audubonii	Dainzu
Herps		
Mexican Tree frog	Hyla baudini	PE
Toad	?	PE
Cricket Frog	Acris gryllus	PE
Spotted Whiptail	Cnemidophorus sacki	PE
Mexican Garter snake	Thamnophis eques	BJ

Shells of Mexico

Yucatan Shells
11-18 Dec 1993

CANCUN ISLAND AND BEACH,
Quintana Roo, Mexico

11-18 Dec 93

Fine, light tan coraline sand with off shore reefs. Dead in drift lines and at bottom of seawall and construction.

"Sea Beans"	
Lucky Bean	(Mucuna sp.)
Sacoglottis sp.	
Sword Bean	[Entada gigas (L.)
Palm	(Elaeis guineensis jacq.)
(Astrocaryum sp.)	
Tropical almond	(Terminalia Catappa L.)
Avocado	(Persea americana Mill)
Anchovy Pear	(Grias sp.)
Navelwort, Navel-seed, Navel spurge.	(Omphalodes sp.)
Mangrove	(Rhizophora Mangle)

Other

Sand dollar (Mellita sp.)

Goose-neck Barnacle (Lepas sp.)
Sea Whip corals

Shells
Class GASTROPODA Cuvier, 1797
subclass PROSOBRANCHIA
FISSURELLIDAE

Fissurella angusta Gmelin,	Pointed Keyhole Limpet
TROCHIDAE	
Tegula livivomaculata C.B. Adams,	West Indian Tegula
ASTRAEINAE	
Astraea tuber Linne, 1758	Green Star-shell
VERNETIDAE	
Petaloconchus mcgintyi Olson & Harbison	McGinty's Worm Shell
Petaloconchus floridanus Olson & Harbison,	Florida Worm Shell
CREPIDALIDAE	
Calyptraea centralis Conrad,	Circular Cup-and-Saucer
CASSIDAE	
Phalium granulatum Born,	Scotch Bonnet
Phalium cicatricosum Gmelin,	Smooth Scotch Bonnet
MURICIDAE	
Murex cellulosus Conrad,	Pitted Murex
OLIVIDAE	
Oliva reticularis Lamarck,	Netted Olive
CONIDAE	
Conus ranunculus Hwass,	Atlantic Agate Cone
Subclass OPISTHOBRANCHIA	
BULLIDAE	
Bulla striata Bruguiere,	Striated-bubble
Subclass PULMONATA	
ELLOBIIDAE	

Melampus monile Bruguiere, Yellowish Melampus

Class PELECYPODA

ARCIDAE

Arca zebra Swainson, Turkey Wing

A. imbricata Bruguiere, Mossy Ark

Anadara notabilis Roding, Eared Ark

MYTILIDAE

Brachidontes exustus Linne, Scorched Mussel

PECTINIDAE

Chlamys imbricata Gmelin, Little Knobby Scallop

C. benedicti Verrill and Bush, Benedict's Scallop

Leptopecten bavayi Dautzenberg, Bavay's Scallop

LIMIDAE

Lima pellucida C.B. Adams, Antillean Lima

L. scabra Born, Rough Lima

OSTREIDAE

Ostrea frons Linne, 'Coon Oyster

CRASSATELLIDAE

Crassinella guadalupensis Orbigny, Guadeloupe Crassinella

LUCINIDAE

Lucina blanda Dall and Simpson, Three-Ridged Lucina

Anodontia alba Link, Buttercup Lucina

CHAMIDAE

Chama sarda Reeve, Red Jewel Box

C. macerophylla Gmelin, Leafy Jewel Box

CARDIIDAE

Trachycardium magnum Linne, Magnum Cockle

VENERIDAE

Pitar fulminata Menke, Lightning Venus

TELLINIDAE

Tellina radiata Linne, Sunrise Tellin

T. laevigata Linne, Smooth Tellin

COZUMEL, QUINTANA ROO, MEXICO

16 DEC 93

Fossil coral/live coral reefs with turtle grass beds. Dead on beach.

Class ANTHOZOA
Family MUSSIDAE
Lobophyllia sp. Blainville — Lobed cup corals

Class GASTROPODA Cuvier,
Family FISSURELLIDAE
Fissurella barbadaensis Gmel — Barbados Keyhole Limpet
Family NERITIDAE Rafinesque,
Nerita fulgurans Gmelin, — Antillean Nerite
Family LITTORINIDAE Gray,
Littorina (Littorinopsis) angulifera
(Lamarck,1822) Angulate Periwinkle
Family COLUMBELLIDAE
Columbella (Pyrene) mercatoria L. — Mottled Dove Shell
Mitrella (Astyris) lunata (Say,) — Lunar Dove Shell
Psarostola monulifera Sowerby — Many Spotted Dove Shell

Class PELECYPODA Golgfuss)
Family MACTRINAE Lamarck
Mulinia lateralis (Say) — Dwarf Surf Clam
Family VENERIDAE Rafinesque,
Dosinia elegans Conrad, 1846 — Elegant Dosinia

Class POLYPLACOPHORA Blainville, 1816 =
[AMPHINEURA Von Ihering, 1876, in part]
Family CHITONIDAE
Chiton marmaratus Gmelin — Marbled Chiton

Isla Mujures, Quintana Roo, Mexico

14 Dec 93

Sandy beaches with off shore reefs and sea grass beds. Dead on beach.

Class GASTROPODA Cuvier, 1797

Family FISSURELLIDAE

Diodora cayenensis Lamarck — Cayenne Keyhole Limpet

Family TROCHIDAE

Tegula fasciata Born — Smooth Atlantic Tegula

Family TURBININAE

Turbo canaliculatus Hermann — Channeled Turban

Family ASTRAEINAE

Astraea tecta Solander — Imbricated Star-shell

Family LITTORINIDAE

Littorina ziczac Gmelin — Zebra Periwinkle

Family NERITIDAE

Nerita tessellata Gmelin — Tessellated Nerite

Family TURRITELLIDAE

Vermicularia knorri Deshayes — Knorr's Worm Shell

Family CERITHIIDAE

Cerithium variable C.B. Adams — Dwarf Cerith

Family CALYPTRAEIDAE

Calyptraea centralis Conrad — Circular Cup-and-Saucer

Family COLUMBELLIDAE

Columbella (Pyrene) mercatoria L — Mottled Dove Shell

Family MITRIDAE

Mitra barbadensis Gmelin — Barbados Miter

Family MARGINELLIDAE

Hyalina avena Kiener — Orange-banded Marginella

Family CONIDAE

Conus jaspideus Gmelin — Jasper Cone

Class BIVALVA Linne, 1758 =(PELECYPODA Golgfuss, 1820
Family CARDIIDAE
Americardia media Linne — Atlantic Strawberry Cockle
Family VENERIDAE
Antogina listeri Gray — Princess Venus

CANCUN ISLAND BEACH,
Quintana Roo, Mexico

21-28 May 94

Fine, light tan coraline sand with off shore reefs. Dead in drift lines and at bottom of seawall and construction.

"Sea Beans"
Coconut (Cocos nutifera)
Elaes guineensis jacq
Anchovy pear (Grais sp)

Shells
Class GASTROPODA Cuvier
subclass PROSOBRANCHIA
Family FISSURELLIDAE
Diodora variegata Sowerby — Variagated Keyhole Limpet
Family HIPPONICIDAE
Chilea equistris L. — False Cup-and-saucer
Class PELECYPODA
Family NUCULIDAE
Yoldia perprotracta Dall — Long Yoldia
Family TELLINIDAE
Tellina mera Say — Mera Tellin

CANCUN ISLAND Bahia de Mujeres
Quintana Roo, Mexico
21-28 May 94

Fine, light tan coraline sand with off shore reefs. On the channel facing Isla Mujeres. Dead in drift lines and at bottom of seawalls.

Shells
Class GASTROPODA Cuvier
subclass PROSOBRANCHIA
Family FISSURELLIDAE

Diodora listeri Orbigny	Lister's Keyhole Limpet
Acamea antillarum Sowerby	Antillean Limpet
Lucapinalla limatula Reese	File Fleshy Limpet

Family VERMETIDAE

Petaloconchus floridanus Olson and Harbison	Florida Worm Shell
Vermicularia knorri Deshayes	Knorr's Worm Shell
Sarpulorbis decussata Gmelin	Decussate Worm Shell

Family OVULIDAE

Cyphoma gibbosum L.	Flamingo Tongue

Isla Mujures, Quintana Roo, Mexico
26 May 94

North Beach. Sandy with off shore reefs and sea grass beds. Dead on beach.

Class GASTROPODA Cuvier, 1797
subclass PROSOBRANCHIA
Family FISSURELLIDAE

Fissurella barbadensis Gmelin	Barbados Keyhole Limpet

Family MURICIDAE

Purpara patula L.	Widemouth Purpura

Family TEREBRIDAE

Terebra protexta Conrad	Fine-ribbed Auger
Family COLUMBELLIDAE	
Columbella mercatoria L.	Common Dove
Class PELECYPODA	
Family MYTILLIDAE	
Branchiodontes exustus L.	Scorched Mussel
Family CHAMIDAE	
Chama congregata Conrad	Little Corrogated Jewel Box

Shells of los Cabos

November 2003

Turbinidae	
Turbo fluctuosus	La Paz
Turritellidae	
Turritella gonostoma	La Paz
Fissurellidae	
Diodora inaequalis	Cabo
Fissurella virescens	Cabo
Vermetidae	
Vermicularia eburnean	Cabo
Hipponidae	
Hipponix antiquatus	Cabo
H. pilosus	Cabo
Calyptraeidae	
Calyptracea subreflexa	La Paz
Crepidula striolata	Cabo, La Paz
Crucibulum spinosum	Cabo, La Paz
Strombidae	
Strombus gracilior	La Paz
Thaididae	
Thais speciosa	Cabo

Fusinidae	
Fusinus ambustus	Cabo
Arcidae	
Arca mutabilis	La Paz
Anadara grandis	La Paz
Barbatia illota	Cabo
Glycmeridae	
Glycymeris gigantea	La Paz
Mytilidae	
Mytella guyanensis	Cabo
Septifer zeteki	Cabo
Spondylidae	
Spondylus calcifer	Cabo
Ostreidae	
Osterea fisheri	Cabo
Pectinidae	
Argopecten circularis	La Paz
Limidae	
Lima pacifica	Cabo
Chamidae	
Chama buddiana	Cabo
Semelidae	
Semele bicolor	Cabo
Sanguinolariidae	
Tagelus californianus	La Paz
Veneridae	
Chione gnidia	Cabo
C. californiensis	Cabo
Dosinia dunkeri	Cabo, La Paz
Tivela planulata	Cabo
Ventricolaria rigida isocardia	Cabo. La Paz

Shells from Puerto Escondido

Purchased Aug 2007

Fissurellidae	
Fissurella gemmata Menkei	
Patellidae	
Patella mexicana Brod. &Sow	Giant Mexican Limpet
Acamaeidae	
Scurria mesoleuca Menke	Half-white Limpet
Turritellidae	
Turritella leucostoma Valencienes	White-mouth Turritella
Vermetidae	
Vermicularia pellucida Brod. & Sow.	Worm shell
V. p. eburnean Reeve	
Crepidulidae	
Crucibulum spinosum Sow.	Spiny Cup-and-saucer
Cypraeidae	
Cypraea albuginose Gray	Albugine Cowrie
Columbellidae	
Columbella fuscata Sow	Burnt Dove Shell
Spondylidae	
Spondylus princeps Brod.	Pacific Thorny Oyster
Carditidae	
Cardita crassicostata Sowerby	Thick-ribbed Cardita
Donacidae	
Donax californicus Conrad	California Donax
Veneridae	
Chione gnidie Brod & Sow	Gnidie Venus
Polyplacophora	
Stenoplex conspicus Dall	Conspicuous Chiton

Shells of Todo Santos

Febrary 08

Fissurellidae Keyhole Limpets
Fissurella gemmata
F. rugosa
Patellidae Patella Limpets
Patella Mexicana
Acmaidae True Limpets
Acmaea fuseicularis
A. strongiana
Neritidae Nerites
Nerita funiculata
Crepidulidae Slipper Shells
Crepidula scutellatum
C. striolata
Olividae Olives
Oliva undatella half inch long olives
Mytillidae mussels
Mytalla falcate juveniles
Veneridae Venus Clams
Tivela byronensis juveniles

Monte Alban

Dainzu

Mitla

Wildflowers

Tule Tree

Surfers